AF799782

Nonlinear Time Series Analysis with Applications to Foreign Exchange Rate Volatility

Contributions to Economics

Gerhard Gehrig/Wladyslaw Welfe (Eds.)
Economies in Transition
1993. ISBN 3-7908-0721-4

Christoph M. Schneider
Research and Development Management: From the Soviet Union to Russia
1994. ISBN 3-7908-0757-5

Bernhard Böhm/Lionello F. Punzo (Eds.)
Economic Performance
1994. ISBN 3-7908-0811-3

Lars Olof Persson/Ulf Wiberg
Microregional Fragmentation
1995. ISBN 3-7908-0855-5

Ernesto Felli/Furio C. Rosati/
Giovanni Tria (Eds.)
The Service Sector: Productivity and Growth
1995. ISBN 3-7908-0875-X

Giuseppe Munda
Multicriteria Evaluation in Fuzzy Environment
1995. ISBN 3-7908-0892-X

Boris Maurer
R & D, Innovation and Industrial Structure
1996. ISBN 3-7908-0900-4

Giovanni Galizzi/Luciano Venturini (Eds.)
Economics of Innovation: The Case of Food Industry
1996. ISBN 3-7908-0911-X

David T. Johnson
Poverty, Inequality and Social Welfare in Australia
1996. ISBN 3-7908-0942-X

Rongxing Guo
Border-Regional Economics
1996. ISBN 3-7908-0943-8

Oliver Fratzscher
The Political Economy of Trade Integration
1996. ISBN 3-7908-0945-4

Ulrich Landwehr
Industrial Mobility and Public Policy
1996. ISBN 3-7908-0949-7

Arnold Picot/Ekkehard Schlicht (Eds.)
Firms, Markets, and Contracts
1996. Corr. 2nd printing 1997.
ISBN 3-7908-0947-0

Karin Peschel (Ed.)
Regional Growth and Regional Policy Within the Framework of European Integration
1997. ISBN 3-7908-0957-8

Thorsten Wichmann
Agricultural Technical Progress and the Development of a Dual Economy
1997. ISBN 3-7908-0960-8

Ulrich Woitek
Business Cycles
1997. ISBN 3-7908-0997-7

Michael Carlberg
International Economic Growth
1997. ISBN 3-7908-0995-0

Massimo Filippini
Elements of the Swiss Market for Electricity
1997. ISBN 3-7908-0996-9

Giuseppe Gaburro (Ed.)
Ethics and Economics
1997. ISBN 3-7908-0986-1

Frank Hoster/Heinz Welsch/
Christoph Böhringer
CO_2 Abatement and Economic Structural Change in the European Internal Market
1997. ISBN 3-7908-1020-7

Christian M. Hafner

Nonlinear Time Series Analysis with Applications to Foreign Exchange Rate Volatility

With 82 Figures
and 29 Tables

Springer-Verlag Berlin Heidelberg GmbH

Series Editors
Werner A. Müller
Peter Schuster

Author
Dr. Christian Hafner
Institut für Statistik und Ökonometrie
Wirtschaftswissenschaftliche Fakultät
Humboldt-Universität zu Berlin
Spandauer Str. 1
D-10178 Berlin, Germany

ISBN 978-3-7908-1041-7

Cataloging-in-Publication Data applied for
Die Deutsche Bibliothek – CIP-Einheitsaufnahme
Hafner, Christian M.: Nonlinear time series analysis with applications to foreign exchange rate volatility; with 29 tables / Christian M. Hafner.
(Contributions to economics)
ISBN 978-3-7908-1041-7 ISBN 978-3-662-12605-9 (eBook)
DOI 10.1007/978-3-662-12605-9

Originally published by Physica-Verlag Heidelberg in 1998

Softcover Design: Erich Kirchner, Heidelberg

SPIN 10633562 88/2202-5 4 3 2 1 – Printed on acid-free paper

To my parents

I can only remember scooping up money in thousands, and I am beginning to remember also that the middle twelve numbers, to which I had become positively attached, turned up most frequently of all. There was a sort of pattern – they appeared three or four times running, without fail, then disappeared for two turns, then again appeared three or four times in succession. This remarkable regularity occurs sometimes in streaks – and this is what throws out the inveterate gamblers, always doing sums with a pencil in their hands. And what terrible jests fate sometimes plays!

FYODOR DOSTOYEVSKY, *The Gambler*

Preface

The present book was accepted as a dissertation at the *Humboldt Universität zu Berlin* in summer 1996. I am very much obliged to thank my advisor, Professor Wolfgang Härdle, for the continuous, always inspiring support and for opening me the world of nonparametric statistics. Without him I probably would have worked on a different, less exciting topic and this book would not exist.

Also, I would like to thank my second advisor, Professor Helmut Lütkepohl, for his excellent introduction to time series analysis and for always helpful comments on my work.

This work was financially supported by the *Deutsche Forschungsgemeinschaft*, in the first stage while I was a member of the *Graduiertenkolleg* "Applied Microeconomics", and later when I came to the Sonderforschungsbereich 373. For an interestingly widespread academic surrounding I want to thank the members of the *Graduiertenkolleg* and the *Sonderforschungsbereich*, especially Stefan Sperlich and Axel Werwatz. For the use of `XploRe` and many other issues I received substantial help from my colleagues Sigbert Klinke, Thomas Kötter, Marlene Müller and Swetlana Schmelzer. Concerning many central topics of this dissertation, helpful and improving comments were given by Jörg Breitung, Helmut Herwartz, Rolf Tschernig and Lijian Yang, who also revised most parts of the manuscript. I have much reason to thank them for their help. Of course, all remaining errors are mine.

Berlin, July 1997 CHRISTIAN M. HAFNER

Contents

List of Tables

List of Figures

1
Introduction

Over the last decades, the dynamic properties of economic and financial time series have increasingly attracted the interest not only of financial econometricians, but also of politicians and publicity. The latter mainly in such periods where financial indicators seemingly drifted away from their fundamental value. Two examples of such 'speculative bubbles', as this phenomenon is called in modern finance literature, are the Dollar–boom in the mid–eighties and the stock market crash in October 1987. – The former, because financial econometrics serves as the basis for many decisions in governments, central banks, private banks, and investment companies, to name just a few. Also, the profit of large industrial companies crucially depends on major financial indicators. For example, a German internationally active company is interested in a high DM/Dollar exchange rate, but faces the uncertainty of a price decline in foreign markets.

In general, "uncertainty" has to be distinguished from "risk", where certain probabilities can be assigned to the different states. Thus, once statistical models are designed to descibe the dynamic behavior of financial series, only the term "risk" will be used.

In theory and practice, there have been mainly two approaches to deal with uncertainty or risk. The first one is the so–called "hedging" of risks and will be discussed later in the context of derivative securities. The second, more direct approach is the attempt to predict financial series. This has a long tradition and continues to be the main point of interest among practioners, along with the rapid development of new and seemingly new prediction methods. However, it is striking that almost hundred years after Louis Bachelier postulated the non–predictability of financial time series (Bachelier (1900)), his results still remain valid. For example, in the field of foreign exchange rate prediction, Meese and Rogoff (1983) tested various models based on economic theory against the simple random walk model. The surprising result was the non–ability of the economic models to outperform naive prediction in out–of–sample forecasts. Other researchers even think that in general economies are too complex to allow for reliable forecasts, as for example a physicist has expressed:

> *If one tries to give a dynamical interpretation of economic phenomena, the ideas of John M. Keynes and his followers come to mind.*

> *Most economists would, however, agree now that these interesting ideas have no great predictive value. In other words, economy (specifically, macroeconomy) cannot be analyzed convincingly as a moderately complex dynamical system, even though it has some some features of such systems. (D. Ruelle, "Chance and Chaos", Princeton University Press, Princeton 1991, pp. 82)*

and later:

> *There is little doubt that economics and finance give us examples of chaos and unpredictable behavior (in a technical sense). But it is difficult to say more, because we do not have here the kind of carefully controlled systems with which physicists like to experiment. Outside events, which the economists call* shocks, *cannot be neglected. Earnest efforts have been made to analyze financial data (which are known with much better precision than economic data) in the hope of isolating a moderately complicated dynamical system. Such hopes, in my opinion, have failed. (pp. 88)*

As one of the pioneers of the chaos literature in the natural sciences, Ruelle is obviously influenced by its paradigms, one of which is the nonpredictability of most complex dynamical systems, even when they are deterministic. In fact, several recent approaches attempted to transfer the achievements of the chaos literature in the natural sciences to economics and finance, see e.g. Hsieh (1991) and Hall, Matthews and Platen (1995). A review is given by LeBaron (1995). However, even though this approach has some potential to *describe* financial series, it lacks the ability to *explain* the observations economically. Except for a small part of Chapter 3, only stochastic models will therefore be discussed throughout this work.

Bachelier (1900) already viewed financial series as the accumulation of independent, identically distributed random variables. About the distribution of price changes or returns, one soon detected a typical deviation from the normal distribution: very small and very large changes occurred more often than would be expected under the normal distribution. Influential works in this direction were Mandelbrot (1963) and Fama (1965). The former paper also first reported another typical property of security price changes, namely the clustering of volatilities. It was observed that large changes of either sign tend to be followed by large ones, and small changes by small ones. In almost all subsequent empirical investigations this result was confirmed. Thus, price changes were no longer considered to be independent, though still uncorrelated.

The two main properties of security price changes or returns – leptokurtic distribution and volatility clustering – are, of course, not necessarily independent (not in a stochastic sense). In fact, the evidence today is that there is a close relationship between both features. Naturally, this relationship can only be quantified with the specification of a statistical model.

The next question was, how the named properties of returns depend on the degree of aggregation of the data, that is, whether a financial series, that may as well be a series in continuous time, is observed e.g. daily, weekly, or monthly. Recent results for many different financial series suggest that the limit distribution for increasing time intervals is normal, see e.g. Guillaume, Dacorogna, Davé, Müller, Olsen and Pictet (1994) for a review about many aspects of the properties of aggregated and dis–aggregated financial series. This stands in contradiction to the early result of Fama (1965), who found a non–normal stable distribution to be a closer description of stock market returns. On the other side, intra–daily 'high–frequency' series revealed new empirical facts about the microstructure and the efficiency of the market.

Turning to the methodology of financial time series analysis, the failure of the classical Box–Jenkins approach (Box and Jenkins (1976)) soon became obvious. Linear ARMA models were not able to cope with the stylized facts of financial series. The important dynamical properties did not show in the mean, but rather in the squares or absolute values of financial series. Thus, *nonlinear* time series models describing the dependence in higher order moments were needed. Within this class, several models in principle have the ability to reflect time–dependence in second moments, the most important of which are the bilinear model, the stochastic variance model, Markov switching regime models, and, last but not least, autoregressive conditional heteroskedasticity (ARCH) models. Chapter 3 is dedicated to an overview of the most important nonlinear models. In the eighties, the ARCH model with its various extensions became the predominant tool for financial time series analysis. One reason for this is the profound theory for maximum likelihood estimation, ARCH tests with an appealing interpretation as Lagrange multiplier tests, and above all the success of model fitting and prediction of volatility. However, some unsolved theoretical questions remain, in particular the consistency of maximum likelihood estimators for some extensions of the ARCH model.

Now that volatility has become the central issue of financial time series analysis, the question arose how the improved understanding of volatility dynamics could be used in practice. In other words, what gains do we have from a successful prediction not of exchange rates, but of a specific function of exchange rates? First to be mentioned, there is the improved possibility to construct prediction intervals for exchange rates, say, at time $t+1$, because standard errors based on information at time t are no longer erroneously assumed to be constant, but time–varying. Second, even more importantly, the pricing of derivative securities, which in general crucially depends on the volatility of the underlying object, can be performed much more accurately. This is important for risk–averse investors who want to avoid – or "hedge" – the risk of their long positions in financial assets by going short in options on that asset and permanently adapting the proportion held in assets and short–selled options according to the movement of the underlying object, thereby constructing a riskless portfolio. This so–called "self–financing" strategy forms the basis of modern option pricing theory, because it does not depend on risk preferences of the investors, but only on arbitrage conditions that need to be fulfilled. To determine the hedge ratios, however, it is necessary to specify a stochastic process for the underlying object. For example, the seminal paper of Black and Scholes (1973) used the continuous–time Brownian motion

$$\mathrm{d}S_t/S_t = \mu \mathrm{d}t + \sigma \mathrm{d}W_t \tag{1.1}$$

with constant drift rate μ, constant volatility rate σ and standard Wiener process W_t to derive a closed form for the price of calls and puts on that asset. However, as the above exposition of the properties of financial assets shows, this might lead to severe under– or overpricing of options due to the misspecification of volatility. In fact, many new approaches in the options literature attempt to extend the Black–Scholes model to allow for stochastic volatility, e.g. Hull and White (1987) and Melino and Turnbull (1990). For example, Hull and White (1987) assume a model as in (1.1), but with σ itself being a Brownian motion with standard Wiener process independent of the Wiener process in (1.1). Only for this special case, they are able to derive a closed form expression for the price of an option. Simulation studies show that stochastic volatility is able to explain some of the empirically observed anomalies of the Black–Scholes model, particularly the so–called "smile"–effect.

Besides these models based on diffusion processes, an alternative and important direction in the literature is the use of jump processes or even a combination of diffusion and jump processes. This is motivated by the fact that security price changes in reality are not smooth, but rather jump between discrete values. For a recent work on this subject see Zhang (1994). The pricing bias of the Black–Scholes model, however, is also likely to be a result of fitting a continuous time model to a process that is in fact a discrete time process. Bossaerts and Hillion (1996) show that this approximation may lead to the "smile" and "wave" effect observed in practice.

Option pricing with discrete time processes seems to become more popular, although still the derivation of closed form expressions is a difficult task.

Extensive simulation studies are needed to give precise and reliable prices. For example, Duan (1995) has used the ARCH model to price options by using the risk–neutral pricing methodology of Cox and Ross (1976). As could be expected, the results are similar to the case of continuous time stochastic volatility models. Recently, Härdle and Hafner (1997) have extended Duan's model to the more flexible threshold ARCH case, allowing for volatility asymmetry.

A general problem in this context is the neglection of specification tests of the volatility equation. Option prices should be analyzed with respect to their sensitivity to changes of volatility specification, for example the use of exponential GARCH (EGARCH) instead of standard GARCH. The practitioner does not know *a priori* which model class fits best. Two famous examples how important correct understanding and pricing of options is for banks and industrial companies are the cases of *Metallgesellschaft* and *Barings Bank*. In the latter case, it was a problem of lacking control mechanism that led the bank into ruin. In the former case a new management did not value the open positions in oil futures correctly and realized heavy losses by clearing the positions, which was against the trading strategy of the old management. In fact, if the positions had been held some more months, they would have been even profitable for the company.

Many recent investigations show that standard GARCH models can be severely misspecified, particularly in the case of stock market data. Observed features such as the "leverage effect" first noted by Black (1976) and Christie (1982) could only be modelled by allowing for asymmetry in the volatility equation. Although, or perhaps even because an uncomprehensible amount of extensions trying to deal with the asymmetry issue appeared in the literature, see Engle and Ng (1993), the situation became worse for the practitioner: now the choice not only of the model, but even of the model class became a difficult job due to dozens of possible alternatives.

The main object of this work is to show that nonparametric ARCH models provide a powerful, flexible, and easy–to–use alternative to conventional parametric ARCH modeling. Since the path–breaking papers of Robinson (1983) and Bierens (1983), nonparametric time series analysis has gained increasing interest of mathematicians, statisticians, and econometricians. At first, application was restricted to conditional mean estimation until Härdle and Vieu (1992) and Härdle and Tsybakov (1997) provided theoretical results of conditional variance estimation for the Nadaraya–Watson and kernel weighted local polynomial estimator, respectively. Härdle, Tsybakov and Yang (1997) also presented results for local polynomial estimation of a multiple time series model with conditional covariance matrix. These papers open the field for application in various dynamic finance models such as the intertemporal capital asset pricing model (CAPM). First results of Bossaerts, Härdle and Hafner (1996) and Hafner (1997) confirm volatility asymmetry of high frequency foreign exchange rates.

The outline of this work is as follows. In Chapter 2, a description of the data used throughout the book is provided. Although the peculiarities of stock market returns and interest rates are briefly sketched, the emphasis will be on high frequency foreign exchange rate series. Some necessary adjustments and transformations of the time scale are discussed. Based on a transformed time scale, the properties of several exchange rate series are demonstrated. Also, the influence of outliers on volatility is shown by tracing back these observations to policy news.

Chapter 3 gives an overview of nonlinear time series analysis with the distinction parametric/nonparametric models. First, various different model classes and some of their properties and peculiarities are sketched. Then, nonlinearity tests are discussed, some of which are applied to the foreign exchange rate series. Finally, the principles of parametric and nonparametric prediction methods are described.

In Chapter 4, the ARCH model class is investigated in greater detail due to their importance for financial time series analysis. Estimation methods are discussed as well as applications to the foreign exchange rate series. These estimation results serve as a benchmark for subsequent nonparametric estimation.

Chapter 5 deals with nonparametric ARCH models. First, a model conditioning on only one lag – the so–called CHARN model – is discussed with its advantages and deficiencies. It is shown that models of higher order are needed to describe foreign exchange rate volatility. Therefore, models of higher order with multiplicative volatility are introduced, and estimation methods and results presented. Also, Markov models allowing for heterogeneous higher order conditional moments, e.g. skewness and kurtosis, are sketched. Estimation results show that especially conditional skewness seems to be an important feature so far neglected in most applications. Instead of specifying nonparametric analogues to ARCH(q) models, it would be more elegant and parsimonious to estimate a nonparametric analogue to a GARCH(1,1) model. This also would avoid the 'curse of dimensionality' of unrestricted nonparametric models of higher order. A possibility to estimate this NGARCH model is given in the last section. A simulation study demonstrates the performance of this estimator for generated GARCH processes.

Finally, Chapter 6 summarizes the results and gives an outlook to future work.

2
Modelling Volatility of Financial Time Series

This chapter starts with some general comments on risk and volatility in financial markets. It gives several examples of financial time series and their peculiarities. Foreign exchange rates, the HFDF93 data set, and the time scale of high frequency data are described in more detail. The results will be used in subsequent chapters.

2.1 Risk and Volatility

In finance theory, the question of finding appropriate risk measures has become increasingly important over past years. Although some intuition tells what 'risk' is, exact statistical measures are needed, and so far no unique measure has evolved as the only risk measure used in theory and practice. The reason is that economic agents, acting in asset or currency markets may have very different utility functions. The link between microeconomics and statistics starts when considering future asset returns as random variables, as it is standard among financial analysts, even though the chaos approach may become more important. Thus, the uncertainty about future returns is reflected by the utility functions of the agents, who may evaluate this uncertainty differently. The expected utility theory, pioneered by Neumann and Morgenstern (1944), is able to define concepts such as risk aversion and risk premium. Of course, the problem is that these concepts only hold for individual utility functions and not for a whole market, because not all of the agent's utility functions are known. That is why empirical investigations of the agent's behaviors are required that tell something about the (weighted) *average* risk attitude and risk premium in the market.

2.1.1 Risk and Volatility in the CAPM

Risk plays a dominant role in equilibrium models such as the capital asset pricing model (CAPM), established independently by Sharpe (1964), Lintner (1965) and Mossin (1966). The CAPM is based on the crucial assumption that either all utility functions are quadratic, i.e. only depend on the first two moments of the return distribution, or the returns are normally distributed, or both. In order to illustrate the meanings of risk and volatility in the CAPM framework, let us introduce some notation. Suppose we have a finite number A of risky assets $a, a = 1, \dots, A$, and one riskless asset. Denote by y^a the *excess* return of asset a, i.e. the return of asset a minus the return of the riskless asset. The excess return of the market portfolio, which can be thought of as a broadly diversified portfolio, is denoted by y^m. The market portfolio is a linear combination of all traded assets, i.e. $y^m = \mathbf{y}'\,\mathbf{w}$, where $\mathbf{y} = (y^1, \dots, y^A)'$ and $\mathbf{w} = (w_1, \dots, w_A)'$ is the weight vector in the CAPM equilibrium. Let $\mu^a \equiv \mathrm{E}[y^a]$ be the expected excess return of asset a, and in vector notation $\mu \equiv \mathrm{E}[\mathbf{y}]$. Also, let $\mathbf{\Sigma} = \mathrm{E}[(\mathbf{y} - \mu)(\mathbf{y} - \mu)']$ be the variance–covariance matrix of $\mathbf{y}$, and σ_{ay} be the ath column of $\mathbf{\Sigma}$. From the definition of the market portfolio it follows for its mean and variance that

$$\mu^m \equiv \mathrm{E}[y^m] = \mu'\,\mathbf{w},$$

and

$$\mathrm{Var}(y^m) = \mathbf{w}'\,\mathbf{\Sigma}\,\mathbf{w}.$$

In a two–period set-up where agents face the investment decisions in the first period and the asset's returns in the second period are random, the CAPM can be written in the well–known form

$$\mu^a = \beta^a\,\mu^m$$

for $a = 1, \dots, A$, with

$$\beta^a \equiv \frac{\mathrm{Cov}(y^a, y^m)}{\mathrm{Var}(y^m)} = \frac{\sigma'_{ay}\,\mathbf{w}}{\mathbf{w}'\,\mathbf{\Sigma}\,\mathbf{w}},$$

or simply

$$\mu = \beta\,\mu^m \tag{2.1}$$

with

$$\beta = (\beta^1, \dots, \beta^A)' = \frac{\mathbf{\Sigma}\,\mathbf{w}}{\mathbf{w}'\,\mathbf{\Sigma}\,\mathbf{w}}.$$

Thus, the expected return of any asset is equivalent to the risk–free rate plus some risk premium that is dependent on the covariance of the asset with the market portfolio. The β determines the risk of assets in the CAPM world. As a consequence of the assumptions, the risk measure is constructed by second order moments only.

In order to clarify the relationship between risk and volatility in the CAPM, assume that we have a multiperiod CAPM where agents face investment decisions at discrete time steps t, $t = 1, 2, \cdots$. Thus, the vector of excess returns can be perceived as a time series, $\mathbf{y}_t$, $t = 1, 2, \cdots$. Now assume that this time series is weakly stationary in the sense that mean and covariance matrix of $\mathbf{y}_t$ do not depend on t. Also, assume that the agents are rational in the sense that for the investment decision at time t they use all relevant information available at time t, which shall be denoted by ψ_t. Now the first two unconditional moments of $\mathbf{y}_t$, i.e. μ and Σ, may still be constants, but the conditional moments, which are relevant for the agent's decision problem, may be time varying. Let $\mathrm{E}[\mathbf{y}_t|\psi_{t-1}] \equiv \mu_t$ and $\mathrm{Var}(\mathbf{y}_t|\psi_{t-1}) \equiv \Sigma_t$. The weights of the market portfolio are adjusted in each period according to the information set. Let $\mathbf{w}_t$ be the weight vector after adjustment in period t. Then the conditional version of the CAPM is written as

$$\mu_t = \beta_t\, \mu_t^m \tag{2.2}$$

with

$$\beta_t = \frac{\Sigma_t\, \mathbf{w}_{t-1}}{\mathbf{w}_{t-1}'\, \Sigma_t\, \mathbf{w}_{t-1}}.$$

The important difference from (2.1) is the fact that the risk factor β_t in (2.2) is not a constant, but allowed to be time-varying. Note that the risk factor depends on the volatility of the individual assets, expressed by the covariance matrix Σ_t. The risk factor, however, is not only a volatility measure, but is dependent also on the weights of the market portfolio in the CAPM–equilibrium. For the econometric specification of Σ_t, the ARCH model discussed in Chapter 4 can be used as in Bollerslev, Engle and Wooldridge (1988). A typical stochastic regression model would be

$$\mathbf{y}_t = \beta_t \mu_t^m + \varepsilon_t, \tag{2.3}$$

with $\mathrm{E}[\varepsilon_t \mid \psi_{t-1}] = 0$ and $\mathrm{Var}(\varepsilon_t \mid \psi_{t-1}) = \Sigma_t$, where the covariance matrix Σ_t is modelled for example by multivariate ARCH. In this model the conditional mean depends on the risk factor β_t, which itself depends on Σ_t. Thus, (2.3) is a special case of the ARCH-in-mean (ARCH–M) model of Engle, Lilien and Robins (1987) that will be discussed in Section 4.6.

If the assumptions of the CAPM are not met, the risk factor in general is dependent not only on second order volatility measures as the conditional covariance matrix, but possibly also on other characteristics of the asset processes. A statistical model that deals with higher order characteristics of the time series is discussed in Section 5.3.

Basically similar arguments hold for other equilibrium models such as the arbitrage pricing theory (APT) of Ross (1976), which states that asset returns usually are highly correlated and linearly depend only on a small number of macroeconomic 'factors'.

Risk not only dominates equilibrium models but also macroeconomic policies and investment decisions. After the breakdown of the Bretton Woods system and the subsequent free–floating period the issue of currency–dependent risk became crucial for international capital investments and the budgeting of involved economies.

In a univariate framework that is considering a single asset price or portfolio series, the standard approach of risk assessment is to use the standard deviation or, equivalently, the variance of the corresponding stationary distribution. Besides the already mentioned assumptions of standard finance models one of the reasons is that for this measure statistical models are analytically better tractable than for other deviation measures. In the following it is shown that this definition is a quite restrictive one, excluding rational expectations of economic agents with certain utility functions that satisfy standard conditions. However, the conclusion will be that there is no unique measure available that captures all requirements.

2.1.2 Generalized Risk

Rothschild and Stiglitz (1970) defined a risk concept that is shown to be more general than the variance measure. It has the appealing property that it can be defined in three equivalent ways:

Definition 2.1 (Generalized Risk) *A random variable X is said to be weakly less risky than a random variable Y in a generalized risk sense, $X \succeq_{GR} Y$, if*

1. $Y \stackrel{\mathcal{L}}{=} X + \varepsilon$, *where ε is a fair game with respect to X, i.e.* $E[\varepsilon|X] = 0$,
2. $E[u(X)] \geq E[u(Y)]$ *for all $u \in \mathcal{U}_1$, where $\mathcal{U}_1$ represents the class of all concave utility functions,*
3. *Y can be obtained by X by applying a series of* mean preserving spreads.

As Rothschild and Stiglitz (1970) showed, all three definitions are equivalent. The first notion says that the risk of X becomes larger when conditionally independent noise is added. Note that conditional independence is stronger than zero correlation but weaker than independence.

The second definition relates risk to the behavior of all economic agents with risk aversion, i.e. with concave utility functions.

In the third definition, a *mean preserving spread* is a function $s(x)$ that puts more weight of X to the tails, with the properties $\int s(x)dx = 0$ and $\int xs(x)dx = 0$.

It follows immediately that the variance criterion is a special case of the GR concept: From 1., $E[\varepsilon|X] = 0 \Rightarrow \text{Cov}(\varepsilon, X) = 0$, so that $\text{Var}(Y) = \text{Var}(X) + \text{Var}(\varepsilon) \geq \text{Var}(X)$. Also, $\mathcal{U}_1$ contains all quadratic utility functions, for which the $\mu - \sigma$ criterion is equivalent.

In fact, this implication is only a special case of a general implication of the GR concept for the L^q norms of the involved random variables.

Proposition 2.1

$$E[\varepsilon|X] = 0 \implies E[|X + \varepsilon|^q] \geq E[|X|^q] \quad \forall q \geq 1. \tag{2.4}$$

Proof:

$$\begin{aligned} E|X + \varepsilon|^q &= E(E[|X + \varepsilon|^q \mid X]) && (2.5)\\ &\geq E(|E[X + \varepsilon \mid X]|^q) && (2.6)\\ &= E|X|^q. && (2.7) \end{aligned}$$

The inequality in (2.6) follows from Jensen's inequality for convex functions, and the equation in (2.7) from the presumption that $E[\varepsilon|X] = 0$.

The GR concept has a close relationship to the concept of second order stochastic dominance (SSD).

Definition 2.2 (Second Order Stochastic Dominance) *Without loss of generality assume two random variables X and Y with bounded support $[a, b]$ and c.d.f. $F(x)$ and $G(y)$, respectively. X weakly stochastically dominates Y, $X \succeq_{SSD} Y$, if and only if*

$$\int_a^k \{G(t) - F(t)\}\, dt \geq 0 \quad \forall k > a.$$

This definition can be shown to be equivalent to the following statements:

1. $X \succeq_{SSD} Y \Leftrightarrow Y \stackrel{\mathcal{L}}{=} X + \xi + \varepsilon$, with $\xi \leq 0$ and $E[\varepsilon \mid X + \xi] = 0$,
2. $X \succeq_{SSD} Y \Leftrightarrow E[u(X)] \geq E[u(Y)]$ for all $u \in \mathcal{U}_2$, where $\mathcal{U}_2$ represents the class of all monotonously increasing and concave utility functions.

The difference to the GR concept becomes obvious: SSD does not adjust for the mean of the distributions, and so a necessary condition for SSD to hold is that the mean of the dominant variable is not less than the mean of the dominated variable. In this respect, SSD is not suited as a risk measure. Consider for example $X \sim N(0, 1)$ and $Y \sim N(1, 100)$. By definition, X cannot dominate Y in the SSD sense, but it does obviously in the GR sense and for the variance criterion. Finally, the GR and SSD concepts are equivalent if X and Y have the same mean.

There are several points to note about the GR concept:

Remark 2.1 *The GR concept is very strong. This rather informal statement is derived by Proposition 2.1, which says that for GR dominance to hold,* every *L^q deviation measure has to give the same result, and also by the definition that* every *concave utility function has to prefer the GR dominating variable, no matter for example how the tails are weighed.*

Remark 2.2 *The GR dominance principle defines only a partial ordering over the set of distribution functions. This means that in general it is possible to have both $E[u_1(X)] > E[u_1(Y)]$ and $E[u_2(X)] < E[u_2(Y)]$. A complete ordering can only be obtained if the class of utility functions is restricted. For example, if only quadratic utility functions are considered, the $\mu - \sigma$ criterion defines a complete ordering over all distributions.*

Remark 2.3 *Among financial analysts it is widely agreed that not only deviation measures tell something about risk, but also odd moments such as the skewness . For example, if two random variables have the same mean and variance, mostly the variable with positive skewness is considered to be less risky than the one with negative skewness. This is merely an informal statement, but is not included into the GR framework.*

Some drawbacks of the GR definition become obvious in the following example.

Example 2.1 *Suppose $X \sim N(0,1)$ and $Y \sim t_5\sqrt{3/5}$. That is, $E[X] = E[Y] = 0$ and $Var(X) = Var(Y) = 1$. Every risk averter with quadratic utility function is indifferent between X and Y. Both random variables are not skewed, but the L^1 and L^4 deviation measures yield different results:*

$$E[|X|] = \sqrt{2/\pi} \approx 0.798 \geq E[|Y|] = \frac{\sqrt{3}}{\sqrt{\pi}\Gamma(5/2)} \approx 0.735,$$

and

$$E[X^4] = 3 \leq E[Y^4] = 9.$$

Thus, following Proposition 2.1, GR cannot order X and Y uniquely for all concave utility functions. Consider for example $u_1(z) = z - c|z|$ and $u_2(z) = z - cz^4$ with some constant $c > 0$. u_1 is concave, u_2 is strictly concave. It is straightforward to show that $E[u_1(X)] = -0.798c < E[u_1(Y)] = -0.735c$, but $E[u_2(X)] = -3c > E[u_2(Y)] = -9c$. The interpretation is that although both utility functions imply risk averse agents, the second agent weighs the tails of the distribution much stronger than the first. Thus, when comparing a standardized Student's t with a normal distribution, the Student's t distribution is rejected by the second because of its fat tails property.

The question remains what an appropiate general risk measure would be. Because there is no unifying theory for this problem available, it seems plausible to use common deviation measures for statistical and time series models. This will be predominantly the variance or standard deviation, but it will be argued later that the mean absolute deviation(MAD), i.e. the L^1 norm, seems to be better able to describe "risk" in financial time series. As a matter of fact, however, models with MAD as volatility measure are less tractable analytically and therefore models with standard deviation are common. For sake of comparison, most models in this work are also formulated in terms of standard deviation.

2.2 Stock Returns

Standard examples of financial time series are the prices of company–shares quoted at major stock exchanges. Unlike foreign exchange rates and interest rates these are assets, because the stock–holder partially owns the company and has certain rights. As a consequence, he is for two reasons interested in an increase of the market value of the stock. First, if he is risk averse he wants a yield that is above the risk–free rate. Second, assume that the market value of the stock decreases. This implies an increase of the debt to equity ratio, which conventionally is considered as an indicator of risk if this ratio is indeed very large. In the finance literature this is the well-known *leverage effect*, where leverage stands for the debt/equity ratio. So there is a basic asymmetry of the risk/return relationship for assets. Large negative returns tend to increase risk more than positive ones. To assess the correct functional form of volatility has important implications for risk analysis and the pricing of derivative securities. Since Black (1976) and Christie (1982) first noted the *leverage effect* for stock returns, it is an empirical fact that volatility of financial assets is asymmetric. Nevertheless, the first models dealing with conditional heteroskedasticity, namely ARCH of Engle (1982) and GARCH of Bollerslev (1986) were symmetric with respect to the conditioning lags. Subsequently, many parametric extensions allowing for asymmetry appeared in the literature, see Engle and Ng (1993) for an overview. Recently, nonparametric approaches were suggested. Pagan and Schwert (1990) compare the performance of parametric and nonparametric estimates using a stock price series, but only consider Nadaraya–Watson estimates. This section deals with the more general local polynomial estimation. For details about this nonparametric estimation technique it is referred to Section 3.4.3, which gives a general overview, and Section 5.2.1.

To give an example, a nonlinear autoregressive model is now anticipated that will be discussed more extensively in Section 5.2. In continuous-time finance, stock price series are traditionally modelled as a geometric Brownian motion, i.e.

$$dS_t/S_t = \mu dt + \sigma dW_t, \tag{2.8}$$

where $(S_t)_{t \geq 0}$ is the stock price series, μ, and σ are the drift and volatility rate, respectively, and W_t denotes the standard Wiener process. This standard model was suggested by Bachelier (1900) already and, for instance, is the basis of Black–Scholes option pricing. Itô's lemma provides that

$$y_t \equiv d(\log S_t) = (\mu - \frac{1}{2}\sigma^2)dt + \sigma dW_t, \tag{2.9}$$

so the return series y_t follows a Brownian motion with drift rate $\mu - \frac{1}{2}\sigma^2$ and volatility rate σ. For the estimation of the parameters in (2.9), a discrete time approximation of the diffusion process, for example the Euler approximation, has to be used. In practice, however, it is often observed that the drift and volatility rate are not constant, but rather depend on past realizations of the process. Therefore, consider the autoregressive model of order one in discrete time

$$y_t = f(y_{t-1}) + \sigma(y_{t-1})\xi_t, \tag{2.10}$$

where $f(\cdot)$ is the conditional mean and $\sigma(\cdot)$ the conditional standard deviation (volatility). Model (2.10) is a *conditionally heteroskedastic autoregressive nonlinear* (CHARN) model. Hafner (1996) applied this model to the returns of the daily closing notations of the Standard and Poor's 500 (S&P 500) stock index of the New York Stock Exchange from August 30, 1993 to December 29, 1995 ($n = 541$). The S&P 500 index is much broader than the Dow Jones industrial index, so that it can be better regarded as a market portfolio. For the estimation of the mean and volatility function, nonparametric local linear estimation as described in Section 5.2.1 is used. In Figure 2.1, the index series s_t is shown together with their returns $y_t = \log(s_t) - \log(s_{t-1})$. Summary statistics of the returns are given in Table 2.1. The null hypothesis of a Gaussian distribution is rejected, because the empirical estimates of kurtosis and skewness are not in accordance with the theoretical values of a Gaussian distribution: The coefficient of kurtosis is significantly larger than three, assuming a standard error of $\sqrt{24/n} = 0.211$. This corresponds to the conditional heteroskedasticity, which induces a fat-tailed distribution of index returns. Also, the coefficient of skewness is significantly different from zero (standard error $\sqrt{6/n} = 0.105$), so the distribution can be assumed to be asymmetric. Considering both coefficients, a significant deviation from a Gaussian distribution is detected. This result is typical for financial time series.

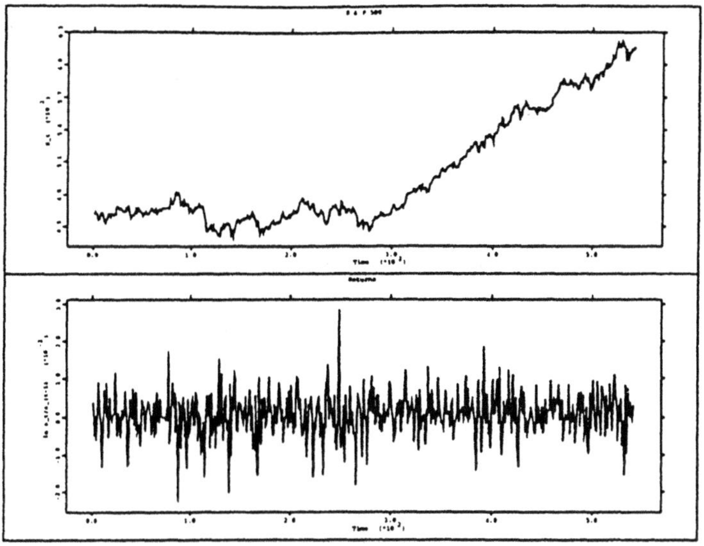

FIGURE 2.1. *Daily closing notations of the S&P 500 stock index from Aug 30, 1993 to Dec 29, 1995, $n = 541$ (upper plot), and corresponding returns (lower plot).*

Period	Min	Max	Mean	Var	Skew	Kurt
08/30/93 – 12/29/95	–.023	.029	5.3E–04	3.2E–05	–.2310	5.20
08/30/93 – 11/29/94	–.023	.029	5.4E–04	3.8E–05	–.1899	5.42
11/30/94 – 12/29/95	–.016	.019	1.1E–03	2.5E–05	–.1207	3.96

TABLE 2.1. *Summary statistics of S&P 500 returns.*

Note from the upper part of Figure 2.1 that there was a distinct upward trend in 1995, whereas in 1993/94 the index remained at about equal level. To see what the trend–behavior implies for the distribution of the returns, the series was divided into two equal parts. The corresponding summary statistics are reported in Table 2.1. Note that the unconditional variance and the coefficient of kurtosis are smaller in the subsample with upward trend.

Autocorrelations of returns, squared and absolute returns are given in Table 2.2. Although not significant, the positive autocorrelation of the returns at the first lag is remarkable. More strikingly, the typically observed highly significant positive autocorrelations of squared and absolute returns are not obtained. Of course this does not imply that the data are conditionally homoskedastic, because there might be other than symmetric functional dependencies. Indeed, this will be the result of nonparametric estimation.

k	$\rho_k(y_t)$	$\rho_k(y_t^2)$	$\rho_k(\|y_t\|)$
1	0.039279	0.006387	-0.003890
2	-0.012534	-0.006006	-0.010675
3	-0.021982	0.008299	0.048371
4	-0.055026	-0.014099	0.000414
5	-0.069647	0.014955	0.020734
6	0.060704	0.040139	0.053635
7	-0.034398	-0.030428	0.005560
8	-0.029333	-0.009197	-0.007555
9	0.002500	0.056853	0.0525430
10	-0.029516	0.124391*	0.052323

TABLE 2.2. *Autocorrelations of S&P 500 returns ($\rho_k(y_t)$), squared ($\rho_k(y_t^2)$) and absolute ($\rho_k(|y_t|)$) returns for the first ten lags k. A star marks asymptotic 5% significance.*

The model (2.10) is estimated by local linear estimation with quartic kernel and the resulting plots for the conditional mean and conditional variance are shown in Figure 2.2 and 2.3, respectively. Bandwidths are required for the estimation of $E[y_t \mid y_{t-1}]$ and $E[y_t^2 \mid y_{t-1}]$. In both cases $h = 0.02$ was chosen according to cross–validation criteria. For calculation of the confidence bands no bias–correction was performed. Experiments with the Linton–Nielsen estimate (Linton and Nielsen (1994)) or smaller bandwidths did not yield substantially different results. For details on bandwidth selection and uniform confidence bands, see Section 5.2.2 and 5.2.3, respectively.

The mean function is nonlinear especially at the boundaries. However, in the part of the plot where there are more than 99% of the returns, i.e. in the interval [-0.018; 0.018], the function is quite linear with positive slope, which corresponds to the previously found positive autocorrelation at the first lag.

The estimate of the volatility function contradicts standard GARCH–type models: volatility is far from being symmetric. Rather, the estimate of volatility is highest for large negative returns (shocks) and declines for higher returns. For large positive returns there is a small increase in volatility but less than the corresponding increase for negative returns. This result underlines the frequently reported leverage effect for stock return data, but it also indicates that standard GARCH models applied to stock return data can be severely misspecified.

Figure 2.4 shows the time plot of estimated volatility over the whole period. Distributional statistics and autocorrelations of the estimated residuals $\hat{\xi}_t$ are given in Table 2.3 and Table 2.4, respectively.

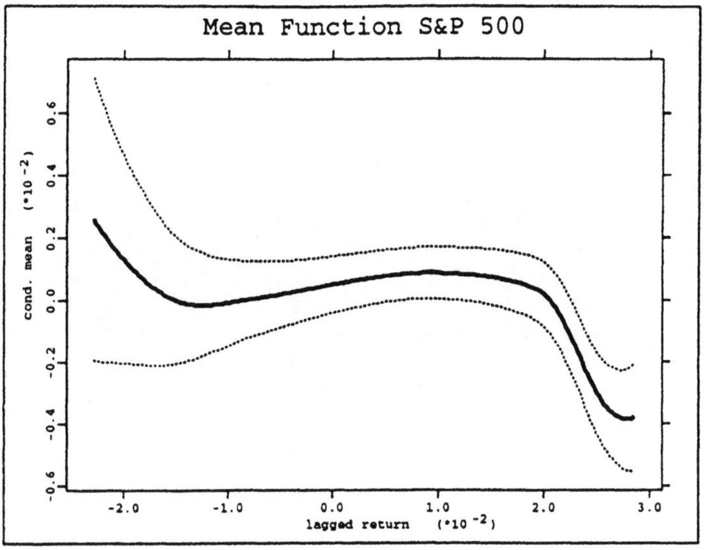

FIGURE 2.2. *S&P 500 returns at t vs. t − 1: local linear estimate of the conditional mean and approximate 95% confidence bands. The bandwidth* $h = 0.02$ *was used.*

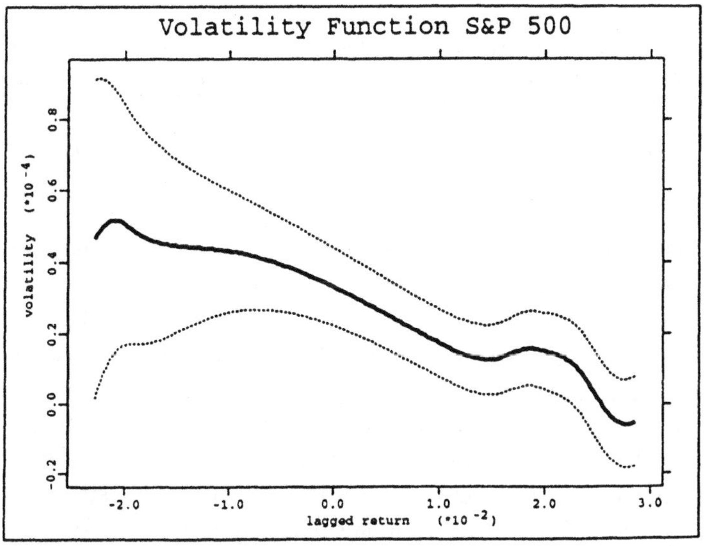

FIGURE 2.3. *S&P 500 returns at t vs. t − 1: local linear estimate of the conditional variance and approximate 95% confidence bands. The bandwidth* $h = 0.02$ *was used for the estimation of the conditional mean and for* $E[y_t^2 \mid y_{t-1}]$.

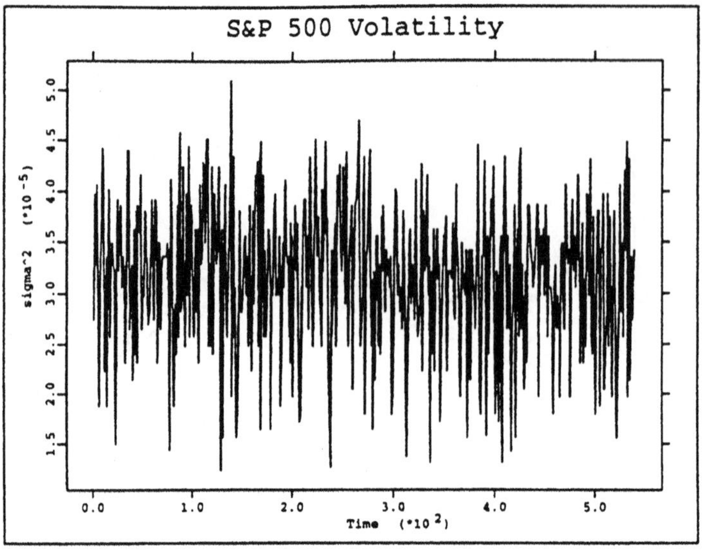

FIGURE 2.4. *Estimated volatility of S&P 500 returns over the period 08/30/93 - 12/29/95.*

Period	Min	Max	Mean	Var	Skew	Kurt
08/30/93 - 12/29/95	-3.77	4.89	.102	1.01	−.09	4.74
08/30/93 - 11/29/94	-3.77	4.89	−.006	1.20	−.02	5.00
11/30/94 - 12/29/95	-2.66	3.21	.206	0.80	−.04	3.69

TABLE 2.3. *Summary statistics of estimated residuals* $\hat{\xi}_t$.

The coefficient of kurtosis of the estimated residuals is still significantly different from three for both subsamples. Thus, not only the unconditional but also the conditional distribution is leptokurtic. On the other hand, the coefficient of skewness is not significantly different from zero, so it is conjectured that skewness is increased by asymmetric conditional heteroskedasticity.

Positive first order autocorrelation has been reduced from 0.039 of y_t to 0.017 of $\hat{\xi}_t$. As the reduction of conditional heteroskedasticity for most lags, however, this result is not significant. Further specification tests would have to compare these results with the residuals of parametric GARCH–type models. Also, parametric and nonparametric tests against asymmetry are called for in future estimation of stock market volatility.

k	$\rho_k(\hat{\xi}_t)$	$\rho_k(\hat{\xi}_t^2)$	$\rho_k(\lvert\hat{\xi}_t\rvert)$
1	0.0169033	-0.0352469	-0.0354939
2	-0.0397547	-0.0007755	-0.0054394
3	-0.0535756	-0.0289742	0.0176977
4	-0.0449123	-0.0090410	-0.0010348
5	-0.0728425	0.0169027	0.0243436
6	0.0286773	-0.027089	-0.0109955
7	-0.0296887	-0.0375203	-0.0158725
8	-0.0309800	-0.0111481	-0.0018047
9	0.0142636	0.0406406	0.0558258
10	-0.0446975	0.0988401*	0.0636360

TABLE 2.4. *Autocorrelations of estimated residuals* ($\rho_k(\hat{\xi}_t)$)*, squared* ($\rho_k(\hat{\xi}_t^2)$) *and absolute* ($\rho_k(|\hat{\xi}_t|)$) *residuals for the first ten lags* k*. A star marks asymptotic* 5% *significance.*

2.3 Interest Rates

Under certainty, the future spot rate has to be equivalent to the corresponding forward rate in order to guarantee absence of arbitrage, so that bond pricing in such an economy is an easy exercise. However, the economy is uncertain and theories about the equilibrium prices of bonds have to be developed. Indeed, an uncomprehensible variety of term structure models exists in the literature. A basic distinction can be made according to how many factors are used to explain the bond prices. The expectations hypothesis with its various expressions claims that the prices of bonds are only determined by expectations of future spot rates. On the other hand, the liquidity preference theory states the existence of a liquidity or risk premium for bonds with longer maturity. This tries to explain the empirically observed 'normal' term structure, i.e. higher yields on long–term bonds than on short–term bonds.

To give an example, a very general class of single-factor models, the so-called *affine* single factor term structure model, can be written as

$$V_t(\tau) = \exp\{a(\tau) + b(\tau)r_t\} \tag{2.11}$$

with r_t denoting the spot interest rate, $V_t(\tau)$ the price of a zero–coupon bond at time t for payment of one Dollar at time $t + \tau$, and $a(\cdot)$ and $b(\cdot)$ differentiable functions in τ. The class is called affine, because the yield-to-maturity $y_t(\tau) = -(1/\tau)\log V_t(\tau)$ is an affine function in the spot rate. The most prominent single factor models are special cases of (2.11). A crucial part is the model for the dynamic behavior of the spot rate. In most models, a diffusion process of the form

$$dr_t = \mu(r_t, t)dt + \sigma(r_t, t)dW_t$$

is assumed. For example, the model of Cox, Ingersoll and Ross (1985) is given by

$$dr_t = \kappa(\mu - r_t)dt + \sigma\sqrt{r_t}dW_t, \tag{2.12}$$

with constant, positive parameters κ, μ and σ. This diffusion process restricts the spot rate to be positive. Unlike a random walk it does not diverge but rather revert to the mean. This appealing *mean reversion* property is diminished, however, by the linear variance rate and the lack of an explicit risk premium. In discrete time, the ARCH literature soon established models allowing for time–varying risk–premia. Engle et al. (1987) formulated an ARCH–M model with log conditional variance as a proxy for risk premium. For general risk premium models in discrete time, see Section 4.6. Ingersoll (1987, pp.407) derives a two-factor model where, written in discrete time, the first difference of the spot rate follows an ARMA(1,1) process. This leads us to suggest a general nonlinear AR(1) model for the spot rate differences allowing for conditional heteroskedasticity, i.e.

$$\Delta r_t = f(\Delta r_{t-1}) + s(\Delta r_{t-1})\xi_t, \tag{2.13}$$

where $\Delta r_t \equiv r_t - r_{t-1}$, and ξ_t is an *i.i.d.* mean zero, variance one innovation. This model is still a Markov chain, but the states are now independent of the level. A technical advantage of (2.13) is the empirical fact that Δr_t can in most cases be considered as a stationary time series, so that standard estimation procedures can be applied. For further details, see Section 5.2.

A different issue concerning interest rates is the prediction of the *levels* of interest rates, which in most empirical contributions could not be rejected to contain a unit root. An example is the competition of various 60–days prediction performances of the yield to ten–year German government loans, as in Breckling and Hillmer (1996). The time series of the levels and first differences are plotted in Figure 2.5 and 2.6, respectively, where the prediction period is emphasized graphically. Standard time series approaches using the stationary first differences, as in Härdle and Hafner (1996), do not seem to be sufficient to give substantial improvement over naive prediction, although nonlinear ARCH effects were detected that in turn may be used for risk premium models. For details about nonlinear prediction and the results of the competition, see Section 3.6.

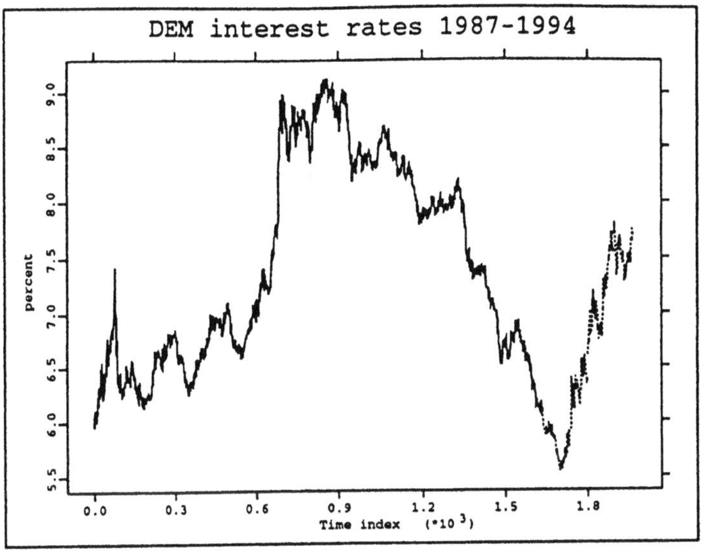

FIGURE 2.5. *Time series of the ten-year DEM interest rates from 87/07/01 to 94/12/23. The prediction period 93/12/23 to 94/12/23 is the dashed part of the line.*

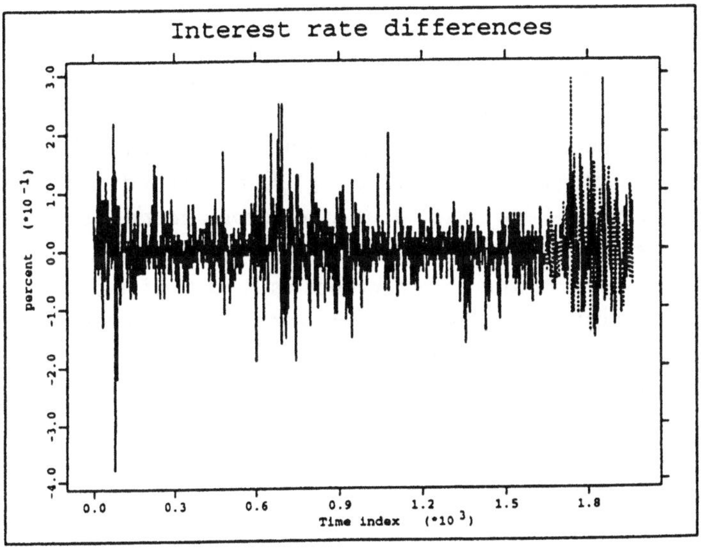

FIGURE 2.6. *Time series of the first differences of the ten-year DEM interest rates from 87/07/01 to 94/12/23. The prediction period 93/12/23 to 94/12/23 is the dashed part of the line.*

2.4 Foreign Exchange Rates

The behavior of foreign exchange (FX) rates has been subject of many recent investigations. A correct understanding of the foreign exchange rate dynamics has important implications for international asset pricing theories, the pricing of contingent claims and policy–oriented questions.

Whether there exists a risk premium in the foreign exchange market is still controversial, but it would explain many empirical observations. Since the literature on market efficiency has tried to shed some empirical light on the rational expectations paradigm (see the reviews of Fama (1970), Fama (1991), and LeRoy (1989)), it became clear that the two hypotheses of market efficency and existence of a risk premium cannot be disentangled: rejection of empirical tests based on the difference of future spot rates and forward rates could mean rejection of either hypothesis, or of both. The empirical findings of Frankel (1986) and Boothe and Longworth (1986), to name just two important papers, is clearly against the joint hypothesis. How models with risk premiums are formulated in the ARCH framework will be discussed in Section 4.6.

2.4.1 The FX Market

The foreign exchange market is by far the largest financial market. According to the Wall Street Journal of March 1 1990, the average daily FX trading volume is about $ 650 billion. Compared to this, the NYSE's largest volume day, Oct. 19 1987, only saw $ 21 billion of volume.

The market is decentralized with the main trading locations being Far East (mainly Tokyo, Singapore and Hong Kong), Europe (London and Frankfurt) and North America (New York). It is an electronic market, active 24 hours a day. Banks act as market makers and place bid– and ask–quotes on the screen. Central information collectors such as Reuters provide the quotes for the market makers. Actual trade takes place over the phone. This is the reason why there is no information about actual prices and trading volume. By far the largest part of trading occurs in US Dollars, which assumes the role of a numéraire for the minor rates. Although there is some important central bank intervention money, by far the largest part of the FX market is speculation by the market makers.

2.4.2 High Frequency Data

High frequency financial data analysis has become a broad research field during the last decade. This is due to improved real–time information systems, relatively cheap data supply by banks and research institutions and improved storing facilities. The first major publication about intra–daily foreign exchange rates was Wasserfallen and Zimmermann (1985), which already reported typical statistical properties, namely negative autocorrelation of the returns at the first lags for time intervals of one to ten minutes. Goodhart and Figliuoli (1991) extended the analysis using one minute intervals. Both papers have the problem that the data sets are not representative, because only single days were selected.

The reason why high frequency data analysis sheds new light on the econometrics of FX markets is twofold. First, after having found that GARCH processes fit daily and weekly FX rates well in most cases (Hsieh (1989), Baillie and Bollerslev (1989)) the topic of temporal aggregation (Drost and Nijman (1993)) arose. It was shown that under suitable conditions the parameters of a model estimated at a given frequency can be uniquely transformed to the parameters of the same model at a different frequency. Recent investigations of research institutes as Olsen & Associates and others revealed that temporal aggregation does not hold for high frequency data. Thus, it is not possible to obtain the parameters of a model based on a weekly scale, say, from parameter estimates based on a 20 minute scale, and vice versa. More evidence on this point will be given in Section 4.9.

Second, by using tick–by–tick data one is able to observe microeconomic features of the market that disappear when the data are aggregated. Two examples are the negative autocorrelation of the returns and the risk–dependent bid–ask spreads. Analyzing these features yields information about the efficiency of the market.

For the estimation of a conditionally heteroskedastic model, an important issue is the correct specification of the conditional density. Since Weiss (1986b) it is known that quasi maximum likelihood estimation (QMLE) of ARCH models provides consistent, although not efficient estimators in the case of misspecification. Engle and Gonzalez-Rivera (1991) simulate relative efficiencies (as variance ratios of MLE and QMLE) for a variety of distributional assumptions. For example, if the true conditional density is a Student's t with five degrees of freedom, the relative efficiency is as low as 41%. This situation becomes worse when dealing with intra-daily data, because the deviation of the unconditional return density from normality increases when the sampling interval is decreased.

The literature on high frequency data is still very scarce. Recently, the first conference on high frequency data in finance (HFDF) was held in Zürich. A review about high frequency data is given by Guillaume et al. (1994).

FX rate	n	Mean	Var	Skew	Kurt	$\rho_1(y)$	$\rho_1(\|y\|)$
CHF/USD	10,171	-5.4E-06	3.4E-08	-0.5423	34.9	-0.096	0.211
CHF/DEM	10,041	-3.1E-08	2.0E-07	-0.0451	13.7	-0.340	0.322
DEM/GBP	12,778	-3.6E-06	2.0E-07	0.3053	22.1	-0.256	0.238

TABLE 2.5. *Summary statistics of the FX returns in five minute intervals, empty intervals skipped. ρ_1 denotes first order autocorrelation.*

2.4.3 The Chemical Bank Data Sets

Basic feature of intra–daily quotes is the irregularity of their occurence. Market activity is usually very low in lunch hours, overnight, and over the weekend. One way of treating the quote arrival process is just neglection of the seasonal structure and observation on a fixed scale in calendar time. For example, one can define discrete time intervals of five minutes, say, take the last observed quote in each interval and skip those intervals that are empty. Another way to interpret this procedure is that implicitly a filter variable 'activity' is used, taking the value one when at least one quote was observed, and zero if not. This was basically the procedure of the Chemical Bank to generate tractable FX rate series. We are indebted to Prof. A. Kirman and the Chemical Bank for generous provision of the data sets. The quotes were taken from Telerate information system screens. Together with the last quote, the highest and lowest quotes are recorded for each interval. Here, some descriptive statistics are given for the Swiss Franken against U.S. Dollar (CHF/USD), Swiss Franken against the Deutsche Mark (CHF/DEM), and Deutsche Mark against British Pound Sterling (DEM/GBP), each one covering about two months in summer 1994 (CHF/USD is recorded for the period 94/06/10 until 94/08/11, CHF/DEM for 94/06/14 until 94/08/16, and DEM/GBP for 94/06/10 until 94/08/14). Summary statistics are given in Table 2.5.

There are at least two drawbacks of these data sets. First, no error filter is used explicitly, such that erroneous data recording is either neglected or removed in a way that is not reconstructable. This applies in principle to all aggregated data of this type. Second, it will be seen in Section 2.4.6 that data aggregated to an equispaced series in calendar time have seasonal volatility. Models based on this scale have to take care of seasonality explicitly, as in Baillie and Bollerslev (1990). An alternative is to remove seasonality, based on tick by tick–data, as will be discussed in Section 2.4.6.

2.4.4 The Data Set HFDF93

The data set HFDF93 was acquired from Olsen & Associates, Zürich. It contains bid and ask quotes for the rates Deutsche Mark against US Dol-

```
; Tick extraction for DEM^USD
; --------------------------
;
;
; Filtering: O&A standard filter for historical tests
;
;   date      time        price     country       filter
;                                      city       Good (1)
;CCYY-MM-DD  (GMT)     bid     ask          bank
1992-10-01 00:00:14 1.4116 1.4121 392 01 0058 1
1992-10-01 00:00:54 1.4108 1.4118 036 02 0130 1
1992-10-01 00:01:00 1.4110 1.4120 392 01 0452 1
1992-10-01 00:01:18 1.4115 1.4120 392 01 0041 1
1992-10-01 00:01:24 1.4107 1.4117 036 02 0130 1
1992-10-01 00:01:30 1.4115 1.4125 036 02 0089 1
1992-10-01 00:01:36 1.4113 1.4123 392 01 0041 1
1992-10-01 00:01:42 1.4110 1.4120 392 01 0053 1
1992-10-01 00:01:54 1.4118 1.4128 392 01 0041 1
1992-10-01 00:02:06 1.4113 1.4123 344 01 0055 1
1992-10-01 00:02:18 1.4115 1.4130 702 01 0126 1
1992-10-01 00:02:24 1.4105 1.4115 036 02 0130 1
```

TABLE 2.6. *An excerpt of the DEM/USD HFDF93 data set.*

lar (DEM/USD), Japanese Yen against US Dollar (JPY/USD) and Japanese Yen against Deutsche Mark (JPY/DEM) during the time Oct 1 1992, 0:00:00 and Sept 30 1993, 23:59:59 GMT. For each pair of bid– and ask–quotes, the time in GMT, the quoting bank and the location of the bank are recorded. The quotes are collected from the Reuters FXFX page, which is considered to be a broad but not 'complete' data supply. For more information about this data set, cf. Dacorogna, Müller, Nagler, Olsen and Pictet (1993) and, generally about FX rate data suppliers and intra–daily FX data, Goodhart and Figliuoli (1991). To illustrate the information of the data set, an excerpt of the DEM/USD data file is given in Table 2.6. the last column contains a filter that indicates erroneous records. The amount of filtered data is unusually low.

We will concentrate on the most liquid market with the smallest bid–ask spreads and therefore the most "efficient" market – DEM/USD. Most analyses also include the Japanese Yen, i.e. the rates JPY/USD and JPY/DEM. European cross rates are of limited comparability to the three major rates because of restrictions in the European Monetary System (EMS), although since the decision to widen the variability bands to 15% in August 1993 the rates have been effectively free–floating. However, there is in general much less volume of these rates than volume of the three major rates.

Also, a 'news' file with major macroeconomic and political news is provided. This will be used in Section 2.4.9 to trace back jumps in the series to news, but before looking for jumps related to news it is necessary to give some definitions and remove those jumps that are an artefact of nontrading hours.

2.4.5 Some Definitions

Before looking at the statistical properties of the FX rates it is necessary to introduce some notation. First, a definition of white noise is given that will be relevant for time series models discussed in subsequent chapters.

Definition 2.3 (White Noise) *The process ε_t is said to be white noise if and only if ε_t has zero mean and covariance function*

$$\gamma(\tau) = \begin{cases} \sigma^2, & \text{if } \tau = 0 \\ 0, & \text{if } \tau \neq 0. \end{cases} \tag{2.14}$$

Note that *i.i.d.* processes with finite variance are white noise, but not necessarily vice versa. Later, it will be useful to distinguish dependent white noise from *i.i.d.* processes. Therefore, the latter will sometimes be called *strict white noise*, the former *weak white noise*.

Let $\{A_t, t \geq 0\}$ and $\{B_t, t \geq 0\}$ denote the ask and bid quote processes in continuous time for some choice of the time unity (20 minutes, say). The logarithmic quote process $\{q_t, t \geq 0\}$ is defined as $q_t \equiv (\log A_t + \log B_t)/2$. This transformation has become standard, since it has the appealing property that the logarithmic quote process of the inverted exchange rate, given by $\{A_t^{-1}\}$ and $\{B_t^{-1}\}$, is just $\{-q_t\}$. If the quotes are observed on a discrete regular time grid and no quote is observed exactly at the grids, the last quote is taken because it is assumed to be the relevant one. This common procedure was first applied by Wasserfallen and Zimmermann (1985). If several quotes arrive per time interval, also the last one is taken. By taking averages one would induce spurious first order autocorrelation, cf. Wasserfallen and Zimmermann (1985).

Returns in continuous time are measured by the process $\{dq_t\}$, but since we observe the quotes in discrete time, returns are defined as the first difference of the logarithmic quotes.

Definition 2.4 (Exchange Rate Return) *Exchange rate returns in discrete time are defined by*

$$y_t \equiv q_t - q_{t-\Delta t}, \quad t = \Delta t, 2\Delta t, \cdots.$$

FX rate	DEM/USD	JPY/USD	JPY/DEM
Number of data	1,472,241	570,814	158,979
Filtered data (%)	0.36	0.54	0.31
Average per day	4034	1564	436
Monday	5415	1993	588
Tuesday	6008	2367	666
Wednesday	5934	2275	633
Thursday	5707	2277	618
Friday	4926	1856	515
Saturday	2	2	1
Sunday	212	164	25
Mean abs value	1.8362E–04	3.0169E–04	4.0590E–04
Mean	9.8945E–08	-2.1651E–07	-1.6916E–06
Variance	8.3468E–08	1.0025E–04	4.5718E–04
Skewness	2.2059E–02	-2.8616E–02	7.9087E–02
Kurtosis	4.2689e+01	3.5569e+04	2.1005e+04

TABLE 2.7. *Summary statistics of the FX returns in calendar time, tick by tick.*

To keep the notation simple, the dependence of y_t on Δt is not written explicitly, but it is important to keep this in mind. Because the time series properties of bid– and ask–quotes are very similar, the loss of information due to the aggregation is small. Attempts to exploit the information contained in the bid–ask spreads for volatility models have not been very successful. We will come back to this point in Section 2.4.8. Summary statistics of the FX returns in transaction time (tick by tick) as reported by Olsen & Associates are given in Table 2.7.

Definition 2.5 (Unconditional Volatility) *For some $\delta > 0$ let*

$$V_\delta(y_t) \equiv (E|y_t - E[y_t]|^\delta)^{1/\delta}$$

be the volatility of the returns depending on Δt.

Two special cases of the volatility definition are the mean absolute deviation for $\delta = 1$ and the standard deviation for $\delta = 2$. For a given sample period S and time interval Δt, the number of observations is given by $n = S/\Delta t$. Mean and volatility of y_t are estimated by $\hat{\mathrm{E}}(y_t) = n^{-1}\sum_{i=1}^n y_{i\Delta t}$ and $\hat{V}_\delta(y_t) = (n^{-1}\sum_{i=1}^n |y_{i\Delta t} - \hat{\mathrm{E}}(y_t)|^\delta)^{1/\delta}$, respectively.

2.4.6 Seasonal Volatility and the Time Scale

At first, it is necessary to deal with the subject of *seasonal volatility*. To see this, consider the following procedure: The quotes are observed every

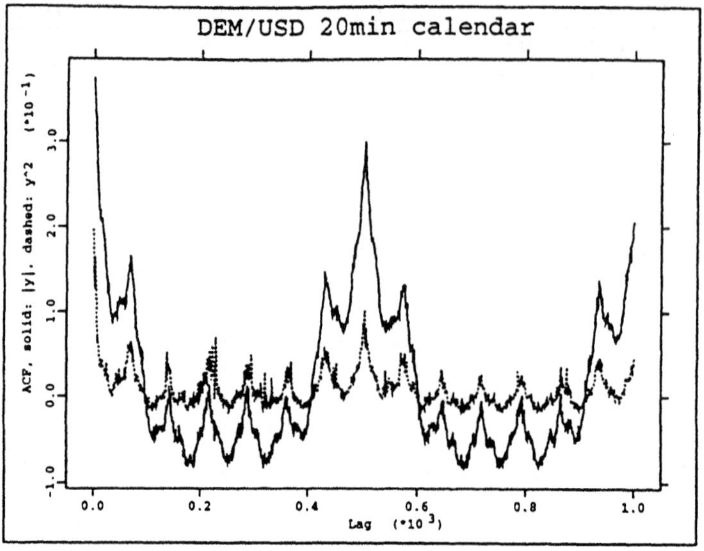

FIGURE 2.7. *Autocorrelation Function of DEM/USD squared returns (dashed) and absolute returns (solid) in calendar time up to lag 1000. The time interval length is 20 minutes.*

twenty minutes, i.e. $\Delta t = 20$min. The returns from this series were calculated according to the definition given above. Figure 2.7 depicts the autocorrelation function of the absolute and squared returns of the DEM/USD rate. The daily and weakly patterns in the ACF are clearly visible and much more distinct for the absolute returns.

Not all autocorrelation plots are shown, but it is worth noting that the Yen rates have much less pronounced seasonality. To see that seasonality is not a peculiarity of DEM/USD, consider the Chemical Bank data sets. Figure 2.8, Figure 2.9, and Figure 2.10 show the ACF of CHF/USD, CHF/DEM, and DEM/GBP, respectively. Skipping empty intervals obviously removes weekly seasonality, but not daily. This holds for all rates.

We will focus on the HFDF93 series, and in particular on the DEM/USD rate, which displays the strongest seasonal effects. A deformed time scale is used, which is more flexible than the dummy–variable method of Baillie and Bollerslev (1990).

Usual time series analysis is based not on a physical time scale, but on a business one. For intra–daily data, we can analogously define the time intervals to be longer in low business periods and shorter in busy ones. This idea is not new: Mandelbrot and Taylor (1967) defined the transaction–based

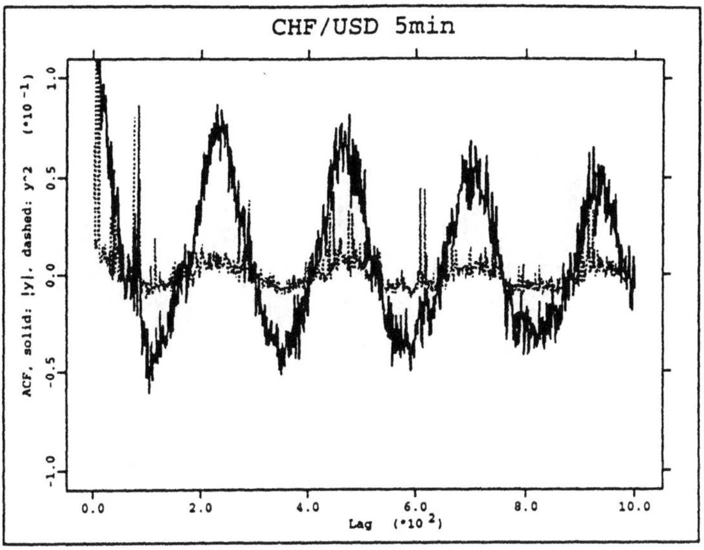

FIGURE 2.8. *Autocorrelation Function of CHF/USD squared returns (dashed) and absolute returns (solid) over the period 94/06/10 to 94/08/11 in five minute intervals and empty intervals skipped. The plot is truncated at lag 1000 and for the first lags at* $|\rho_k(\cdot)| \approx 0.1$.

'clock' referring to the transaction volume in stock markets, using the fact that volume and volatility are highly correlated. Without information about volume in FX markets, it is necessary to refer to some other 'activity' measure that is closely related to volatility. For this, several procedures seem to be possible:

- Pick every k^{th} (50th, say) observation of the tick–by–tick data.
- Define a time interval Δt (e.g. 20 minutes) and a seasonality period (one week). Count the number of quotes in each time interval. Construct subsamples consisting of all time intervals belonging to the same season, for example 12:00 – 12:20 GMT. Finally, average the number of quotes in each subsample.
- Same procedure as before, but instead of the number of quotes calculate volatility directly for each time interval and average over the subsamples. A useful specification of volatility, i.e. choice of δ in Definition 2.5, has to be applied.

Figure 2.11 and Figure 2.12 show the ACF of squared and absolute returns for the first procedure with $k = 50$, for DEM/USD and JPY/DEM,

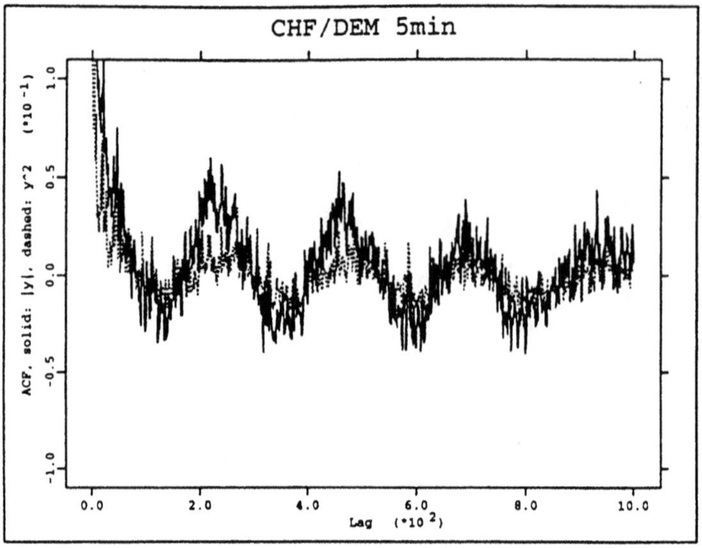

FIGURE 2.9. *Autocorrelation Function of CHF/DEM squared returns (dashed) and absolute returns (solid) over the period 94/06/14 to 94/08/16 in five minute intervals and empty intervals skipped. The plot is truncated at lag 1000 and for the first lags at* $|\rho_k(\cdot)| \approx 0.1$.

respectively. Fifty ticks correspond on average to about eighteen minutes for DEM/USD, and about 165 minutes for JPY/DEM. Obviously, this procedure is able to remove weekly seasonality, that is mainly the weekend effect, but not daily seasonality for DEM/USD. The seasonal patterns of JPY/DEM are much less pronounced.

The same applies to the second procedure when the average number of quotes, as plotted in Figure 2.13, is used to rescale the time intervals proportionally. This was done in Bossaerts, Hafner and Härdle (1996).

An important drawback of the number of quotes as an 'activity' measure is the crucial dependence on the data supplier. Comparison of the HFDF93 data set (recall from Section 2.4.4 that the quotes are taken from Reuters screens) with the one of Chemical Bank (Telerate screens) revealed that especially in low–business hours, e.g. overnight, there are many 'missing observations' in the HFDF93 data set. This is likely to be a consequence of different market observations of the data supplier. For example, Reuters concentrates on the opening hours of Europe and America, whereas Telerate dominates the Far East region. However, the number of quotes is a biased estimate of volatility as can be seen by comparing Figure 2.13 with Figure 2.15: The second intra–day peak, i.e. Europe's opening hours, is higher for the number of quotes

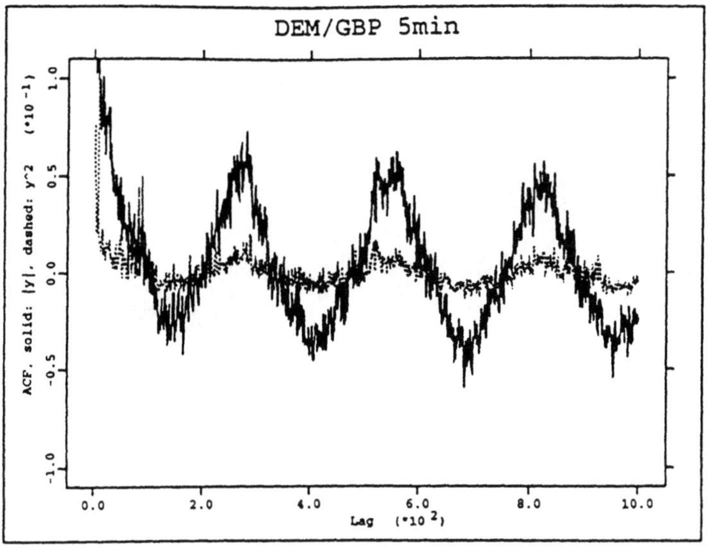

FIGURE 2.10. *Autocorrelation Function of DEM/GBP squared returns (dashed) and absolute returns (solid) over the period 94/06/10 to 94/08/14 in five minute intervals and empty intervals skipped. The plot is truncated at lag 1000 and for the first lags at* $|\rho_k(\cdot)| \approx 0.1$.

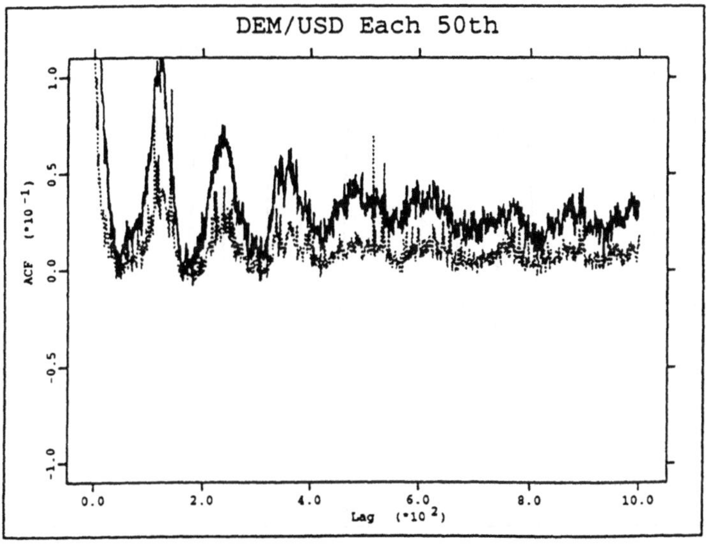

FIGURE 2.11. *Autocorrelation Function of DEM/USD squared returns (dashed) and absolute returns (solid) up to lag 1000. The data were generated by picking every* 50th *quote of the HFDF93 data file.*

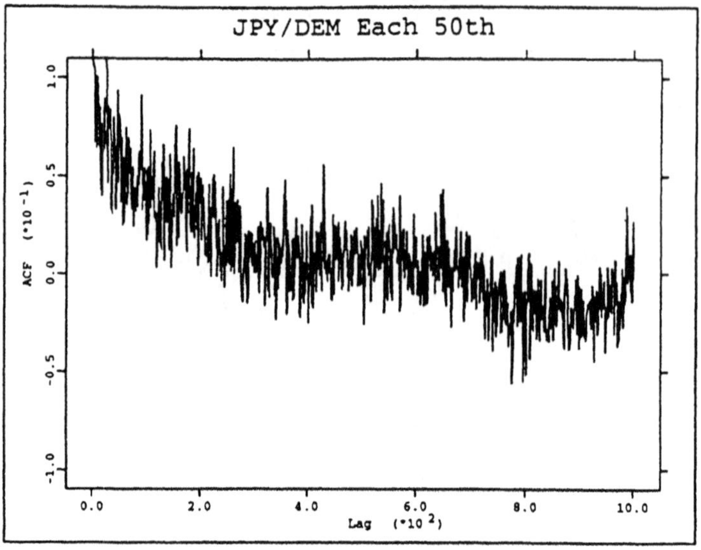

FIGURE 2.12. *Autocorrelation Function of JPY/DEM absolute returns up to lag 1000. The ACF of squared returns is quite similar. The data were generated by picking every* 50th *quote of the HFDF93 data file.*

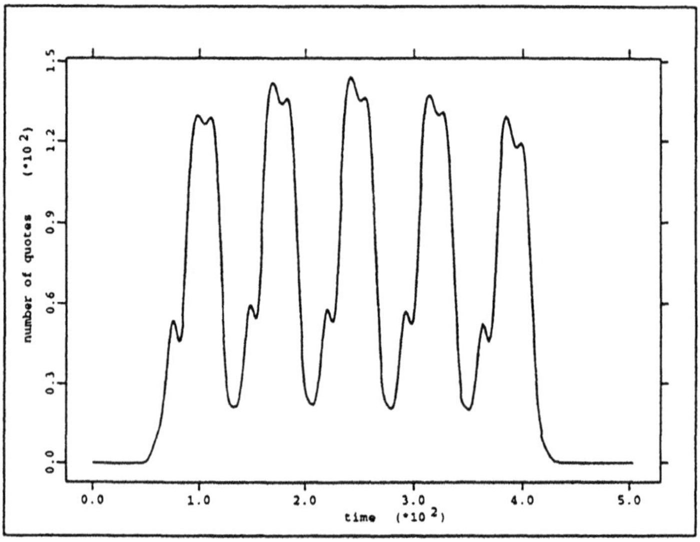

FIGURE 2.13. *Number of quotes as a function of 20-minute intervals during a week for the DEM/USD rate. The function was smoothed with the Nadaraya–Watson smoother, quartic kernel, and bandwidth* $h = 5$.

than for activity, which is a power transformation of volatility, see Definition 2.6 below. Thus, although the numbers of quotes on the Reuters FXFX page for DEM/USD are approximately equal for the opening hours of Europe and America, the impact on volatility is stronger for the quotes recorded in late afternoon GMT.

The third procedure was tested by using two measures of volatility, the first being a sometimes used alternative to Definition 2.5 above, i.e. (i) highs - lows, and (ii) mean absolute returns for each time interval. After proportional adjustments of the time scale, both measures failed to remove daily seasonality satisfactorily. The problem is that volatility does not depend linearly on the time interval. This is plausible: In continuous time the standard deviation of a Wiener process over a small time interval dt is proportional to $\sqrt{dt}$, and analogously in discrete time the standard deviation of a Gaussian process is proportional to $\sqrt{\Delta t}$. Now, the FX returns are not Gaussian, so it cannot be followed that their volatility is proportional to the square root of the time interval. The easiest way is to estimate the scaling exponent. The empirical "scaling law" first noted by Müller, Dacorogna, Olsen, Pictet, Schwarz and Morgenegg (1990) relates the time interval Δt, over which the returns are measured, to volatility, i.e.

$$V_\delta(y_t) = C_1(\Delta t)^{\alpha_\delta}, \tag{2.15}$$

with a constant C_1 depending on the FX rate. The scaling exponent α_δ is estimated by OLS of the equation

$$\log \hat{V}_\delta(y_t) = \log C_1 + \alpha_\delta \log(\Delta t) + u \tag{2.16}$$

where u is a mean zero error term with variance that depends on the time interval. For estimation, a medium range of time intervals should be chosen, because (i) for large time intervals n is small such that the 'statistical' variance increases, and (ii) for small time intervals the 'statistical' variance is small but the returns are of the order of the spreads, which induces a 'microeconomic' variance due to the uncertainty about the true returns. Details on this point are given by Müller, Dacorogna and Pictet (1995). For calculation of the volatilities, μ was neglected here as in Müller et al. (1990) due to the small value compared to the standard deviation, i.e. $\hat{\mathrm{E}}(y_t)/\hat{V}_2$ =3.4E–04 and $\hat{\mathrm{E}}(y_t)/\hat{V}_1$ of the same order for DEM/USD.

According to Müller et al. (1990), the estimates of α_1 and α_2 are 0.58 and 0.52, respectively, for most foreign exchange rate series, indicating a substantial deviation from a Gaussian random walk. The scaling law for $\delta = 1$ is visualized in Figure 2.14, which plots the OLS regression of (2.16) with confidence intervals derived by the variance expression given by Müller, Da-

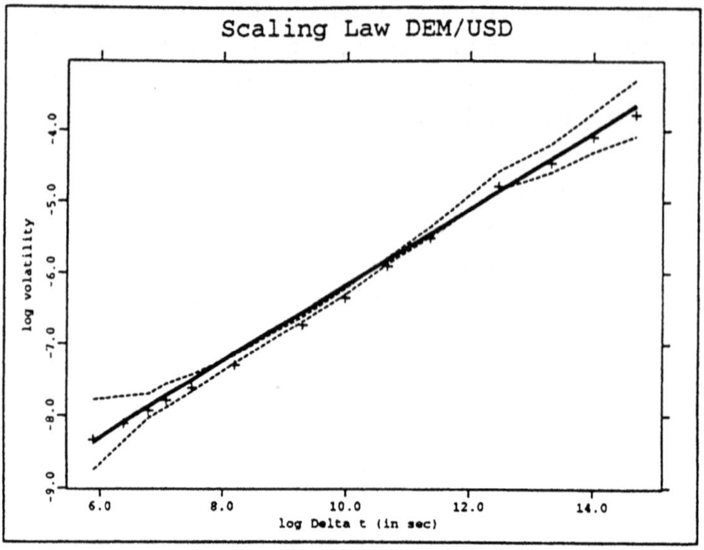

FIGURE 2.14. *Scaling law for the DEM/USD rate. On the abscissa the log time intervals measured in seconds are given, on the ordinate the log volatilities for $\delta = 1$. The thick line represents the OLS fit, the dotted lines 2σ–confidence intervals.*

corogna and Pictet (1995). Here, the confidence intervals are taken to be twice the estimated standard deviation above and below the regression line.

Estimation of (2.16) was performed by OLS and choice of time intervals that are neither too small nor too large for the reason of increasing variances mentioned above. The intervals chosen were 6 min, 10 min, 15 min, 20 min, 30 min, 1h, 3h, 6h, 12h, 1 day, 3 days, 1 week, 2 weeks, and 4 weeks. Our estimate of α_1 for DEM/USD was 0.534, but as can be seen in Figure 2.14 the estimate is larger when the boundaries are skipped. Olsen & Associates use a larger database covering several years, so their estimates are more reliable. For the sake of comparison and consistency, 0.58 as an estimate of α_1 is adopted here for subsequent analyses. Experiments with 0.534 did not yield substantially different results. Our estimate of α_2 was 0.48.

Recall from Figure 2.7 that there is both a daily and weekly seasonal pattern of the FX rates, so the period P is in this case one week. Based on a regular time scale one period consists of J time intervals, i.e. $P = J\Delta t$. For instance, if the time unity is 20 min, then $P = 504$.

In analogy to the whole sample we define volatility for each season separately as

$$V_{\delta,j}(y_t) = V_\delta(y_t \mid t \bmod P = j-1), \quad j = 1,\ldots,J, \tag{2.17}$$

which is estimated straightforwardly by calculating the volatility conditional on the seasons.

Rearranging the scaling law (2.15) and substituting the volatility of the whole sample by the volatility of season j now gives the definition of activity in season j:

Definition 2.6 (Activity) *The activity a_j in season j, $j = 1,\ldots,J$, is defined as*

$$a_j = \frac{1}{\Delta t}\left(\frac{V_{\delta,j}(y_t)}{C_1}\right)^{1/\alpha_\delta}, \quad j = 1,\ldots,J. \tag{2.18}$$

Due to the pronounced seasonal patterns of absolute returns and to the findings of Ding, Granger and Engle (1993), $\delta = 1$ will be used in the following.

If market activity at a certain point t in calendar time is of interest, the estimate a_j is rather crude if large time intervals were used. Because the sample period is fixed, however, it is no solution to use very small time intervals due to the larger variance. To get a continuous activity function nevertheless, $\Delta t = 20$min was used and the resulting function was smoothed with a Nadaraya–Watson kernel smoother, quartic kernel, and bandwidth $h = 5$. This was seen as a compromise between too small and too large bandwidths. Too small bandwidths yield too wiggly curves with large variances and thus highly unstable activity functions. Too large bandwidths, on the other hand, do not capture all detailed patterns of activity. The importance of balancing these two effects is obvious for our in–sample analysis, and even more so for out–of–sample prediction.

Figures 2.15, 2.16 and 2.17 show the activity functions.

For DEM/USD, activity clusters are clearly visible. Typical is a trimodal intraday pattern, corresponding to the openings of the major markets in Far East, Europe and America. Moreover, the activity at the weekend is negligibly small. Similar seasonal patterns are obtained for the Yen rates.

The new time scale ϑ based on the smoothed, continuous activity function $a(t)$ is defined such that time intervals with high activity are shortened and time intervals with small activity are enlarged. More precisely, after transformation of the time scale the same activity is to be expected in each time interval. There is a one–to–one deterministic relationship between calendar

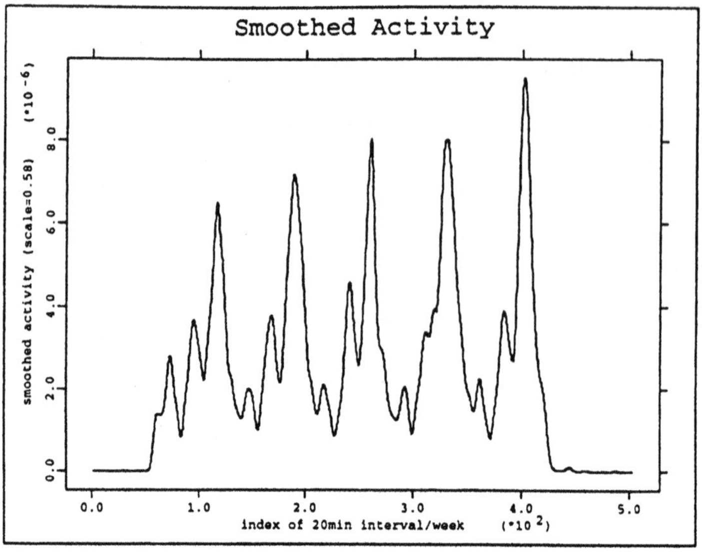

FIGURE 2.15. *Smoothed activity as a function of 20–minute intervals during a week for the DEM/USD rate. A Nadaraya–Watson smoother with quartic kernel and bandwidth* $h = 5$ *was used.*

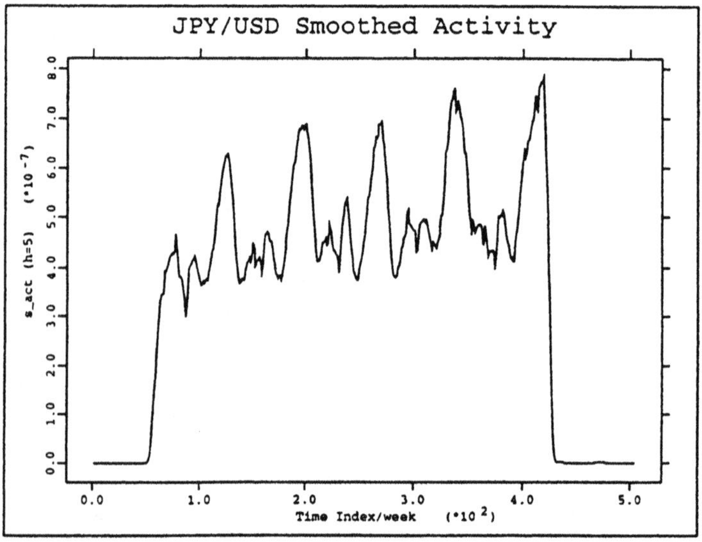

FIGURE 2.16. *Smoothed activity as a function of 20–minute intervals during a week for the JPY/USD rate. A Nadaraya–Watson smoother with quartic kernel and bandwidth* $h = 5$ *was used.*

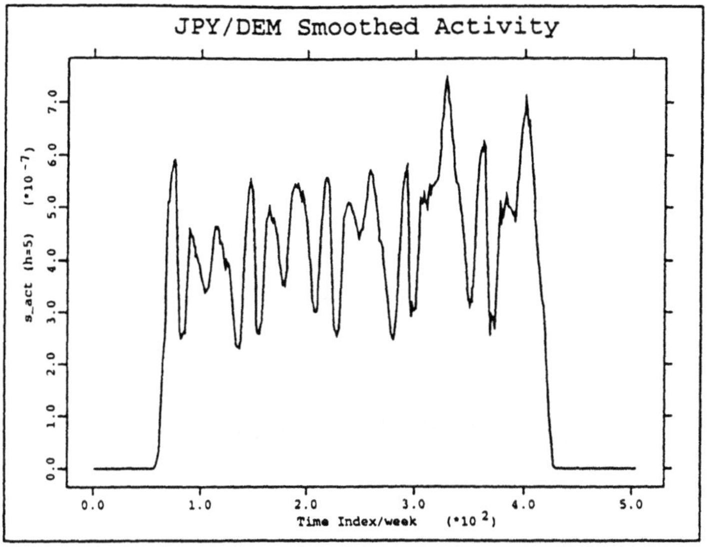

FIGURE 2.17. *Smoothed activity as a function of 20–minute intervals during a week for the JPY/DEM rate. A Nadaraya–Watson smoother with quartic kernel and bandwidth $h = 5$ was used.*

time t and operational time ϑ, and the mapping function $\vartheta(t)$ is

$$\vartheta(t) = \frac{P}{C_2} \int_0^t a(t')dt' \tag{2.19}$$

with constant

$$C_2 = \int_0^P a(t')dt',$$

so that one period P in ϑ–time corresponds exactly to one period in calendar time. Note that this is a deterministic mapping function based on the seasonality in the volatility of returns. It can be regarded as a deseasonalization technique.

Because the activity function is merely an average measure, there is sometimes no quote in the new time interval. In these cases the next occurring quote is taken and empty intervals are skipped. The numbers of records are thus reduced from 26,280 20–minute intervals per year to 25,476 for DEM/USD, 24,838 for JPY/USD, and 23,265 for JPY/DEM. All subsequent analyses are based on the ϑ–scale. Despite the risk of confusion, however, the time indices ϑ are renamed t and numbered as an equispaced scale, i.e. $t = 1, 2, \ldots, n$.

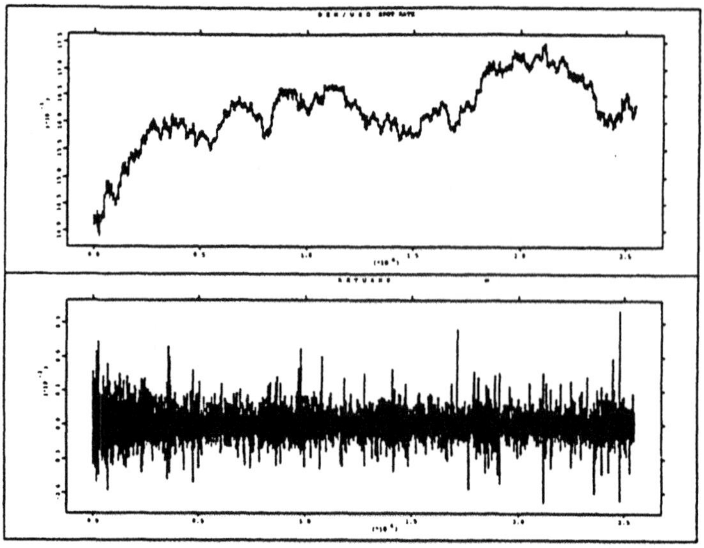

FIGURE 2.18. *DEM/USD spot rate and returns in ϑ-time. The time scale covers 10/01/1992 - 09/30/1993.*

FX rate	DEM/USD	JPY/USD	JPY/DEM
spot rate	−3.4357	−0.6172	−1.7586
return	−71.6939	−73.0813	−69.2669

TABLE 2.8. *Augmented Dickey Fuller statistics for the test of a unit root in the FX spot rates and returns. The 1% critical value of each test is* −3.4338.

2.4.7 Properties of the FX Rates in ϑ–Time

Time series plots of the spot rates and returns for the FX rates are shown in Figure 2.18, 2.19 and 2.20. To test whether the spot rates and returns contain unit roots, augmented Dickey Fuller (ADF) tests were performed. The test statistics are reported in Table 2.8. For each test, the 1% McKinnon critical value for the rejection of the null hypothesis of a unit root was −3.4338.

For the spot rates, the ADF test slightly rejects the null hypothesis of a unit root in the DEM/USD rate at the 1% level, whereas it failed to reject for the Yen rates. All tests applied to the returns clearly rejected the null hypothesis of a unit root. This standard result suggests to consider the FX rates as being integrated and their returns as stationary. More details about the ADF tests are available.

In Table 2.9 summary statistics about the FX returns in ϑ–time are given.

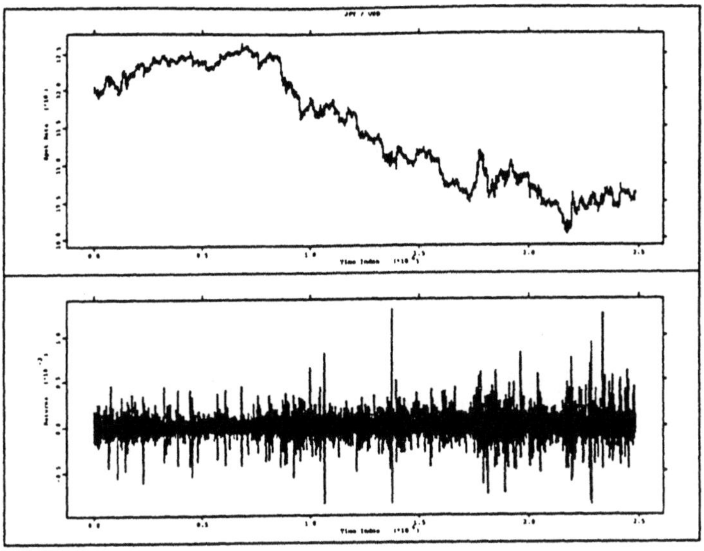

FIGURE 2.19. *JPY/USD spot rate and returns in ϑ-time. The time scale covers 10/01/1992 - 09/30/1993.*

FX rate	Δt	n	Mean	Variance	Skew	Kurt
DEM/USD	20 min	25,476	5.7E-06	6.5E-07	0.24	9.40
JPY/USD	20 min	24,838	-4.9E-06	6.7E-07	0.18	17.30
JPY/DEM	20 min	23,265	-1.1E-05	7.0E-07	-0.17	8.71
DEM/USD	10 min	52,412	2.6E-06	3.4E-07	0.17	42.12
JPY/USD	10 min	52,388	-2.5E-06	3.0E-07	0.03	16.08

TABLE 2.9. *Summary statistics of the FX returns in ϑ-time. 20 minute returns were obtained as described in the text, the 10 minute series were provided by Olsen & Assiociates*

The coefficient of kurtosis reveals substantial differences from normality. Even more striking are the values of the skewness. Considering standard errors of $\sqrt{6/n}$ under the null of normality, these are highly significantly different from zero. Thus, the distributions of the FX returns appear to be significantly asymmetric in ϑ-time. Also reported are the statistics of the DEM/USD and JPY/USD 10 minute returns in ϑ-time, generously provided by Olsen & Associates. They used a slightly refined procedure taking care about geographical components of the activity function, see Dacorogna et al. (1993) for more details.

To assess the degree of leptokurtosis of the 20 minute returns, a kernel den-

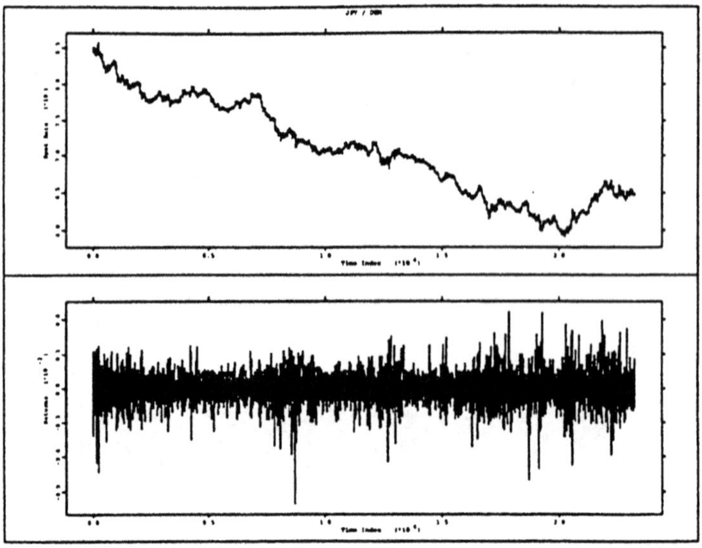

FIGURE 2.20. *JPY/DEM spot rate and returns in ϑ-time. The time scale covers 10/01/1992 – 09/30/1993.*

sity estimate with $h = 0.3$ is given in Figure 2.21. In order to see the difference to low–frequency FX densities, a density estimate of weekly DEM/USD returns using the same data set HFDF93 and $h = 0.9$ is given as well. Recall that for weekly data no transformation of the time scale is necessary under the presumption of daily and weekly seasonality. Both return series were standardized, and the picture is truncated at four standard deviations on each side. To compare the densities with the normal density, 25,476 normally distributed random variables were generated and smoothed with the same bandwidth $h = 0.3$. Except for the high positive skewness (0.3065 with a standard deviation of 0.336) of the weekly data, which is not significant for this small sample of 53 observations, it is seen that low–frequency, i.e. highly aggregated data come close to a normal distribution, whereas the 20 minute returns obviously have much more probability mass in the centre and – not in the picture – for large outliers.

Another way to look at this empirical fact is the QQ plot of 20 minute DEM/USD returns in Figure 2.22, where the quantiles of the FX distribution are plotted against the quantiles of a normal distribution. The deviation from the normal distribution is obvious.

Consider the autocorrelations of returns, squared and absolute returns in Table 2.10. The Dollar rates have significant negatively autocorrelated re-

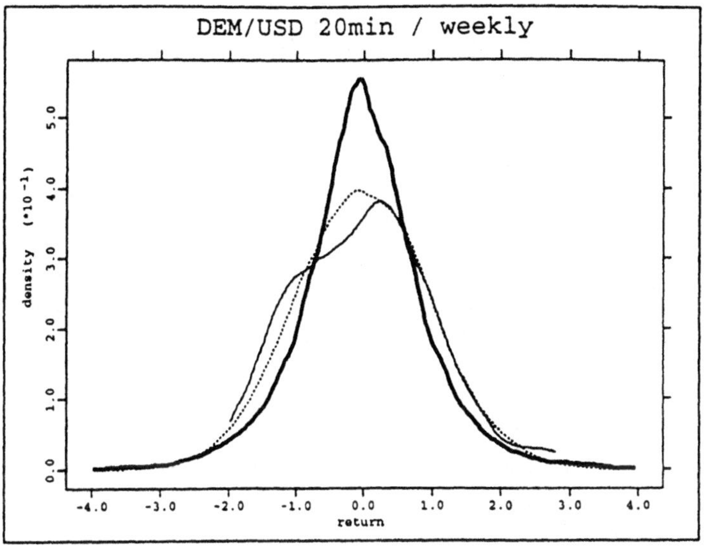

FIGURE 2.21. *Density estimate of 20 min DEM/USD returns in* ϑ*–time (solid thick), weekly DEM/USD returns (solid thin), and a smoothed normal density (dashed).*

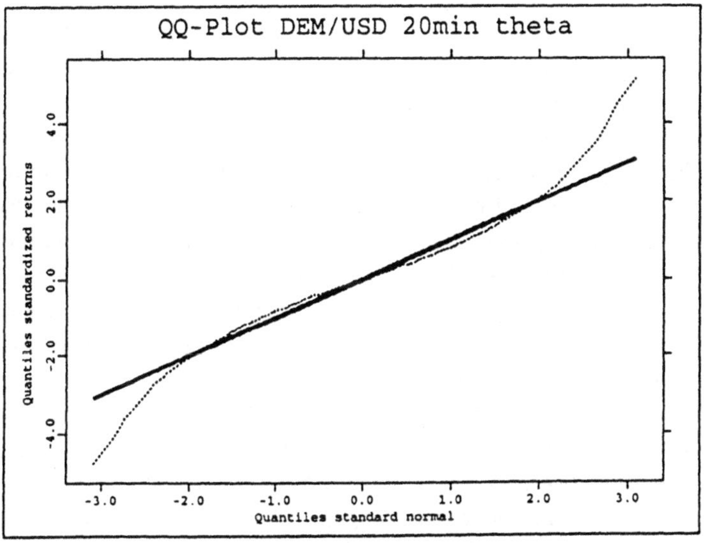

FIGURE 2.22. *QQ plot of 20 min DEM/USD returns in* ϑ*–time. Quantiles of a standard normal distribution are given on the abscissa, corresponding quantiles of the standardized FX returns on the ordinate. The straight line is the identity.*

	DEM/USD			JPY/USD			JPY/DEM		
k	y_t	y_t^2	$\lvert y_t \rvert$	y_t	y_t^2	$\lvert y_t \rvert$	y_t	y_t^2	$\lvert y_t \rvert$
1	−.079*	.204*	.207*	−.101*	.256*	.262*	−.008	.108*	.169*
2	−.015*	.098*	.141*	−.012	.084*	.164*	−.010	.076*	.128*
3	−.024*	.075*	.134	.003	.042*	.134*	−.001	.070*	.112*
4	−.003	.089*	.128*	−.020*	.043*	.126*	.016*	.051*	.097*
5	.006	.076*	.119*	.006	.031*	.111*	−.001	.049*	.094*
6	−.005	.068*	.103*	.009	.034*	.107*	−.010	.051*	.095*
7	.015*	.049*	.095*	.006	.055*	.120*	.006	.074*	.100*
8	.011	.043*	.087*	−.010	.051*	.117*	.016*	.075*	.101*
9	.006	.058*	.095*	.004	.049*	.110*	−.002	.063*	.091*
10	.013*	.056*	.091*	−.007	.037*	.100*	−.003	.031*	.069*
25	.013*	.030*	.057*	−.001	.026*	.085*	−.004	.028*	.050*
50	.010	.023*	.048*	−.006	.025*	.076*	−.010	.029*	.045*
100	−.009	.026*	.067*	.008	.021*	.080*	−.005	.023*	.060*
250	.004	.011	.025*	−.007	.014*	.055*	−.007	.017*	.034*
500	−.005	.018*	.036*	.000	.006	.036*	.005	.013	.021*
1000	−.002	.007	.023*	.001	.006	.027*	−.003	.007	.020*

TABLE 2.10. *Autocorrelations of 20 minute FX returns, squared and absolute returns in ϑ–time for selected lags k. The asterisk marks asymptotic 5% significance.*

turns at the first lags. Goodhart and Figliuoli (1991) and Guillaume et al. (1994) report similar results for ultra–high frequencies. Two economic explanations are possible. The first is that traders have at the same time different information sets (this would imply market ineffficency) or interpret the same news differently. This, however, can hardly be tested, and thus, other reasons were looked for, the most prominent being a microeconomic structural explanation based on the bid–ask spread. Banks have to perform inventory rebalancing if they hold open positions longer than just a few minutes. This explanation is confirmed by the fact that negative autocorrelation disappears when the data are aggregated to about more than one hour time intervals.

Note that the autocorrelations of the much less liquid JPY/DEM returns are not significant at the first lags. This indicates the commodity status of the Dollar rates, which banks use for inventory rebalancing instead of rates with less volume and thus larger bid–ask spreads, resp. transaction costs. The most significant autocorrelation of the DEM/USD is at the first lag. Therefore, it would be worthwhile to look at the scatterplot of $[y_t, y_{t-1}]$ to visualize whether the dependence structure is linear, as the autocorrelation suggests, or if the significance is a spurious artefact of a nonlinear dependence structure. However, the scatterplot does not convey substantially more information than a density contour plot, which is given in Figure 2.23. The left panel displays the density contour lines of DEM/USD with outliers removed. Nonparametric twodimensional density estimation and bandwidths chosen according to Silverman's rule of thumb were used. No significant non-

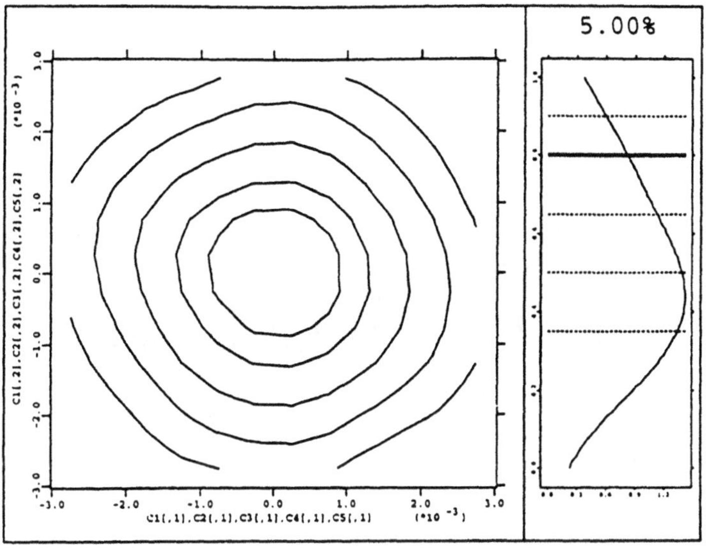

FIGURE 2.23. *Density contour plot of 20 minute DEM/USD returns in ϑ-time. The lagged return y_{t-1} is reported on the X-axis, y_t on the y-axis. A kernel density estimate with quartic kernel and bandwidth $h = 0.001$ in each direction was used. The ranges on both axes cover more than 99% observations, see Table 5.1.*

linear dependence structure can be detected besides the apparent negative linear dependence. The right panel gives information about the distribution of density function values. This curve is relatively flat, because outliers were removed in the plot.

Turning to the subject of time-dependent volatility, recall that conventional linear ARMA models assume conditional homoskedasticity. This implies that the information set, containing past returns, cannot be exploited to obtain a better prediction of future volatility than the unconditional variance. Since Mandelbrot (1963) and Fama (1965), however, it is a well known empirical fact that financial series exhibit significant clustering of volatilities, i.e. large returns tend to be followed by large ones and small returns by small ones. In the econometrics literature, this feature is known since the seminal work of Engle (1982) as *conditional heteroskedasticity*. Figure 2.24 shows the autocorrelations for the DEM/USD squared and absolute returns up to lag 1000. Absolute returns are clearly higher autocorrelated than squared returns. Ding et al. (1993) showed that models of the ARCH type are able to produce such behavior. The ACF of absolute returns declines very slowly, so that a hyperbolic rather than an exponential decline seems to be plausible. This

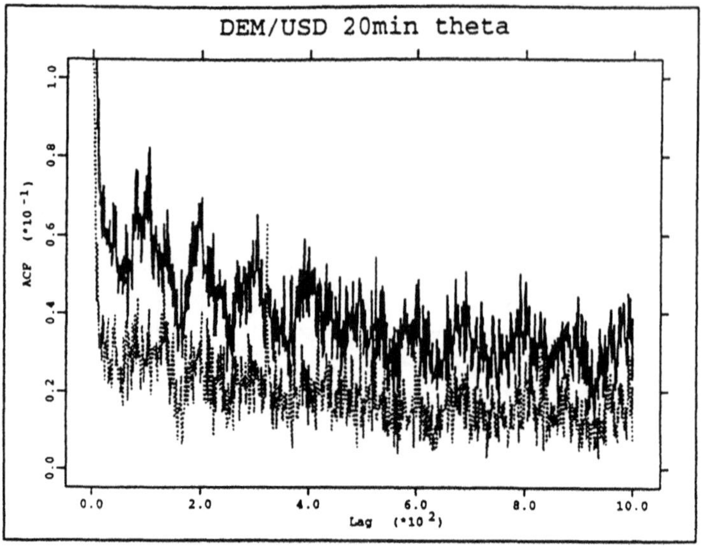

FIGURE 2.24. *Autocorrelation Function of DEM/USD squared returns (dashed) and absolute returns (solid) in ϑ–time up to lag 1000.*

gives some motivation for the fractionally integrated GARCH (FIGARCH) model of Baillie, Bollerslev and Mikkelsen (1996), compared with the exponential decline implied by GARCH or the persistence in IGARCH. Indeed, the long memory in volatility is striking: There is still significant positive autocorrelation in absolute returns at lag 1000, approximately two weeks of time lag. For a discussion of volatility persistence in the ARCH framework, see Section 4.4.

In order to evaluate how well the above described activity–based time transformation works compared to the refined ϑ–time of Olsen & Associates, a plot of 10 minute DEM/USD returns for the same data set HFDF93 but with a time scale generated by Olsen & Associates using additional geographical components is given in Figure 2.25. Note that the doubled amount of lags is given on the X–axis, so that the same time horizon, approximately two weeks, is covered by Figure 2.24 and Figure 2.25. No systematical, structural differences can be detected. Thus, it is concluded that the time transformation described above performs relatively well in removing seasonality in volatility. Throughout the work, the main data set used will therefore be the 20 minute DEM/USD returns as based on our own calculations. In some cases, however, the results will be compared with the 10 minute series of Olsen & Associates.

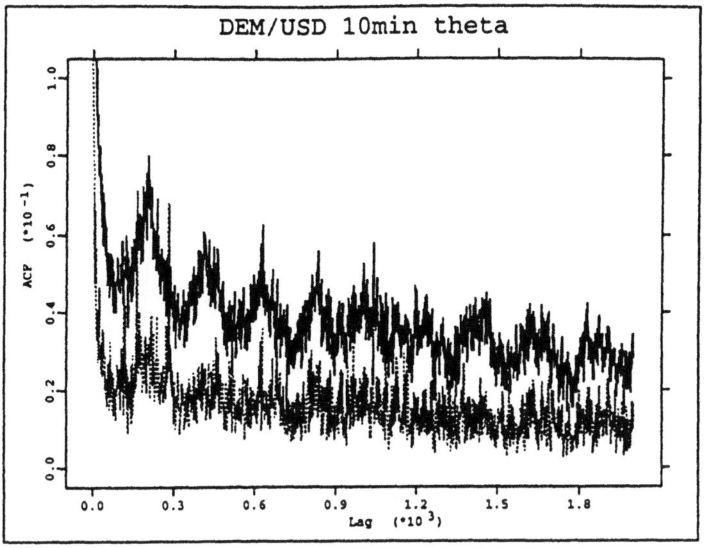

FIGURE 2.25. *Autocorrelation Function of DEM/USD squared returns (dashed) and absolute (solid) 10 minute returns in ϑ-time up to lag 2000. The data set was provided by Olsen & Associates.*

2.4.8 The Role of Bid–Ask Spreads

Each quote consists of the price at which the bank wants to buy, i.e. the bid quote, and to sell, i.e. the ask quote. In less liquid markets the difference between both quotes is usually higher because the bank takes the risk of having an open position for a longer period of time. Thus, the bid–ask spread can be considered as transaction costs that are closely related to 'risk' in the market. Following Stoll (1989), the transaction costs consist of three components: order processing costs, inventory holding costs, and adverse information costs.

As a convention among market makers, bid–ask spreads usually take only a few discrete values, but Glassman (1987) already found that the spreads are time–varying and related to both volume and volatility. Not surprisingly, the bid–ask spreads also show intra–daily and intra–weekly seasonal patterns, as can be seen in Figure 2.26 for the DEM/USD rate. If no quote occurs within a time interval the spread is set to zero. Clearly, the spreads are highest when market volume is low, especially Sunday evening GMT with the opening of Tokyo. The peaks within the week are associated to the time before the East Asian markets open.

Under suitable conditions, this regular behaviour of the bid–ask spreads can be exploited for volatility models. For a promising first step in this direction,

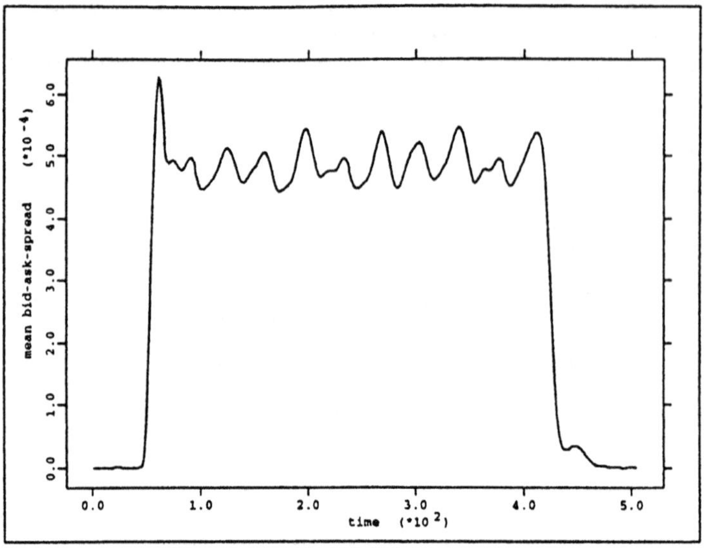

FIGURE 2.26. *Bid–ask spreads of DEM/USD as a function of 20–minute intervals per week. The function is smoothed with a Nadaraya–Watson smoother, quartic kernel, and bandwidth $h = 5$. If no quote was reported for a time interval, the spread was set to zero.*

see Bossaerts, Hafner and Härdle (1996). A recent review of the bid–ask spread literature is given by Bessembinder (1994).

2.4.9 How are Major Jumps Related to News?

As already noted, it is possible to trace back major shifts of the FX rates to news recorded in the news file. Now the advantage of the ϑ–time scale becomes obvious: Because each interval on the new scale amounts to the same mean activity, jumps in the series are no longer spurious.

In Table 2.11 jumps of the DEM/USD rate larger than 0.0045, i.e. more than five and a half standard deviations, are reported together with calendar time and the corresponding news that are conjectured to have caused the jumps. For this to find out, two criteria were used: (i) if the news arrived within five minutes before or within the time interval over which the jump occurred, and (ii) if the news appeared frequently in subsequent 'news'.

Several points are of importance. First, the clustering of volatilities can be seen by the occurrence of three pairs (y_t, y_{t+1}) of outliers. In all cases the second outlier is smaller than the first with sign reverted. This corresponds to *mean reversion* and negatively autocorrelated returns reported previously.

t	y_t	y_{t+1}	Date	$(t-1;t]$	$t(news)$	cat
4	4.7	1.6	92/10/01	01:14/01:36	01:15	A
BOJ OFFERS TO BUY 250 BLN YEN						
144	−4.9	0.4	92/10/02	11:50/12:00	11:49	C
GERMANY LOWERS YIELD ON 5-YEARS NOTES						
148	6.5	−1.9	92/10/02	12:15/12:32	12:22	B
BUBA RATES TO STAY STEADY FOR "TIME BEING"						
281	7.4	2.8	92/10/05	16:43/16:53	16:42	A
GEORGIA ACCUSES RUSSIA SHOOTING HELICOPTER						
669	5.4	−2.7	92/10/09	15:01/15:07	15:03	A
CITICORP PLANS ASSET SALES						
699	−5.7	0	92/10/10	00:01/+		D
multiple						
1276	4.5	0.8	92/10/19	18:47/19:07	18:55	A
US INTEREST RATES HIGHER IN OCT						
3510	−4.8	0.7	92/11/19	14:28/14:34	14:29	A
UK STOCK EX: PRICES NO LONGER INDICATIVE						
3575	6.9	−3.8	92/11/20	08:17/08:29	08:24	A
DUTCH BONDS CLIMB EARLY ON EMS WORRIES						
3641	6.0	−4.2	92/11/20	17:43/17:58	17:47	A
FRENCH FARMERS DENOUNCE EC-US TRADE						
4725	−5.1	1.6	92/12/07	17:04/17:15	17:02	B
FED: US ECONOMIC GROWTH STILL ANEMIC						
4730	4.8	−1.6	92/12/07	18:10/18:28	18:18	D
ARGENTINE CENTRAL BANK BUYS $72.3 MILLION						
9688	5.0	−2.1	93/02/18	11:56/12:05	11:49	C
BUBA LEAVES INTEREST RATES UNCHANGED						
9803	6.7	−2.6	93/02/19	13:12/13:18	13:27	C
GERMAN M3 CONTRACTED 2.3% IN JAN						
10795	6.0	0.6	93/03/05	13:28/13:35	13:33	C
US FEB JOBLESS RATE 7.0%						
14118	4.9	−2.0	93/04/22	13:16/13:29	13:26	C
BUBA CUTS DISCOUNT, LOMBARD RATES						
17142	8.4	0.4	93/06/04	12:28/12:35	12:32	C
US MAY JOBLESS RATE 6.9%						
17639	−5.7	−0.6	93/06/11	12:28/12:35	12:32	C
US MAY PPI UNCHANGED						
17934	4.7	0.2	93/06/16	12:36/12:47	12:35	B
INST: GERMAN INVESTMENT CLIMATE IMPROVING						
19129	−5.2	4.6	93/07/02	12:28/12:35	12:32	C
US JUNE JOBLESS RATE 7.0%						
19130	4.6	−1.9	93/07/02	12:35/12:42	12:40	C
US PAYROLLS SHOW SLIGHT GAIN						
21159	−6.9	4.6	93/08/02	23:54/00:11	00:05	D
EC AGREES 15% BANDS FOR 6 ERM CURRENCIES						
21160	4.6	0	93/08/02	00:11/00:28	00:17	B
EC MINIST SEE CURRENCIES BACK TO PARITIES						
23568	−6.1	2.0	93/09/03	12:28/12:35	12:31	C
US AUG JOBLESS RATE 6.7%						
24450	5.9	−2.0	93/09/16	13:16/13:22	13:18	C
US AUG INDUSTRIAL OUTPUT ROSE 0.2%						
24773	10.1	−6.7	93/09/21	16:17/16:25	16:18	B
US BANK GROUP CALLS IMF TO AID G7 PROCESS						
24774	−6.7	2.5	93/09/21	16:25/16:33	16:27	A
US FOREX UNIMPRESSED BY JAP RATE CUT						

TABLE 2.11. *Jumps of the DEM/USD rate greater than 0.0045 and the time of their occurence in ϑ–time (first column) and calendar time (GMT, fifth column). For each jump, the subsequent row associates the jump to news appearing at time t(news), GMT time on the Reuters screen, as reported in the Olsen & Associates news file. cat is the suggested category of news. Returns are measured on a* $E-03$ *scale. A + indicates a gap of more than one day.*

Category	Description	Number of news
A	Not Related Decisions and Statements	8
B	Related Statements	5
C	Related Decisions	11
D	Extraordinary Events	3

TABLE 2.12. *News categories and number of news per category.*

Second, in at least two cases the jump occurred *before* the news that very likely caused it was reported. For example, on 93/08/01, 23:50 GMT the DEM/USD began to run into a trend, but the news about broader ERM bands was reported fourteen minutes later. Similarly, at 93/02/19, the news about contracted German money supply occurred after the jump. In this case no other news was reported before or within the corresponding time interval. This paradox can only have two explanations: Either some market makers are insiders who give signals to the rest of the market, or the news in the Reuters database are recorded with a time delay of up to several minutes. The latter explanation appears to be more plausible.

An attempt was made to classify the obtained news into four categories. Table 2.12 gives a brief characterization of the categories. Basic criterion to categorize news was not the *contents* but rather the *type* of news. In category A, all news are summarized that could only indirectly be regarded as having caused the jump, because there was no direct relationship to the DEM/USD rate. So there are many other equally vague news that could have been chosen as well. However, in some cases there appear some basic news that have persisted in the market. For example, for $t = 3,575$ this is 'EMS worries', for $t = 3,641$ it is 'EC–U.S. Trade Deal', and for $t = 24,774$ 'Japanese Rate Cut'. These can be seen as the basic sources of turbulence, but having occurred longer before the jump, in the last case almost one day.

Category B collects news that are statements of politicians, central banks and business institutes related to the DEM/USD rate. In this sample the FED, the German Bundesbank, a German economic research institute, EC ministers, and the U.S. Bankers Group gave statements that caused the jumps with a higher likelihood than those in category A.

Category C includes announcements and decisions having a direct impact on the DEM/USD rate. In most cases these are either decisions of the FED or the Bundesbank to change interest rates or official announcements about economic indicators. A major characteristic of this category is that the time of the news can be predicted: For example, U.S. economic indicators are announced on Fridays at 12:30 GMT, and the Bundesbank meets on Thursdays,

Category	$m(\lvert y_t \rvert)$	$m(\lvert y_{t+1} \rvert)$	$m(\lvert y_{t+1} \rvert)_{y_t>0}$	$m(\lvert y_{t+1} \rvert)_{y_t<0}$
all	5.86	2.03	2.11 (18)	1.87 (9)
A	5.81	2.38	2.66 (6)	1.56 (2)
B	6.21	2.08	2.20 (4)	1.60 (1)
C	5.75	1.75	1.67 (7)	1.89 (4)
D	5.82	2.07	1.60 (1)	2.31 (2)

TABLE 2.13. *Average of absolute values of DEM/USD returns for categorized outliers. Number of observations of each subsample are reported in parentheses.*

tending to announce interest rate decisions around noon.

Last but not least, category D is reserved for extraordinary news. The first one at $t = 699$ is a weekend–effect: The 'jump' occurred from the last observation on Saturday morning to the first observation on Sunday evening, so it is very likely to be spurious because of missing observations, as already mentioned above. Many news were reported at this weekend, so no single one could be identified. The second record in this category at $t = 4,730$ is the information that the Argentine central bank bought a large amount of Dollars. Because this event is not regular and cannot be anticipated by outside traders it was chosen not to be included in category C. Finally, at $t = 21159$ the decision of the EC to widen the variability bands from 2.25% to 15% for six European currencies is recorded. Although it does not have the highest impact on the immediate return, this news persisted for a long time in the FX markets and was most important for this sample.

In order to discuss the impact of different types of news on volatility, the averages of the absolute values of the returns, $m(|y_t|)$, were calculated for each category. Anticipating what will be the issue of Chapter 4 and 5, also the corresponding values for the next interval, $m(|y_{t+1}|)$, are given in order to shed some light on how persistent the news are. Another issue discussed in Chapter 4 and 5 is asymmetry of news impact on volatility, i.e. does a negative shock have the same impact as a positive one of same size? Therefore, $m(|y_{t+1}|)$ is calculated only for those cases where $y_t > 0$ and $y_t < 0$, respectively. The results are reported in Table 2.13. Note that statistical inference cannot be made due to the small numbers of observations, so the different results for the categories need to be treated carefully. Generally, news had a positive impact also on the next interval's volatility, although much less distinct: on average two and a half standard deviations. Substantial differences across the categories cannot be detected, although category C includes news with slightly smaller impacts on volatility. Considering the last two columns, there seem to be asymmetric effects apparent. For the average of all categories, a positive shock to DEM/USD has a higher impact on volatility than a negative one. This is consistent with the findings in Chapter 5, where nonparametric models are used. However, for categories A and B this asymmetry seems to be inverted. It is refrained from interpreting these results, which should be underlined by larger data sets allowing for larger subsamples of outliers. The only point one can make is that category C seems to be of minor importance compared to those types of news that cannot be anticipated. So although regular announcements and decisions create outliers immediately, the impact on volatility is not extreme and they tend to persist less in the market.

Concluding, it can be stated that the FX market reacts to news almost immediately such that the new 'equilibrium' is found after a few minutes. This is one aspect of an efficient market, which, in a general definition, is a market that reflects all available and relevant information through the prices at any time.

2.5 Conclusions

In this chapter, a relationship was drawn between financial volatility in finance theory and the econometric modelling of typical financial time series. The conditional standard deviation was adopted as the standard risk measure. A stock return index series was analysed and the typical leverage effect detected. The emphasis laid on the description of the foreign exchange market and on the high frequency FX return series used throughout the work. Intra-day and intra-week seasonal volatility was shown to be a typical phenomenon, and a redefinition of the time scale served as deseasonalization. Based on this scale, the FX return series properties are illustrated, the main findings being highly significant negative autocorrelation at the first lags (based on original 20 minute intervals), heavy tails of the densities, and long memory in volatility, measured either by squared or – even stronger – absolute returns. Bid-ask spreads are shown to have a similar seasonal pattern as volatility. Finally, extreme outliers are traced back to macroeconomic and political news headlines. It was found that regular announcements of relevant economic indicators creates volatility that is less persistent than volatility caused by irregular events.

3
Nonlinear Time Series Analysis

3.1 Introduction

The recent development of nonlinear time series analysis is primarily due to the efforts to overcome the limitations of linear models such as autoregressive moving-average (ARMA) models of Box and Jenkins (1976) in real applications. Two examples of such limitations are the non-ability to model sudden outbursts and the restriction to symmetry in the sense of reversible processes, whereas many processes observed in reality reveal irreversibility, well-known examples being the sunspot numbers and the Canadian Lynx data, see Tong (1990) for a discussion of these data sets with respect to nonlinearity and irreversibility. The increasing popularity of nonlinear time series models is also attributed to the development of nonlinear and nonparametric regression techniques which provides many useful tools. Advanced computational power and easy–to–use advanced softwares and graphics such as S–Plus(Venables and Ripley (1994)) and XploRe(Härdle, Klinke and Turlach (1995)) contribute to the increasing application of nonlinear time series analysis.

In most empirical research fields in the natural sciences and in econometrics, it is important and essential to formulate simple nonlinear models that are sufficient for handling most nonlinear phenomena observed in practice such as limit cycles, amplitude-dependent frequency, modulation efforts, chaos, etc. However, there is no unified theory applicable to all nonlinear models because of the many different nonlinear functions and model structures. A general classification of time series models can be made according to whether the process is in continuous or discrete time. With the theoretical background of stochastic differential equations, the dynamics of continuous time stochastic processes are sometimes better tractable. However, for estimation one has to use discrete time approximations analogous to discrete models in regression analysis. Because this chapter will focus on the practical aspects of nonlinear time series models, only processes in discrete time are considered.

Using the terminology of Priestley (1988, ch.3), the most general non-anticipative time series model is

$$h(y_t, y_{t-1}, \dots) = \varepsilon_t, \tag{3.1}$$

where h is a prescribed function. This model merely says that y_t is an implicit function of lagged values y_{t-j}, $j > 0$, and a stochastic disturbance ε_t. For the degenerated case that ε_t is a constant, (3.1) is a deterministic process. This will not be of practical importance, unless the function $h(\cdot)$ has properties under which the process would be called *chaotic*. Section 3.2 will discuss some properties of chaotic processes.

If the stochastic process in (3.1) is *invertible*, it can be written as

$$y_t = g(\varepsilon_t, \varepsilon_{t-1}, \ldots). \tag{3.2}$$

Obviously, without some further restrictions, neither (3.1) nor (3.2) can be used in practice. An important restriction is to write y_t as an explicit function of a finite number of lagged values and an additive error term, i.e.

$$y_t = f(y_{t-1}, \ldots, y_{t-p}) + \varepsilon_t, \quad t = 1, 2, \ldots. \tag{3.3}$$

The error term $\{\varepsilon_t\}$ is a white noise series according to Definition 2.3, but not necessarily *i.i.d.*. Similarly, ε_t is uncorrelated with, but not necessarily independent of y_s for all $s < t$. Thus, the nonlinear autoregressive model of order p in (3.3) is general enough to incorporate many of the model specifications discussed in Section 3.3 and 3.4. Note that (3.3) can be regarded as a Markov chain of order p. There are two ways to apply this model. The first approach is to formulate a certain parametric function $f(\cdot)$ for the model, presumably based on the physical dynamic background, economic theory, or other substantive information of the data. The second approach is to use nonparametric techniques to estimate the function. Then, based on the estimated nonparametric function, one can either make inference directly or formulate a parametric function, and hence, build a parameterized nonlinear model for the process.

General conditions for *stationarity* and *ergodicity* of the process (3.3) are available. Intuitively, stationarity refers to the property of the process not to explode, whereas ergodicity is the property that characteristics of the stationary distribution, such as the mean, are consistently estimated by the corresponding sample estimates. The following proposition gives sufficient conditions for the process to be stationary. Here, the error term is not necessarily additive, so a very general process is considered.

Proposition 3.1 (Lasota and Mackey, 1989) *The general nonlinear process*

$$y_t = f(y_{t-1}, \ldots, y_{t-p}, \varepsilon_t)$$

is stationary, if

1. $f(x, \varepsilon)$ *is continuous in* x,

2. $\{\varepsilon_t\}$ is a white noise process,

3. $E[|f(x_1, \varepsilon_t) - f(x_2, \varepsilon_t)|] < \| x_1 - x_2 \|$,

4. $E\left[f(x, \varepsilon_t)^2\right] < \sigma^2 \| x \| + \beta$ for $\| x \| < 1$,

with $\sigma > 0$, $x_1 \in I\!R^p$, $x_2 \in I\!R^p$, $x \in I\!R^p$, and $\| \cdot \|$ an arbitrary norm in $I\!R^p$. Proof: see Lasota and Mackey (1989).

For ergodicity conditions, consider the important example of a conditionally heteroskedastic autoregressive (CHARN) model, which will be discussed in Section 5.2. It takes the form

$$y_t = f(y_{t-1}) + \sigma(y_{t-1})\xi_t \tag{3.4}$$

with stochastic innovations ξ_t that are independent, identically distributed with mean zero and variance one. Ango Nze (1992) has shown that (3.4) is ergodic, if

$$|f(x)| \leq C_1(1 + |x|),$$

$$|\sigma(x)| \leq C_2(1 + |x|),$$

and

$$C_1 + C_2 E|\xi_t| < 1,$$

where C_1 and C_2 are some positive finite constants.

Under these conditions, (3.4) is geometrically ergodic, so convergence to the stationary distribution is fast.

The purpose of this chapter is to give an overview of the most important nonlinear time series models. For the sake of brevity and clarity, not many technical details are given. Rather, the peculiarities and (dis-)advantages of the processes for the application shall be addressed.

The chapter is organized as follows. Before continuing on stochastic nonlinear processes, Section 3.2 considers deterministic chaotic processes. Section 3.3 discusses the most important existing parametric nonlinear time series models. Section 3.4 focuses on nonparametric approaches to time series analysis, and Section 3.5 surveys some existing nonlinearity tests. Section 3.6 presents basic nonlinear prediction methods, and Section 3.8 concludes.

3.2 Deterministic Systems and Chaos

The issue of deterministic chaos has been examined extensively in the natural sciences over the past decade. An increasing part of the literature also comes from the field of social sciences and economics. An overview of the latter is given e.g. by LeBaron (1995).

The general deterministic dynamic system can be written as a difference equation:

$$y_t = f(\theta; y_{t-1}, \ldots, y_{t-p}), \tag{3.5}$$

where θ denotes a parameter set. Typical questions are whether a system has one or more fixed points or limit cycles. One reason why it is relevant for statisticians to consider this class of models is that chaotic processes often reveal a similar behavior as stochastic processes and thus can be used for descriptive models as well. Also, in computational statistics, 'pseudo' random number generators are in fact deterministic, 'chaotic' processes of high dimension that for practical purposes can be treated as stochastic, because the behavior in low dimensions is very similar. Here, 'dimension' can be defined in different ways, one of which will be followed below.

Consider for example the famous "tent map":

$$y_t = \begin{cases} 2y_{t-1} & \text{if } \ y_{t-1} < 0.5, \\ 2(1 - y_{t-1}) & \text{if } \ y_{t-1} \geq 0.5. \end{cases} \tag{3.6}$$

In the upper part of Figure 3.1, y_t is plotted against y_{t-1} for a generated tent map with $n = 500$. In the lower part, the series y_t is plotted against time. From this plot it would be difficult to decide whether it is a stochastic or deterministic process. In fact, the autocorrelations of y_t are not significant at the first lags, so that from a statistical viewpoint this process would be considered as a weak white noise process.

How can one detect chaos for a given series? Tests as the in Section 3.5.6 discussed BDS Test are based on the definition of ***dimension*** for a chaotic process. In general, a series is defined to have dimension m, if the m–dimensional space is filled out, but the $(m+1)$–dimensional is not. Clearly, the tent map has dimension one, as can be seen in Figure 3.1: The process y_t fills out the unit interval $[0, 1]$, but the sequences $\{y_t, y_{t-1}\}$ do not fill out the unit square $[0, 1] \times [0, 1]$. As far as only the first m dimensions are regarded, the series looks like a random process, but in the $(m+1)^{th}$ dimension a deterministic dependence becomes observable. For higher dimensions, of course, this is difficult to find out graphically, but Grassberger and Procaccia (1983) found another way to display m–dimensional dependence in a $2d$–space: ***m-histories*** y_t^m are defined to be m-vectors of subsequent values of y, i.e. $y_t^m = (y_{t-m+1}, \ldots, y_t)$. Now, the *correlation integral* $C_m(\varepsilon)$ is defined as the fraction of pairwise m-histories that are close together with respect to the sup–norm, i.e.

$$C_m(\varepsilon) = \lim_{n \to \infty} \#\{(t,s), 0 < t, s < n : \| y_t^m - y_s^m \| < \varepsilon\}/n^2, \tag{3.7}$$

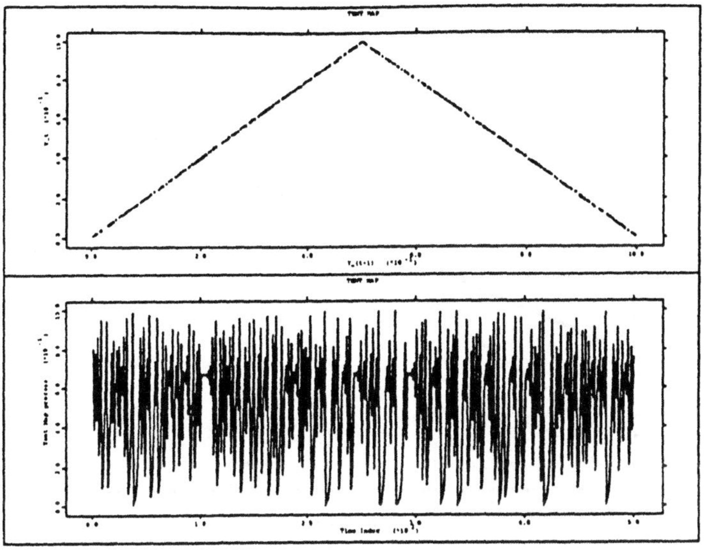

FIGURE 3.1. *The Tent Map. The upper panel shows* y_t *against* y_{t-1} *and the lower one* y_t *against* t, $t = 1, \ldots, 500$. *Both ordinates range from zero to one.*

where $||\cdot||$ denotes the sup-norm in $\mathbb{R}^m$.

The procedure of Grassberger and Procaccia (1983) is to plot $\log C_m(\varepsilon)$ against $\log \varepsilon$ for small ε and to compute the slope s_m as

$$s_m = \lim_{\varepsilon \to 0} \frac{\log C_m(\varepsilon)}{\log \varepsilon}. \tag{3.8}$$

s_m is monotonically increasing in $\log \varepsilon$. The *correlation dimension* d is now defined as $d \equiv \lim_{m\to\infty} s_m$. Deterministic and thus also chaotic processes have finite, random processes infinite correlation dimension. Intuitively, this means that for a random process, $C_m(\varepsilon)$ is expected to increase more for larger dimension when ε is increased than for a smaller dimension. Contrarily, for a chaotic process the increase of $C_m(\varepsilon)$ stays constant for sufficiently large dimension.

A graphical test can be based on shuffling the series and thus destroying any possible chaotic dependence. If the slope of the shuffled series is significantly larger than that of the original series, the latter can be considered as being dependent, although this does not necessarily imply chaotic dependence. Following Brock, Hsieh and LeBaron (1991), this plot is called the "Grassberger and Procaccia Plot" or simply GP Plot. The scale of ε is in terms of standard deviations $\hat{\sigma}$ of the series. Brock et al. (1991) suggest val-

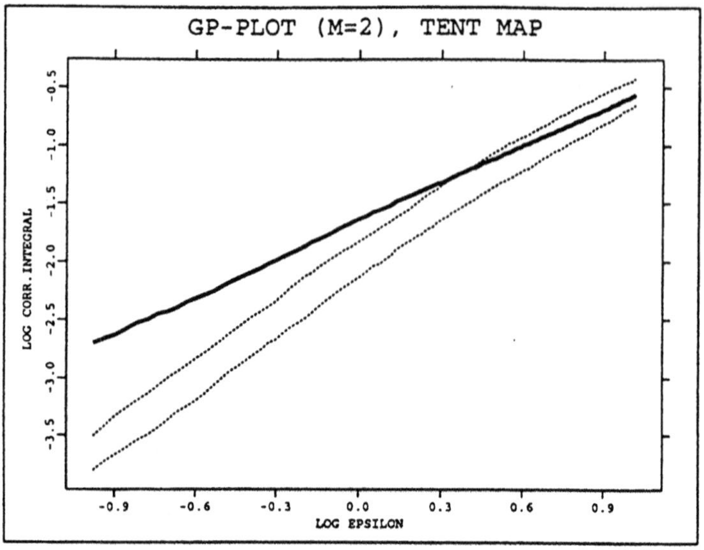

FIGURE 3.2. *GP Plot of the simulated tent map data, $n = 500$. The embedding dimension m is equal to two. Log ε is measured on a $\log_2 \hat{\sigma}$ scale. The thick line represents $\log C_2(\varepsilon)$ against $\log \varepsilon$ for the original series, the dotted lines the corresponding upper and lower boundaries of 50 shuffles of the series.*

ues between 0.5 and 2 times the standard deviation to be reliable and without too much noise. So the $\log_2$ scale used in the following pictures goes from -1 for $0.5\hat{\sigma}$ to 1 for $2\hat{\sigma}$.

Figure 3.2 shows the GP Plot for the simulated tent map series analysed above. The embedding dimension is chosen to be two. Recall that the tent map has dimension one, so $m = 2$ is sufficient to find out any structure. It clearly can be seen that the slope of the curve is higher for the fifty shuffled series than for the original series. Thus, the nonlinear dependence is detected.

Now consider the GP Plot for the 20 minute DEM/USD returns in ϑ–time, described in Section 2.4. Because the computation of the correlation integral is intensive, only the first 1000 observations are used. The series is more complex than the tent map, so in the first dimensions the series looks like an *i.i.d.* sequence. In Figure 3.3, the GP Plot is shown for $m = 8$. Still, there is not enough evidence for a rejection of the *i.i.d.* hypothesis. Unlike Brock et al. (1991), we conclude that the GP Plot alone does not yield reliable results, because it is known that financial series in general are not *i.i.d.* Therefore, a statistical test is required. A test based on the notion of correlation integral is discussed in Section 3.5.6.

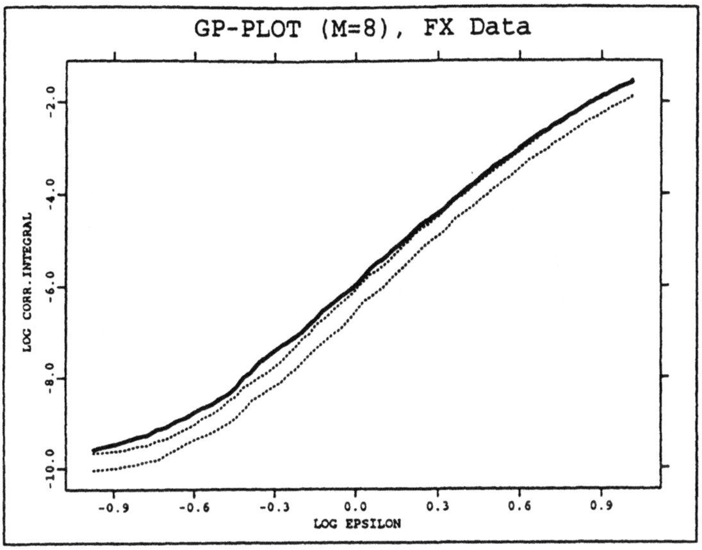

FIGURE 3.3. *GP Plot of the first thousand 20 minute DEM/USD returns in ϑ-time. The embedding dimension m is equal to eight. Log ε is measured on a* $\log_2 \hat{\sigma}$ *scale. The thick line represents* $\log C_8(\varepsilon)$ *against* $\log \varepsilon$ *for the original series, the dotted lines the corresponding upper and lower boundaries of 10 shuffles of the series.*

A general critique is the failure of dimension estimation in the case where the observed series consists both of a chaotic and a stochastic component, even if the structure is additive. In this situation, the chaotic series cannot be isolated unless the noise is unrealistically small and hence the process is 'almost' deterministic. Because usually the amount of noise in financial series is too large, one should refrain from estimating the 'dimension' of such real time series. This is underlined by the result for the DEM/USD return series.

3.3 Parametric Stochastic Models

Many successful nonlinear parametric models for time series have been developed and analysed extensively. For recent surveys, see the monographs by Granger and Teräsvirta (1993), Priestley (1988) and Tong (1990).

Unless otherwise stated, in all subsequent models $\{\varepsilon_t\}$ denotes a white noise sequence according to Definition 2.3.

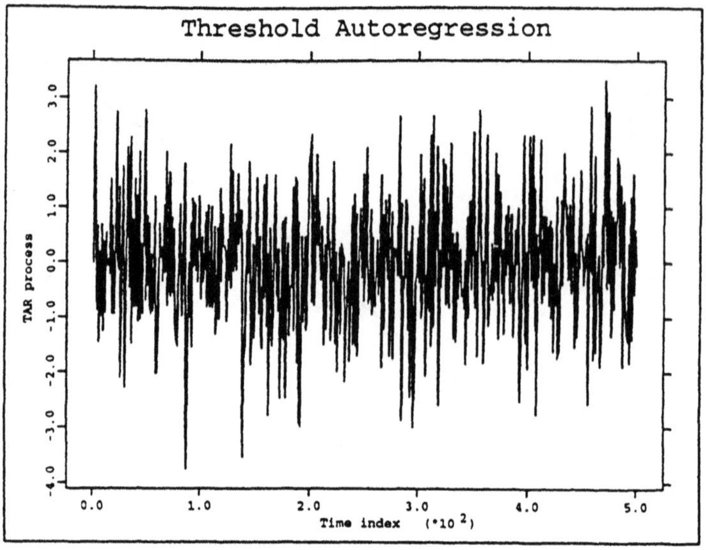

FIGURE 3.4. *Realization of the TAR process in (3.10),* $\varepsilon_t \sim N(0,1)$ *and* $n = 500$.

3.3.1 Threshold Autoregressive Models

Tong (1978) and Tong (1983) proposed a *threshold autoregressive* (TAR) model which is of the form

$$y_t = \phi_0^{(i)} + \phi_1^{(i)} y_{t-1} + \ldots + \phi_p^{(i)} y_{t-p} + \varepsilon_t^{(i)} \tag{3.9}$$

if $y_{t-d} \in \Omega_i$, $i = 1, \ldots, k$, where the Ω_i's are disjoint intervals on the real line with $\bigcup_{i=1}^{k} \Omega_i = I\!R$, and d is called the threshold lag (or delay parameter). Basically, this model can be regarded as a piecewise linear approximation to the general nonlinear AR model of (3.3). One important feature of the threshold models is that they can produce various limit cycles. Hence, if the process under study has an asymmetric cyclical form, the TAR model might be useful in providing a good description of the series and meaningful forecasts. Figure 3.4 shows a realization of the TAR process

$$y_t = \begin{cases} 1 + 0.6 y_{t-1} + \varepsilon_t & \text{if} \quad y_{t-1} \le 0 \\ -1 + 0.4 y_{t-1} + \varepsilon_t & \text{if} \quad y_{t-1} > 0. \end{cases} \tag{3.10}$$

The abrupt change in the regimes may be too restrictive in some cases. Therefore, a smooth transition autoregressive model (STAR) was proposed in the time series context by Teräsvirta, see e.g. Teräsvirta (1994). A simple model takes the form

$$y_t = \alpha_0 + \alpha_1 y_{t-1} + (\beta_0 + \beta_1 y_{t-1})F(y_{t-1} - \mu) + \varepsilon_t, \tag{3.11}$$

with $F(\cdot)$ being a continuous transition function. For example, $F(\cdot)$ can be the monotonously increasing logistic function with $\lim_{z\to-\infty} F(z) = 0$ and $\lim_{z\to\infty} F(z) = 1$. This implies a smooth trade–off between the two autoregressions for extreme values:

$$y_t = \alpha_0 + \alpha_1 y_{t-1} + \varepsilon_t,$$

and

$$y_t = (\alpha_0 + \beta_0) + (\alpha_1 + \beta_1)y_{t-1} + \varepsilon_t.$$

For economic applications of various extensions and refinements of the STAR model, see Granger and Teräsvirta (1993, ch. 9).

3.3.2 Exponential Autoregressive Models

Haggan and Ozaki (1981) proposed an *exponential autoregressive* (EXPAR) model, which assumes the form

$$y_t = \left\{a_1 + b_1 \exp(-c_1 y_{t-d}^2)\right\} y_{t-1} + \ldots + \left\{a_p + b_p \exp(-c_p y_{t-d}^2)\right\} y_{t-p} + \varepsilon_t. \tag{3.12}$$

where $c_i \geq 0, i = 1, \ldots, p$. Research has shown that this model is capable of reproducing nonlinear phenomena like limit cycles, amplitude-dependent frequency and jump phenomena. Thus, it has been applied to the Canadian Lynx data and the sunspot numbers, but also to economic business cycle data, see Tong (1990). A realization of the simplest model

$$y_t = \left\{0.5 + \exp(-y_{t-1}^2)\right\} y_{t-1} + \varepsilon_t. \tag{3.13}$$

is shown in Figure 3.5.

3.3.3 Bilinear Models

A bilinear time series model assumes the form

$$y_t - \sum_{i=1}^{p} \phi_i y_{t-i} = \mu + \varepsilon_t + \sum_{i=1}^{q} \theta_i \varepsilon_{t-i} + \sum_{i=1}^{r}\sum_{j=1}^{s} \beta_{ij} y_{t-i}\varepsilon_{t-j}, \tag{3.14}$$

It was first studied by Granger and Anderson (1978) and subsequently by Subba Rao (1981) and Subba Rao and Gabr (1980). It can be considered as a second order nonlinear time series model since it is constructed simply by

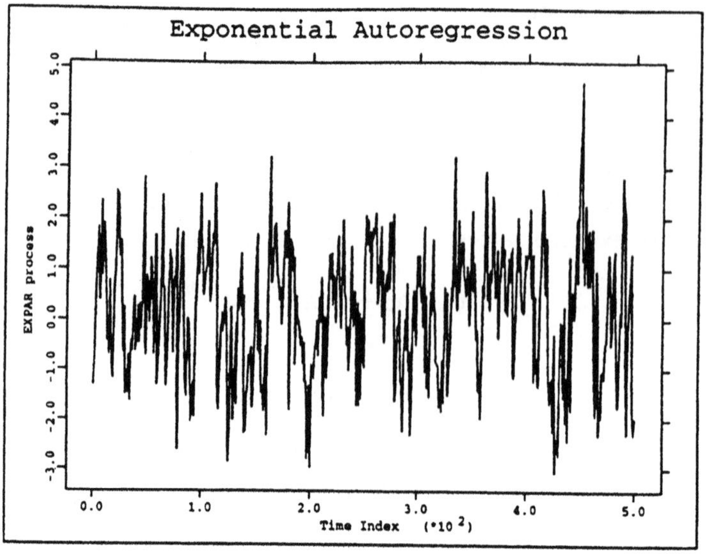

FIGURE 3.5. *Realization of the EXPAR process in (3.13),* $\varepsilon_t \sim N(0,1)$ *and* $n = 500$.

adding the cross-product terms of y_{t-i} and ε_{t-j} to a linear ARMA model. The bilinear model cannot reproduce the limit cycle phenomenon. However, it is able to reflect some other nonlinear phenomena. Subba Rao (1981) showed that with large bilinear coefficients β_{ij} a bilinear model can have sudden large amplitude bursts and is suitable for some kinds of seismological data sets like earthquakes and underground nuclear explosions. It has a clear indication of non-Gaussian structure and may have unbounded moments of marginal distributions.

A realization of the process

$$y_t = \beta\, y_{t-2}\, \varepsilon_{t-1} + \varepsilon_t. \tag{3.15}$$

for $\beta = 0.9$ is shown in Figure 3.6. This process is stationary and ergodic, if $\beta^2\sigma^2 < 1$, and $\sigma^2 \equiv \mathrm{E}[\varepsilon_t^2] < \infty$. It can be seen in Figure 3.6 that the variance of the process is time–dependent. In fact, it can be shown that the conditional variance of y_t, given information at $t-2$, is equal to $\sigma^2(1+\beta^2 y_{t-2}^2)$. This feature enables bilinear processes to be used also for financial data, as e.g. Maravall (1983) and Rothman (1994) show. Because of the typical sudden burst–outs, however, bilinear processes have been more successful in describing seismological data. A comparison and combination of bilinear and ARCH processes is given by Weiss (1986a).

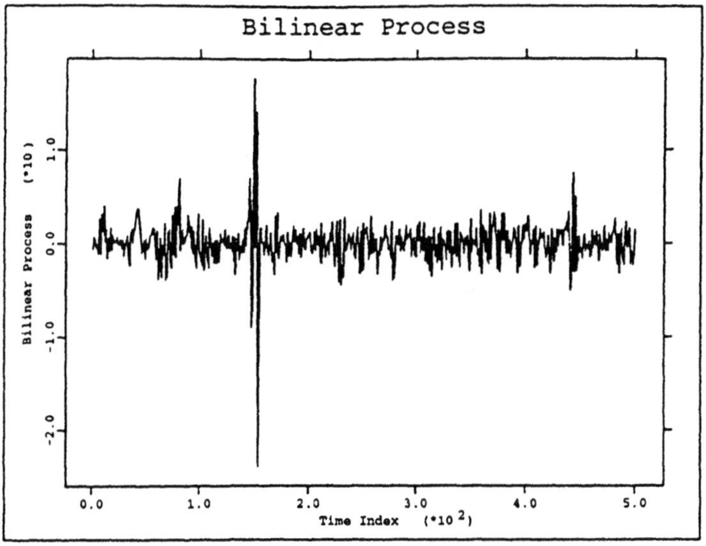

FIGURE 3.6. *Realization of the bilinear process in (3.15),* $\varepsilon_t \sim N(0,1)$ *and* $n = 500$.

3.3.4 Models with Autoregressive Conditional Heteroskedasticity

Within the class of models with time-varying conditional variance, the models with autoregressive conditional heteroskedasticity (ARCH), introduced by Engle (1982), have played the dominant role in the field of financial applications. ARCH-type models are mainly used to handle the following stylized facts which are commonly seen in financial time series:

1. the marginal distribution of returns has fat tails,
2. large changes tend to be followed by large ones and small changes by small ones, and
3. outliers tend to cluster.

Consider a standard regression or time series model with error term ε_t, which exhibits time-varying conditional variance:

$$\begin{aligned} \varepsilon_t \mid \psi_{t-1} &\sim N(0, \sigma_t^2) \\ \sigma_t^2 &= \omega + \sum_{i=1}^{q} \alpha_i \varepsilon_{t-i}^2, \end{aligned} \tag{3.16}$$

where ψ_{t-1} is the σ-field generated by $\{\varepsilon_{t-1}, \varepsilon_{t-2}, \ldots\}$, $\omega > 0$, and $\alpha_i \geq 0$ for $i = 1, \ldots, q$. Thus, the variance of the current disturbance is a linear function of lagged squared disturbances. The normality assumption can be relaxed. It can be shown that for each stationary ARCH(q) process there exists a random coefficient autoregressive process (RCAR), examined by Nicholls and Quinn (1982), such that both processes are equivalent with respect to the first two moments.

A *generalized autoregressive conditional heteroskedastic* (GARCH) process, introduced by Bollerslev (1986), is defined as (3.16) with additional autoregressive terms:

$$\sigma_t^2 = \omega + \sum_{i=1}^{q} \alpha_i \varepsilon_{t-i}^2 + \sum_{i=1}^{p} \beta_i \sigma_{t-i}^2. \tag{3.17}$$

For the GARCH(p,q) model, a sufficient but not necessary condition for the positivity of σ_t^2 is $\omega > 0$, $\alpha_i \geq 0, \beta_i \geq 0$ for all $i > 0$. Realizations of the ARCH(1)

$$\varepsilon_t = \sqrt{0.2 + 0.8\varepsilon_{t-1}^2}\, \xi_t \tag{3.18}$$

and GARCH(1,1)

$$\begin{aligned} \varepsilon_t &= \sigma_t \xi_t \\ \sigma_t^2 &= 0.1 + 0.1\varepsilon_{t-1}^2 + 0.8\sigma_{t-1}^2 \end{aligned} \tag{3.19}$$

processes with $\xi_t \sim N.i.d(0,1)$ are shown in Figure 3.7.

Surveys of the theory and applications in finance are provided by Bollerslev, Chou and Kroner (1992) and Bera and Higgins (1993). ARCH models and a variety of extensions are examined in more detail in Chapter 4.

3.3.5 Stochastic Volatility Models

In ARCH models, the conditional variance is exactly determined by lagged disturbances. An alternative approach is to formulate a stochastic process for the volatility, e.g. an AR(1) process:

$$y_t = \exp(\sigma_t^2/2)\xi_t \tag{3.20}$$

$$\sigma_t^2 = \alpha + \beta\sigma_{t-1}^2 + \eta_t, \tag{3.21}$$

where ξ_t and η_t are mean zero processes with variance one and σ_η^2, respectively, and $|\beta| < 1$. The usual assumption is that ξ_t and η_t are independent and normally distributed. The AR(1) process is written in the exponent to ensure that the variance is positive.

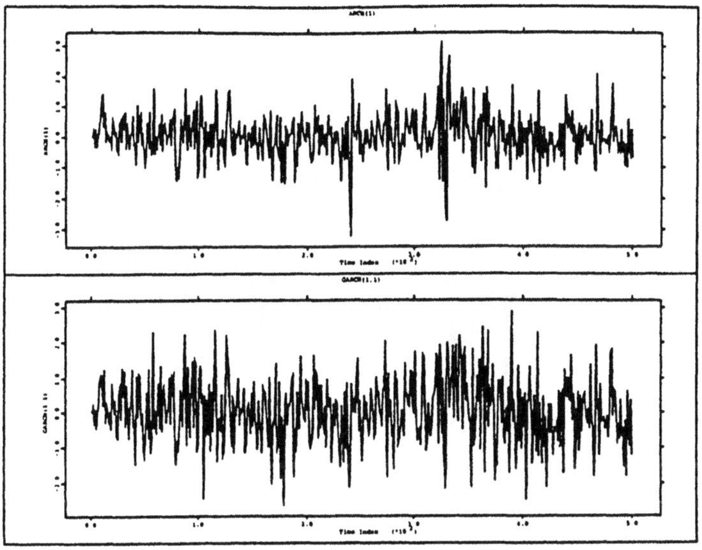

FIGURE 3.7. *Realization of the ARCH(1) process in (3.18) (upper panel) and of the GARCH(1,1) process in (3.19) (lower panel) with* $n = 500$. *The ordinates cover the interval [-3, 3] (upper panel) and [-2.5, 3] (lower panel).*

The distribution of y_t is fat–tailed because of the mixing distributions of ξ_t and η_t. In fact, the kurtosis is equal to $3\exp(\sigma_\eta^2)$. This enables stochastic volatility (SV) models to be used for modelling the dynamic behavior of speculative prices. Examples for foreign exchange rates are given by Gallant, Hsieh and Tauchen (1995) and Mahieu and Schotman (1995).

Besides the ARCH models, which will be discussed in more detail in Chapter 4, the SV model class is most relevant for financial time series, because it is the discrete time analogue to stochastic volatility models in continuous time finance, where log-volatility is modelled as a diffusion process. Because of the importance of SV models, some hints for estimation are given now in addition to the general remarks in Section 3.3.7.

Estimating a SV model by exact likelihood methods is difficult, because σ_t^2 is not observed. Writing (3.20) in the linear state space form

$$y_t^* = \sigma_t^2 + \xi_t^*, \tag{3.22}$$

with $y_t^* = \log y_t^2$ and $\xi_t^* = \log \xi_t^2$, allows the model to be estimated by the quasi maximum likelihood (QML) method, replacing the $\log \chi^2$ distribution of ξ_t^* by the normal distribution with adjusted first and second moment. This can lead to inefficient parameter estimates. The drawbacks of QML are

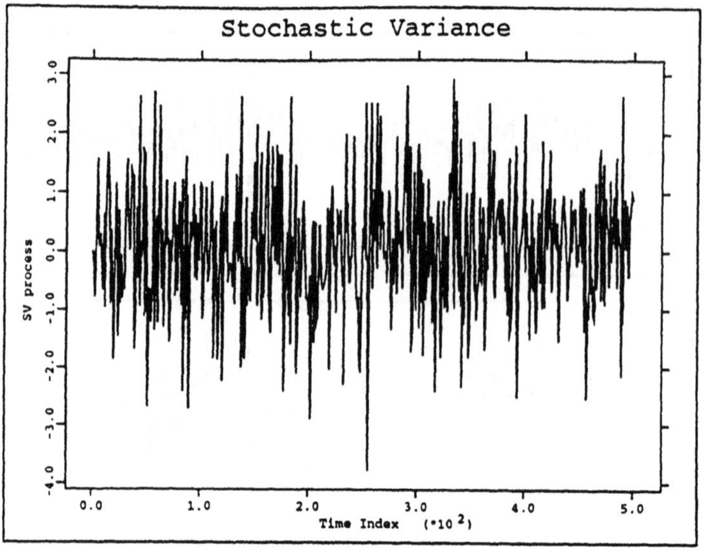

FIGURE 3.8. *Realization of the SV process* $y_t = \exp(\sigma_t^2/2)\xi_t$, *with* σ_t^2 *generated as in (3.23), and* $n = 500$.

listed by Andersen (1994). Other methods such as the generalized method of moments (GMM) also are not without problems.

A realization of the SV AR(1) process (3.20) with $\sigma_\eta^2 = 0.01$ and

$$\sigma_t^2 = 0.1 + 0.9\sigma_{t-1}^2 + \eta_t \tag{3.23}$$

is shown in Figure 3.8.

3.3.6 Markov Switching Regimes

Hamilton (1989) has proposed a model based on a hidden Markov chain, which determines the state, or regime, of the process. In intercept–form, a general form of the model can be written as

$$y_t - \mu(s_t) = \sum_{i=1}^{p} \phi_i \{y_{t-i} - \mu(s_{t-i})\} + \sigma(s_t)\xi_t, \tag{3.24}$$

where both mean and variance depend on the unobserved Markov chain s_t, ϕ_i, $i = 1, \ldots, p$ are parameters, and $\xi_t \sim N.i.d.(0,1)$. In the simplest case, s_t is a first order Markov chain with two regimes and transition probabilities

$$P(s_t = 1 \mid s_{t-1} = 1) = p \tag{3.25}$$

$$P(s_t = 0 \mid s_{t-1} = 0) = q. \tag{3.26}$$

The duration in a given regime is $(1-p)^{-1}$ and $(1-q)^{-1}$, respectively.

Markov switching regime models are mostly applied in the field of business cycles. Pagan and Schwert (1990) provide estimates for US stock index data, comparing various nonlinear models, and Engel and Hamilton (1990) estimate a Markov switching regime model for quarterly exchange rates.

3.3.7 Parameter Estimation

In general, estimation of finite parametric nonlinear time series models can be done by three standard techniques, i.e. maximum likehood, conditional least squares and generalized method of moments. With stationary ergodic Markov chains, Basawa and Prakasa Rao (1980), and Hall and Heyde (1980) provided consistency and asymptotic normality of the maximum likelihood estimates under mild conditions. However, in practice it is usually difficult to find the exact likelihood function for nonlinear time series processes. The conditional least-squares method minimizes the sum of squares of residuals and is very easy to use for appropriately parameterized nonlinear autoregressive models. Klimko and Nelson (1978) proved that under mild conditions the least-squares estimates are consistent and asymptotically normally distributed. More references can also be found in Tjøstheim (1986), Robinson (1977), Hinich and Patterson (1980), and Lai and Wei (1983). Lastly, from a Bayesian viewpoint, with simple formulation and appropriate prior (usually conjugate prior), the posterior distribution of the parameters can be found through numerical integrations or Markov Chain Monte Carlo methods.

3.4 Nonparametric and Semiparametric Models

Nonlinear time series analysis has become one of the most active research fields during the last years. The reason for this is the obvious disability of linear ARMA models to describe many time series in reality, particularly in finance. Many parametric nonlinear models have been investigated. For reviews with practical examples see e.g. Tjøstheim (1994) and Härdle, Lütkepohl and Chen (1997). An overview that focuses on the implementation in XploRe is given by Chen and Hafner (1995). In spite of the improved understanding of the theoretical properties of nonlinear models, the situation for the practitioner has not become easier, because he has to choose a model out of an ocean of different functional forms. If he does not have substantial knowledge about the process under study, i.e. the physical law, the dynamic nature or the deterministic behavior, etc., he may follow the principle of "letting data speak for themselves". Along with the rapid development of nonparametric regression techniques, many nonparametric nonlinear time series model building techniques have been developed.

Historically, nonparametric methods have been developed for the case of independent, identically distributed (*i.i.d.*) regressors. For many different estimators, consistency and asymptotic normality have been proved. In general, the rate of convergence is slower for nonparametric estimation than for parametric. This is the price for obtaining more flexible models.

Since the beginning of the eighties, many researchers have generalized nonparametric regression results for dependent data, allowing for different 'degrees' of dependence. The mathematical concept is that of the *mixing conditions*, which can be interpreted as the speed at which the series becomes independent asymptotically. They are motivated by the fact that for two independent events A and B, the probability of both events occurring together is equal to the product of the two marginal probabilities. So $|P(A \cap B) - P(A)P(B)|$ can be considered as a measure of dependence beween A and B. Let $y_t, t = 1, 2, \ldots$, be a time series and $\mathcal{F}_i^j$ the σ–algebra generated by $y_i, \ldots, y_j$. Then, y_t is called to be α–mixing, if

$$\sup_{A \in \mathcal{F}_1^n, B \in \mathcal{F}_{n+k}^\infty} |P(A \cap B) - P(A)P(B)| \leq \alpha_k$$

and $\alpha_k \to 0$ as $k \to \infty$. The name 'strong mixing' for this concept, introduced by Rosenblatt (1956) is somewhat misleading, because it is weaker than the so–called ϕ–mixing condition of Billingsley (1968),

$$\sup_{A \in \mathcal{F}_1^n, B \in \mathcal{F}_{n+k}^\infty} |P(A \cap B) - P(A)P(B)| \leq \phi_k P(A)$$

with $\phi_k \to 0$ as $k \to \infty$.

These are the most important conditions, but others have been used as well. For a detailed discussion of mixing conditions, see Györfi, Härdle, Sarda and Vieu (1989, ch. II). Bierens (1983) and Collomb and Härdle (1986) provided uniform consistency results of kernel estimators for the ϕ–mixing case. It is known, however, that for example simple parametric AR(1) processes are not ϕ–mixing. Robinson (1983) derived asymptotic normality of nonparametric estimators under the weaker α–mixing condition. Note that generally these conditions are difficult to check. However, if the process follows a stationary Markov chain, then geometric ergodicity implies absolute regularity, which in turn implies α–mixing. There are developed techniques for checking the geometric ergodicity, see Tweedie (1975), Tjøstheim (1990), Pham (1985) and Diebolt and Guégan (1993).

Consider a general nonlinear autoregressive model of order p:

$$y_t = f(y_{t-1}, \ldots, y_{t-p}) + \sigma(y_{t-1}, \ldots, y_{t-p})\xi_t, \tag{3.27}$$

where $\xi_t \sim i.i.d.(0,1)$, $\mathrm{E}[y_t \mid \psi_{t-1}] = f(\cdot)$ is the conditional mean or *mean function*, and $Var(y_t \mid \psi_{t-1}) = \sigma^2(\cdot)$ is the conditional variance or *variance function*. Here and in the following, ψ_t denotes the information set available at time t. Thus, model (3.27) allows for both nonlinear mean and variance functions, also incorporating conditional heteroskedasticity. For a formal treatment of nonparametric estimation of this general models, it is referred to Masry and Tjøstheim (1995), who provide strong convergence and asymptotic normality results under mild conditions. In the very general form (3.27), the model can be estimated only for small dimensions p, due to the so-called 'curse of dimensionality'. Purely nonparametric estimation techniques are based on a locally weighted averaging method. This method collapses, however, if there are locally not enough data. As a consequence, the 'smoothing parameter' or bandwidth would have to be chosen reasonably large, thereby averaging out local structure in the data. To overcome these difficulties, restricted models have been proposed recently in the time series context, based on well-known properties in the regression case. After discussing purely nonparametric estimators, restricted models such as additive models, functional coefficient models and adaptive spline threshold AR models are investigated.

3.4.1 Local Conditional Mean (Median) Estimation

Consider the general nonlinear homoskedastic AR(p) process

$$y_t = f(y_{t-1}, \ldots, y_{t-p}) + \varepsilon_t.$$

Let $\mathbf{Y}_{t-1} = (y_{t-1}, \ldots, y_{t-p})'$, and choose $\delta_n > 0$. For any $x \in \mathbb{R}^p$, let $I_n(x) = \{t : 1 < t < n \text{ and } \| \mathbf{Y}_{t-1} - x \| < \delta_n\}$, where $\| \cdot \|$ is an arbitrary norm in $\mathbb{R}^p$, and $N_n(x) = \#I_n(x)$. The conditional mean function estimator is given by

$$\hat{f}_n(x) = \frac{1}{N_n(x)} \sum_{t \in I_n(x)} y_t,$$

and the local conditional median estimator is given by

$$\tilde{f}(x) = \text{median}\{y_t,\, t \in I_n(x)\}.$$

Under α-mixing conditions, Truong (1993) provides the optimal rate of convergence.

3.4.2 Nadaraya-Watson Estimation

Robinson (1983) and Auestad and Tjøstheim (1990), among others, used a kernel estimator to estimate the conditional mean. Härdle and Vieu (1992) extended the result to simultaneous estimation of conditional mean and variance in (3.27).

Let us write $\mathrm{E}[y_t \mid y_{t-1} = x_1, \ldots, y_{t-p} = x_p] \equiv f(x_1, \ldots, x_p)$. The function $f(x_1, \ldots, x_p)$ is estimated by the Nadaraya–Watson estimator. For $p = 1$ and $x_1 \equiv x$ this can be written as

$$\hat{f}(x) = \frac{\sum_{t=2}^{n} K\{(x - y_{t-1})/h_n\} y_t}{\sum_{t=2}^{n} K\{(x - y_{t-1})/h_n\}}, \tag{3.28}$$

where $h_n > 0$ denotes the bandwidth and $K(\cdot)$ a kernel function satisfying $\int K(u)du = 1$, $K(\cdot) \geq 0$ and $\int u^2 K(u)du < \infty$. The conditional variance, $\mathrm{Var}(y_t \mid y_{t-1} = x_1, \ldots, y_{t-p} = x_p) \equiv \sigma^2(x_1, \ldots, x_p)$ can be estimated by using

$$\begin{aligned} \mathrm{Var}(y_t \mid \psi_{t-1}) &= \mathrm{E}\left[(y_t - \mathrm{E}[y_t \mid \psi_{t-1}])^2 \mid \psi_{t-1}\right] \\ &= \mathrm{E}[y_t^2 \mid \psi_{t-1}] - (\mathrm{E}[y_t \mid \psi_{t-1}])^2, \end{aligned}$$

so that

$$\hat{\sigma}^2(x) = \frac{\sum_{t=2}^{n} K\{(x - y_{t-1})/h_n\} y_t^2}{\sum_{t=2}^{n} K\{(x - y_{t-1})/h_n\}} - \{\hat{f}(x)\}^2. \tag{3.29}$$

In nonparametric estimation, there is a general trade-off between a large variance for small bandwidths and large bias for large bandwidths. Thus, the choice of h_n has proven to be much more crucial than the choice of the kernel. Asymptotically, some measure of discrepancy between regression curve and estimate, for example the average squared error (ASE), is minimized by balancing the squared bias and the variance term. Härdle and Vieu (1992) proved that the result in the *i.i.d.* case, $h \sim n^{-1/5}$, holds under suitable conditions in the time series context. Plugging this into the expressions of asymptotic bias and variance, one obtains an MSE-convergence rate of $n^{-4/5}$, which is slower than the n^{-1}-convergence of parametric estimation and is a standard result for most nonparametric estimates. This holds for the estimation of both $\mathrm{E}[y_t \mid \psi_{t-1}]$ and $\mathrm{E}[y_t^2 \mid \psi_{t-1}]$.

For finite samples, some data–driven bandwidth selection techniques have been developed in the regression context. Härdle and Vieu (1992) also showed that cross-validation using a leave–one–out estimate yields an asymptotic optimal estimate in the sense that ASE converges in probability to its infimum. For more information on bandwidth–selection and cross–validation, see Section 5.2.2.

If $p > 1$, estimation becomes more difficult. A multivariate version of (3.28) is easily established, but the sparseness of data in high dimensions, say $p > 5$, makes the problems in most cases not tractable. In many cases, however, the data can be considered as being in some sense 'locally independent', which allows the reduction of one multidimensional kernel to the product of p univariate kernels. The Nadaraya–Watson estimator with product kernels is thus given by

$$\hat{f}(x_1,\ldots,x_p) = \frac{\sum_{t=p+1}^{n}\prod_{i=1}^{p} K\{(x_i - y_{t-i})/h_{n,i}\} y_t}{\sum_{t=p+1}^{n}\prod_{i=1}^{p} K\{(x_i - y_{t-i})/h_{n,i}\}}. \tag{3.30}$$

The conditional variance $\sigma^2(x_1,\ldots,x_p)$ in (3.27) is estimated by

$$\hat{\sigma}^2(x_1,\ldots,x_p) = \frac{\sum_{t=p+1}^{n}\prod_{i=1}^{p} K\{(x_i - y_{t-i})/h_{n,i}\} y_t^2}{\sum_{t=p+1}^{n}\prod_{i=1}^{p} K\{(x_i - y_{t-i})/h_{n,i}\}} - \{\hat{f}(x_1,\ldots,x_p)\}^2. \tag{3.31}$$

In this general form, $h_{n,i}$, $i = 1,\ldots,p$, is allowed to differ for each lag. In practice, however, it will in most cases suffice to use the same bandwidth.

3.4.3 Local Polynomial Estimation

Tsybakov (1986) and Härdle and Tsybakov (1997) used local polynomial nonparametric regression techniques to estimate the conditional mean and conditional variance in time series. They considered the conditionally heteroskedastic autoregressive nonlinear model (CHARN) $y_t = f(y_{t-1}) + \sigma(y_{t-1})\xi_t$ where ξ_t is an *i.i.d.* error with mean 0 and variance 1. For estimation of $f(x)$ and $\sigma^2(x)$ with local polynomials of degree l, the following weighted least squares problems are solved:

$$\hat{\beta}(x) = \arg\min_{\beta\in\mathbb{R}^{l+1}} \sum_{t=2}^{n}\left(y_t - \sum_{j=0}^{l}\beta_j(y_{t-1}-x)^j\right)^2 K_h(y_{t-1}-x) \tag{3.32}$$

and

$$\hat{s}(x) = \arg\min_{s\in\mathbb{R}^{l+1}} \sum_{t=2}^{n}\left(y_t^2 - \sum_{j=0}^{l}s_j(y_{t-1}-x)^j\right)^2 K_h(y_{t-1}-x). \tag{3.33}$$

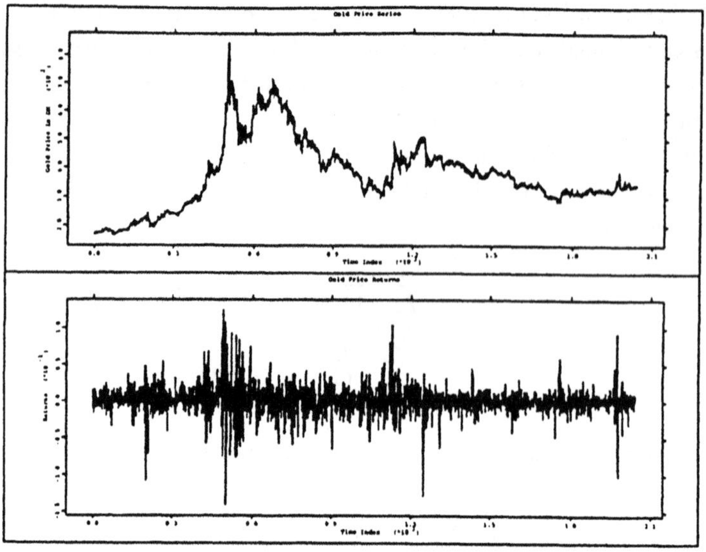

FIGURE 3.9. *Daily gold prices in DM (upper panel) and returns (lower panel), 1978 to 1986 (n = 2040). The ordinates cover approximately the interval [200, 800] (upper panel) and [-0.15, 0.1] (lower panel).*

The estimators $\hat{f}(x)$ and $\hat{\sigma}^2(x)$ are then given by

$$\hat{f}(x) = \hat{\beta}_0(x) \quad \text{and} \quad \hat{\sigma}^2(x) = \hat{s}_0(x) - \{\hat{\beta}_0(x)\}^2.$$

Härdle and Tsybakov (1997) proved asymptotic normality of these estimators under conditions satisfying the assumptions of Tweedie (1975) and Diebolt and Guégan (1993). Again, the MSE-convergence rate is $n^{-4/5}$. For details about nonparametric estimation of the CHARN model, see Section 5.2.

Example 3.1 (Gold Price Returns) *The performances of the Nadaraya-Watson estimate and the local linear estimate shall be compared graphically by applying both estimators to the gold price series analysed in Härdle and Vieu (1992). The data set consists of the daily recorded price of one ounce gold in DM, 1978 to 1986 (n = 2041). In Figure 3.9, the price series p_t is shown together with the returns, defined as $y_t = \log(p_t) - \log(p_{t-1})$.*

The model

$$y_t = f(y_{t-1}) + \sigma(y_{t-1})\xi_t$$

is estimated by the Nadaraya-Watson and local linear estimator and the resulting plots for the conditional mean and variance are shown in Figure 3.10 and 3.11, respectively. It can be seen that the local linear estimate is more flexible at the boundaries.

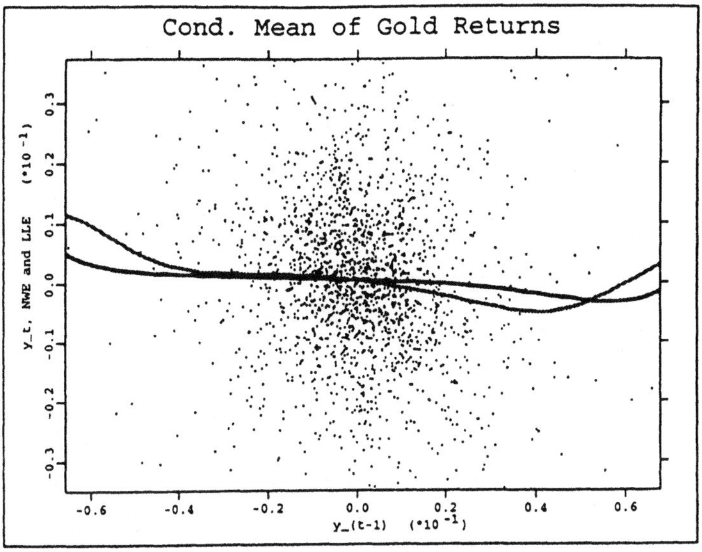

FIGURE 3.10. *Gold price returns at t vs. t − 1, Nadaraya-Watson (black) and local linear estimates (grey) of the conditional mean. In both cases,* $h = 0.05$ *was used. Boundaries were skipped in the picture.*

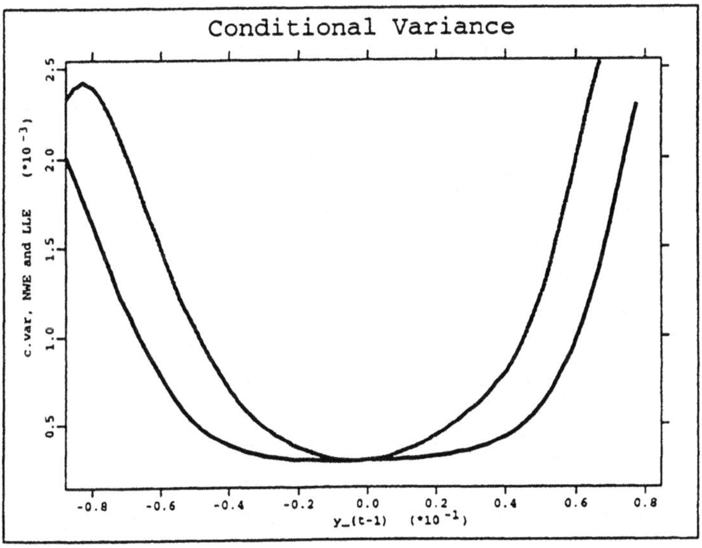

FIGURE 3.11. *Nadaraya-Watson (black) and local linear estimates (grey) of the conditional variance of the gold price returns. In both cases,* $h = 0.05$ *was used. Boundaries were skipped in the picture.*

3.4.4 k-Nearest Neighbor Estimation

Yakowitz (1987) provided convergence results for a k-Nearest Neighbor (kNN) estimator for dependent observations. Under the assumption of a stationary ergodic Markoc chain, he proves the same convergence rate of the MSE as in the regression context, namely $n^{-4/5}$.

Define the index set $J_x = \{t : y_t \text{ is one of the } k \text{ nearest neighbors of } x\}$. Consider again the model (3.27). Then the kNN estimator can be written in the general linear representation of a nonparametric estimator

$$\hat{f}_k(x) = n^{-1} \sum_{t=1}^{n} W_{kt}(x) y_t, \tag{3.34}$$

where the weights $W_{kt}(x) = n/k$, if $t \in J_x$, and zero otherwise. The kNN estimator can be interpreted as a kernel estimator with uniform kernel and adaptive bandwith equal to the distance between x and its kth nearest neighbor. Therefore, the variance of the estimator is no more dependent on the density of the data. Yakowitz (1987) provided an application to the hydrological Bird Creek data. In economics, Diebold and Nason (1990) use kNN estimates to predict foreign exchange rates, and in the semiparametric GARCH framework of Sentana and Wadhwani (1991) the kNN estimator is used to model Japanese stock market returns with respect to exogenous variables.

3.4.5 Functional Coefficient AR Model

A *functional coefficient autoregressive* (FAR) model can be written as

$$y_t = f_1(y_{t-d})y_{t-1} + f_2(y_{t-d})y_{t-2} + \ldots + f_p(y_{t-d})y_{t-p} + \varepsilon_t.$$

The model is general enough to include TAR models (when the coefficient functions are step functions) and EXPAR models (when the coefficient functions are exponential functions) along with many other models (e.g., sine function models, logistic function models).

Chen and Tsay (1993a) use an *arranged local regression* procedure (ALR) to roughly identify the shapes of the nonlinear functions. For $x \in I\!R$ and $\delta_n > 0$, let $I_n(x) = \{t : 1 < t < n, |y_{t-d} - x| < \delta_n\}$. If we regress y_t on $y_{t-1}, \ldots, y_{t-p}$ using all the observations y_t such that $t \in I_n(x)$, then the estimated coefficients can be used as estimates of $f_i(x), i = 1, \ldots, p$. Note that the window width δ_n can be interpreted as the smoothing parameter.

Example 3.2 (Chickenpox Data) *For an illustration of the ALR implementation consider the chickenpox data used by Chen and Tsay (1993a) and described by Sugihara and May (1990) with* 533 *observations. Natural logarithms are taken for variance stabilization. In the implementation, the sample*

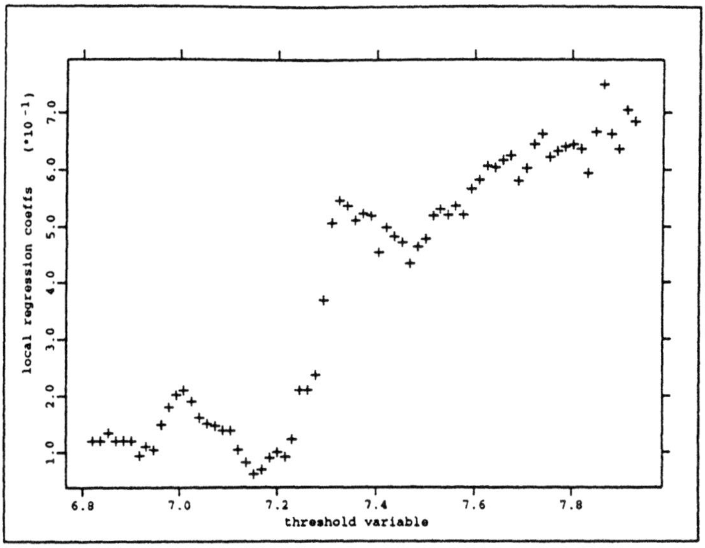

FIGURE 3.12. *In the ALR procedure, the local regression coefficients $\beta_1(\cdot)$ are used as estimates of $f_1(\cdot)$ for the FAR model (chickenpox example).*

size within each window is required to be at least k ($> p$) to ensure the accuracy of the coefficient estimates. Lacking an optimal selection criterion, the structure parameters are selected heuristically to be $k = 30$ and the window width $c = (x_{max} - x_{min})/10$. Several nonlinearity tests indicate strong nonlinearity for the threshold lag $d = 12$, which is plausible because we have monthly data with strong seasonality. The most significant lags are 1 and 24. Thus, the resulting model is

$$y_t = f_1(y_{t-12})y_{t-1} + f_2(y_{t-12})y_{t-24} + \varepsilon_t. \tag{3.35}$$

At first, the values need to be sorted for the window shifting. The number of iterations is computed such that the whole range $x_{max} - x_{min}$ is covered. At each step the time indices of those values that are within the current window are calculated. Finally, the least squares estimation of the first and second coefficient, i.e. function value, is performed for each window.

The estimates of $f_1(\cdot)$ and $f_2(\cdot)$, which represent the local coefficients $\beta_1(\cdot)$ and $\beta_2(\cdot)$, are shown in Figures 3.12 and 3.13, respectively.

One can now formulate parametric models based on the forms of the estimated nonlinear functions. There seems to be a level shift around the value $y_{t-12} = 7.2$, so a TAR model with threshold value 7.2 is suggested. For details see Chen and Tsay (1993a).

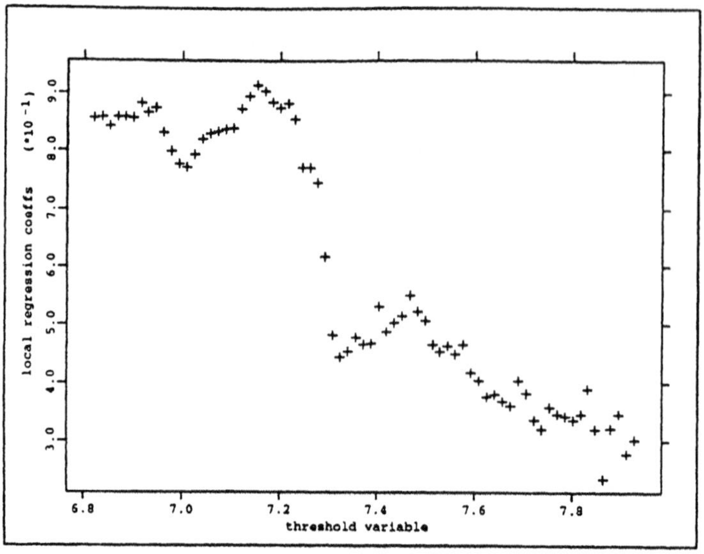

FIGURE 3.13. *In the ALR procedure, the local regression coefficients $\beta_2(\cdot)$ are used as estimates of $f_2(\cdot)$ for the FAR model (chickenpox example).*

Note that a procedure similar to the local weighted regression of Cleveland and Devlin (1988) can be used here as well.

3.4.6 Nonlinear Additive AR Model

A *nonlinear additive autoregressive* (NAAR) model can be written as

$$y_t = f_1(y_{t-1}) + f_2(y_{t-2}) + \ldots + f_p(y_{t-p}) + \varepsilon_t.$$

Similar models have been studied extensively in the regression context, see Hastie and Tibshirani (1990) and the references therein. Chen and Tsay (1993b) used the alternating conditional expectation) (ACE) algorithm of Breiman and Friedman (1985) to specify the model. The basic idea is to estimate the transformations $f_1(y_{t-1}), \ldots, f_p(y_{t-p})$ such that the fraction of variance not explained by a regression of y_t on $\sum_{j=1}^{p} f_j(y_{t-j})$ is minimized. Unlike in the general ACE algorithm, the response variable y_t is not transformed.

Example 3.3 (Riverflow Data) *The ACE algorithm was applied to the riverflow data of the river Jokulsa Eystri in Iceland. This is a multiple time series data set, consisting of daily riverflow (y_t), precipitation (z_t), and temperature (x_t) from January 1, 1972, to December 31, 1974 ($n = 1096$). For*

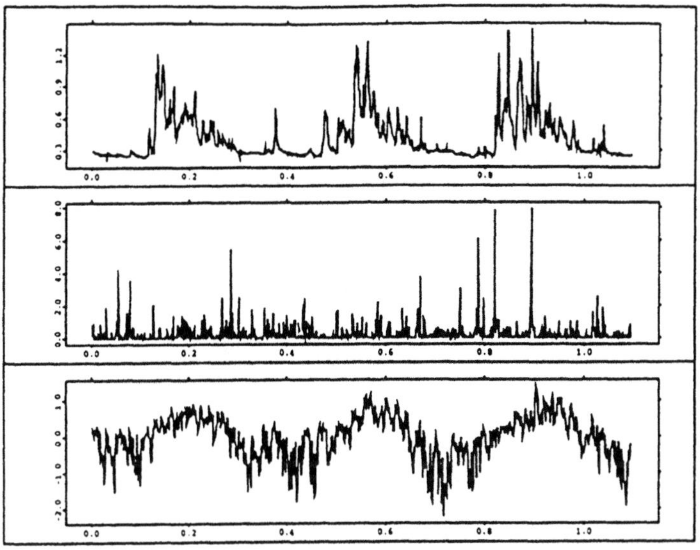

FIGURE 3.14. *Time plots of riverflow data; from top to bottom: daily riverflow y_t (30 to 120 m^3/s), daily precipitation z_t (0 to 800 mm/day) and daily temperature x_t (-20 to 10 C°); time index: $t = 1, \ldots, 1096$.*

further information see Tong (1990), who used threshold autoregressive models. The time series are plotted in Figure 3.14.

A procedure similar to the best subset regression is suggested by Chen and Tsay (1993b) to select the lag variables in the model. They found $\{y_{t-1}, y_{t-2}, z_t, z_{t-1}, x_{t-1}, x_{t-3}\}$ to be an appropriate explanatory set for the response variable y_t. The transformations $f_1(y_{t-1})$, $f_2(y_{t-2})$, $f_3(z_t)$, $f_4(z_{t-1})$, $f_5(x_{t-1})$, $f_6(x_{t-3})$ are shown in Figure 3.15.

Linear functions are suggested for the precipitation and piecewise linear functions for the lagged riverflow and temperature variables. In comparison to Tong's threshold model, the obtained model improves out-of-sample prediction and is preferred by the Akaike information criterion (AIC).

Note that the *additivity and variance stabilization* (AVAS) algorithm of Tibshirani (1988) can also be used here.

3.4.7 Projection Pursuit Model

Friedman and Stuetzle (1981) developed the semiparametric projection pursuit model, which can be written as

$$y_t = f(\gamma' \mathbf{Y}_{t-1}) + \varepsilon_t, \tag{3.36}$$

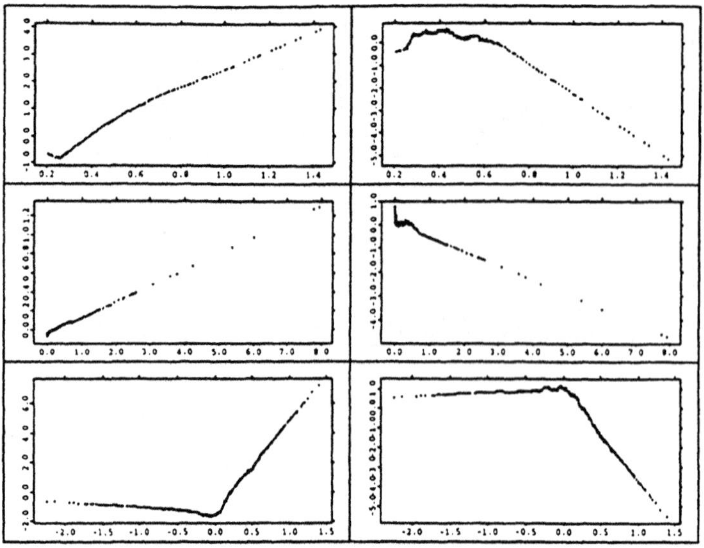

FIGURE 3.15. *Results of the ACE algorithm for the riverflow data. The plots show the suggested transformations. First row: y_{t-1} and y_{t-2}, second row: z_t and z_{t-1}, third row: x_{t-1} and x_{t-3}, where y_t indicates the riverflow series, z_t the precipitation, and x_t the temperature.*

where $\mathbf{Y}_{t-1} \equiv (y_{t-1}, \ldots, y_{t-p})'$, $f(\cdot)$ is a nonparametric unknown function, and γ denotes a parameter vector. This model reduces the dimension of the nonparametric estimation to one by projecting the lagged variables to an 'index', $\gamma'\mathbf{Y}_{t-1}$. The estimates of γ and $f(\cdot)$ are only identified up to scale and sign. The estimation procedure is iterative and thus computer intensive. Granger and Teräsvirta (1993) give some simulation results. They conclude that projection pursuit works well if the underlying function is nonlinear, otherwise the fit may be poor. This suggests to test first if nonlinearity is indeed apparent. For tests against nonlinearity see Section 3.5.

3.4.8 Neural Network Model

In some sense a completely different approach comes from the neural network literature, although these models are similar to projection pursuit models, discussed in Section 3.4.7. A neural network model with one *hidden layer* and q *units* can be written as

$$y_t = \alpha + \sum_{j=1}^{q} \beta_j \Phi(\gamma_j' \mathbf{Y}_{t-1}) + \varepsilon_t, \tag{3.37}$$

where $\Phi(\cdot)$ is a monotonically increasing function such as the logistic function, γ_j, $j = 1, \ldots, q$ denote parameter vectors, and $\mathbf{Y}_{t-1} \equiv (y_{t-1}, \ldots, y_{t-p})'$.

The main difference to projection pursuit models is that $\Phi(\cdot)$ is known. Statistical problems arise because a model of the form (3.37) is not identified due to the exchangeability of parameters. Thus, it is not always possible to note standard errors for the parameters, depending on the model and the training procedure used. Also, in most applications the model will be overparameterized, giving good in-sample fits, but poor out-of-sample predictions.

3.5 Testing Linearity

Nonlinear modelling is apparently useful in time series analysis. A nonlinear model, however, may give a spuriously good fit even when it is misspecified. In this case, out-of-sample predictions may be very poor. Heuristically, predictions based on linear models are more robust against model misspecification than predictions based on nonlinear models. It certainly follows that statistical methods are needed to ascertain whether a process is nonlinear. In the following we will discuss some of the time domain tests available in the literature. For frequency domain tests, see Subba Rao and Gabr (1980) and Hinich (1982). An excellent overview on general linearity tests is given by Granger and Teräsvirta (1993, ch. 6).

3.5.1 Lagrange Multiplier Tests Against an Unspecified Alternative

Among the three classical test procedures, the Lagrange multiplier (LM) test has been the most important one for testing against nonlinearity, covering a variety of tests against specific alternatives. A general test for linearity against an unspecified alternative is the classical regression error specification test (RESET) of Ramsey (1969). It consists of three steps:

1. Fit a linear AR(p) model to y_t and calculate the fitted values $\hat{y}_t$ and the residuals $\hat{\varepsilon}_t$ for $t = p+1, \ldots, n$, where n is the sample size. Denote the residual sum of squares by SSR_0.

2. Regress $\hat{\varepsilon}_t$ on the set of regressors $\{1, y_{t-1}, \ldots, y_{t-p}, \hat{y}_t^2, \ldots, \hat{y}_t^q\}$. Denote the residual sum of squares by SSR.

3. The test statistic is

q	2	3	4	5	6
F_{RESET}	1.59	29.45	21.01	15.99	14.7
$F^{q-1}_{n-p-q;0.99}$	6.63	4.61	3.78	3.32	3.02

TABLE 3.1. *Results of the RESET test applied to the 20 minute DEM/USD exchange rate returns in ϑ–time; $q = 2, \ldots, 6$.*

$$F = \frac{(SSR_0 - SSR)/(q-1)}{SSR/(n-p-q)}. \tag{3.38}$$

Under the null hypothesis of linearity, the statistic has an asymptotic F distribution with $(q-1)$ and $(n-p-q)$ degrees of freedom.

Example 3.4 (DEM/USD) *The RESET test was applied to DEM/USD exchange rate returns based on 20 minute intervals in ϑ–time, as described in Section 2.4, for $q = 2, \ldots, 6$. Based on model selection criteria, an AR(3) model was fitted (see Section 4.7) and the obtained residuals and fitted values were used for the test statistic. The results are given in Table 3.1 and show that the linearity assumption is rejected for $q > 2$.*

The RESET test is equivalent to the F-test of Keenan (1985) for $q = 2$. Several improvements of the original RESET test have been proposed, see e.g. Tsay (1986). Luukkonen, Saikkonen and Teräsvirta (1988) consider modifications particularly suited for the smooth transition AR model (STAR) discussed in Section 3.3.1.

3.5.2 Lagrange Multiplier Tests Against Conditional Heteroskedasticity

Engle (1982) adopted the general test against heteroskedasticity by Breusch and Pagan (1979) to the case of conditional heteroskedasticity with parametric autoregression, i.e. the ARCH(q) case. Basic assumption is the correct specification of the mean function. Thus, a rejection of the ARCH–test is not necessarily evidence against constant conditional variance, but might also be the result of a misspecification of the mean function.

The null hypothesis is that in (3.16), $\alpha_1 = \cdots = \alpha_q = 0$. Denote the constant variance under the null by σ_0^2. Let $z_t = (1, \varepsilon_{t-1}^2, \ldots, \varepsilon_{t-q}^2)$ and $z = (z_1, \ldots, z_n)'$, where ε_t, $t = 1-q, \ldots, n$ are for example the residuals of an ARMA model. Thus, the matrix z is of dimension $[n \times (q+1)]$. Then the Lagrange multiplier test can be written as

$$\lambda = (1/2)\, f_0' z(z'z)^{-1} z' f_0, \tag{3.39}$$

where $f_0 = \left(\frac{\varepsilon_1^2}{\sigma_0^2} - 1, \ldots, \frac{\varepsilon_n^2}{\sigma_0^2} - 1\right)'$.

Under the null hypothesis, $\text{Cov}(\varepsilon_t^2, \varepsilon_{t-\tau}^2) = 0$ for $\tau \neq 0$. Thus, the covariance matrix in (3.39) is asymptotically diagonal, and it can be shown that the statistic is asymptotically equivalent to

$$\lambda^* = nR^2, \tag{3.40}$$

where R^2 denotes the squared multiple correlation between f_0 and z, which is equivalent to the coefficient of determination of the regression

$$\varepsilon_t^2 = a_0 + a_1 \varepsilon_{t-1}^2 + \ldots + a_q \varepsilon_{t-q}^2 + v_t.$$

Under the null hypothesis, (3.40) is asymptotically equivalent to

$$\lambda^{**} = n \sum_{\tau=1}^{q} r_{\tau,2}^2, \tag{3.41}$$

where $r_{\tau,2}$ denotes the empirical τ–order autocorrelation of the squares of ε_t. Thus, the ARCH–LM statistic can be interpreted as a standard portmanteau test for the squares of a series.

The asymptotic distribution of λ, λ^*, and λ^{**} under the null is χ^2 with q degrees of freedom. An extension to the GARCH case was provided by Bollerslev (1986).

3.5.3 Portmanteau Tests

Portmanteau tests are based on asymptotic normality of the empirical autocorrelations of ε_t under the null of *i.i.d.* The theoretical autocorrelations of ε_t^j, $j = 1, 2, \ldots$ are obviously zero if ε_t is an independent sequence, such that general portmanteau tests for higher powers of ε_t are possible, testing for a stronger notion of linearity. McLeod and Li (1983) have derived the same asymptotic result for the squares of a series, ε_t^2.

Denoting the mean of ε_t^2 by σ_ε^2, the ACF of ε_t^2 can be written as

$$\rho_{\tau,2} = \frac{\text{E}[(\varepsilon_t^2 - \sigma_\varepsilon^2)(\varepsilon_{t-\tau}^2 - \sigma_\varepsilon^2)]}{\text{E}[(\varepsilon_t^2 - \sigma_\varepsilon^2)^2]} \tag{3.42}$$

for $\tau = 0, 1, 2, \cdots$.

The test statistic is based on $r_{\tau,2}$, the empirical counterpart of $\rho_{\tau,2}$, where expectations in (3.42) are replaced by sample means. Based on the results of Ljung and Box (1978) which showed that standard portmanteau tests tend to

q	1	2	3	4	5	7	10
ARCH–LM	805	898	961	1064	1119	1159	1194
$Q(q)$	805	1017	1159	1359	1515	1692	1883
$\chi^2_{q;0.99}$	6.63	9.21	11.34	13.28	15.09	18.47	23.21

TABLE 3.2. *Results of the ARCH–LM and portmanteau tests applied to the DEM/USD exchange rate returns;* $q = 1, \ldots, 5, 7, 10$.

accept the null hypothesis too often in small samples, McLeod and Li (1983) modified (3.41) to

$$Q(q) = n(n+2)\sum_{\tau=1}^{q}(n-\tau)^{-1}r^2_{\tau,2}, \tag{3.43}$$

which is, of course, asymptotically equivalent to (3.41).

Under the null hypothesis of *i.i.d.*, $Q(q)$ is asymptotically distributed as χ^2_q. As the Ljung–Box statistic, this test can be applied to the residuals of a fitted model as well as to the original series.

Example 3.5 (DEM/USD) *The asymptotically equivalent ARCH-LM test (3.40) and portmanteau test (3.43) were applied to the residuals of a fitted AR(4) model to the 20 minute DEM/USD exchange rate returns, see Section 2.4. Table 3.2 reports the statistics for* $q = 1, \ldots, 5, 7, 10$. *In both cases, the critical values are* $\chi^2_{q;0.99}$. *For* $q = 1$, *both tests are equivalent also for small samples. It is seen that both tests strongly reject the linearity assumption. This is evidence for a second order dependence structure in the data.*

3.5.4 Tests Against Threshold Nonlinearity

In Section 3.3.1 threshold autoregressive models (TAR) were introduced. There are several tests designed for testing linearity against threshold nonlinearity. Some of them are briefly sketched in the following.

3.5.4.1 CUSUM Test

The CUSUM test is based on rearranged observations. It estimates a linear AR model sequentially according to the increasing order of the value of a given threshold variable. The idea is to construct cumulative sums (CUSUMs) of the standardized prediction errors (also called *predictive residuals*). If the process is linear, the standardized predictive residuals are asymptotically independent normal random variables. The test statistic is formed by the maximum of the absolute CUSUMs. Petruccelli and Davies (1986) provide expressions for the asymptotic distribution. For an overview on CUSUM tests it is referred to Tong (1990, pp.249) and Granger and Teräsvirta (1993, pp.83).

3.5.4.2 Likelihood Ratio Test

For the threshold model

$$y_t = \begin{cases} \mu^{(1)} + \sum_{i=1}^{p_1} \phi_i^{(1)} y_{t-i} + \varepsilon_t^{(1)} & y_{t-d} \leq c \\ \mu^{(2)} + \sum_{i=1}^{p_2} \phi_i^{(2)} y_{t-i} + \varepsilon_t^{(2)} & y_{t-d} > c, \end{cases}$$

the null hypothesis of the likelihood ratio test for testing linearity is H_0: $p_1 = p_2 = p$ and $\phi_i^{(1)} = \phi_i^{(2)}$ for $i = 1, \ldots, p$ and $\mu^{(1)} = \mu^{(2)}$. Denote by $RSS_{TAR(c)}$ the residual sum of squares of a fitted TAR model with threshold c, and by RSS_{AR} the residual sum of squares of the restricted AR model. The asymptotic distribution of the test statistic

$$\lambda(c) = \frac{RSS_{AR} - RSS_{TAR(c)}}{RSS_{TAR(c)}/n} \tag{3.44}$$

is non-standard and given by Chan (1990).

3.5.4.3 TAR–F Test

The TAR–F test of Tsay (1989) combines the idea of CUSUM and F tests. The F–statistic is obtained by regressing the predictive residuals of the arranged autoregression (as in CUSUM) on the regressors $\{1, y_{t-1}, \ldots, y_{t-p}\}$. A large F–statistic implies that there are model changes in the series.

3.5.5 New–F Test

The New–F test of Tsay (1991) modifies the TAR–F test to test linearity against threshold nonlinearity, exponential nonlinearity, and bilinearity. The F–statistic is obtained by regressing the predictive residuals on the regressors $\{1, y_{t-1}, \ldots, y_{t-p}\}$, $\{y_{t-1} \exp(-y_{t-1}^2/\gamma)$, $G(z_{t-d})$, $y_{t-1}G(z_{t-d})\}$, $\{y_{t-1}\hat{e}_{t-1}$, $\ldots$, $y_{t-p}\hat{e}_{t-p}\}$, $\{\hat{e}_{t-1}\hat{e}_{t-2}, \ldots, \hat{e}_{t-p}\hat{e}_{t-p-1}\}$, where $\gamma = \max_t |y_{t-1}|$, and $z_{t-d} = (y_{t-d} - \bar{y}_d)/S_d$ with $\bar{y}_d$ and S_d being the sample mean and standard deviation of y_{t-d}, respectively, and $G(\cdot)$ is the cumulative distribution function of the standard normal random variable. The F–statistic of this regression follows asymptotically an F–distribution if the process is a linear AR(p) process.

3.5.6 BDS Test

The Test of Brock, Dechert and Scheinkman (1987), usually called BDS Test, is a test for independence and is based on the correlation integral, see Section 3.2. Recall from (3.7) the notation $C_m(\varepsilon)$ for the correlation integral with respect to embedding dimension m and given $\varepsilon > 0$. Now, the test is motivated by the fact that for an *i.i.d.* sequence, $C_m(\varepsilon) = \{C_1(\varepsilon)\}^m$. In Brock et al. (1987) it is shown that the test statistic

$$W_{m,n} = n^{1/2}\left\{C_{m,n}(\varepsilon) - C_{1,n}(\varepsilon)^m\right\}/\sigma_{m,n}(\varepsilon) \tag{3.45}$$

converges in distribution to N(0,1) under the null of *i.i.d.* Here, $\sigma_{m,n}(\varepsilon)$ denotes an estimate of the standard deviation under the null hypothesis.

As shown by Brock et al. (1991) and Hsieh (1991), the test has power against various linear and nonlinear processes, including for example GARCH and EGARCH processes. Brock et al. (1991) also provide power comparisons of the BDS test, Engle's ARCH test and Tsay's F test against five nonlinear processes. They conclude that the BDS test is performing well. One might criticize that the tests are designed for completely different purposes. The BDS test can also be used as a specification test, but not for all model classes. As shown in Brock and Dechert (1988) and Brock et al. (1991, pp. 235), under regularity conditions the test has the same asymptotic distribution when applied to the residuals of some time series models. Unfortunately, however, this does not hold for ARCH-type models, as their simulations show. The simulated size of the BDS test for the residuals of ARCH models has only been simulated, and no exact asymptotic results are available yet.

3.5.7 Nonparametric Tests

Hjellvik and Tjøstheim (1995) proposed a nonlinearity test based on the distance between the best linear and a nonlinear predictor of the conditional mean and conditional variance of y_t, given y_{t-k}. Having standardized the series, the best linear predictor of $M_k(y_{t-k}) = \mathrm{E}[y_t \mid y_{t-k}]$ is the autocorrelation between y_t and y_{t-k}, whereas a nonlinear predictor can be obtained by local polynomial estimation. For example, the Nadaraya–Watson estimate of $M_k(x)$ is

$$\hat{M}_k(x) = \frac{\sum_{t=k+1}^{n} K_h(x - y_{t-k})y_t}{\sum_{t=k+1}^{n} K_h(x - y_{t-k})}. \tag{3.46}$$

The distance index is defined as

$$L(M_k) = \mathrm{E}[(M_k(y_{t-k}) - \rho_k y_{t-k})^2],$$

which is estimated by

$$\hat{L}(M_k) = \frac{1}{n}\sum_{t=1}^{n}\left\{\hat{M}_k(y_t) - \hat{\rho}_k y_t\right\}^2 w(y_t),$$

where $w(x)$ is a weighting function with compact support.

A test against conditional heteroskedasticity can be based on the distance of an estimate of $V_k(y_{t-k}) = \text{Var}(y_t \mid y_{t-k})$ and the variance of the estimated residuals $\hat{\varepsilon}_t$ of an AR(p) model, $\hat{\sigma}^2_{\hat{\varepsilon}}$.

Hjellvik and Tjøstheim (1995) showed that the test statistics are consistent estimates of their theoretical values. A proof of asymptotic normality under the null hypothesis of linearity, however, is missing, but they argue that in the *i.i.d.* case tests based on the difference of parametric and nonparametric regression fits require very large data sets to have reliable approximation of the asymptotic distribution, as shown by Härdle and Mammen (1993). The situation is worse in the case of dependent observations. Therefore, Hjellvik and Tjøstheim (1995) recommend a bootstrap–based test procedure. The idea is to form bootstrap replicas and obtain a distribution of the test indices for the bootstrap replicas. The empirical size of the bootstap test was shown to be closer to the nominal size than the corresponding test based on the conjectured asymptotic normality for various sample sizes.

Example 3.6 (DEM/USD) *The functions $M_k(y_{t-k})$ and $V_k(y_{t-k})$ of the 20 minute DEM/USD returns in ϑ-time, see Section 2.4, were estimated for $k = 1,\ldots,4$ by local linear estimation. The results with the corresponding linear estimates are depicted in Figure 3.16 and 3.17, respectively. In both cases, boundaries were skipped in the pictures, and quartic kernels with $h =$ 0.5 were used for the standardized series. Note that the straight lines in Figure 3.16 correspond to the reported autocorrelations in Section 2.4.*

3.6 Nonlinear Prediction

Although some new approaches in the econometrics literature distinguish between 'prediction' and 'forecasting', it will be used synonymously in the following. Prediction of nonlinear time series models is a tedious exercise for multi–step forecasts. As was seen already in the deterministic chaos case in Section 3.2, for some nonlinear functions it is not possible to predict accurately over a given time horizon, no matter how precisely the initial values are measured. The situation tends to become worse when a stochastic error term is introduced, and the noise variance is relatively large compared with

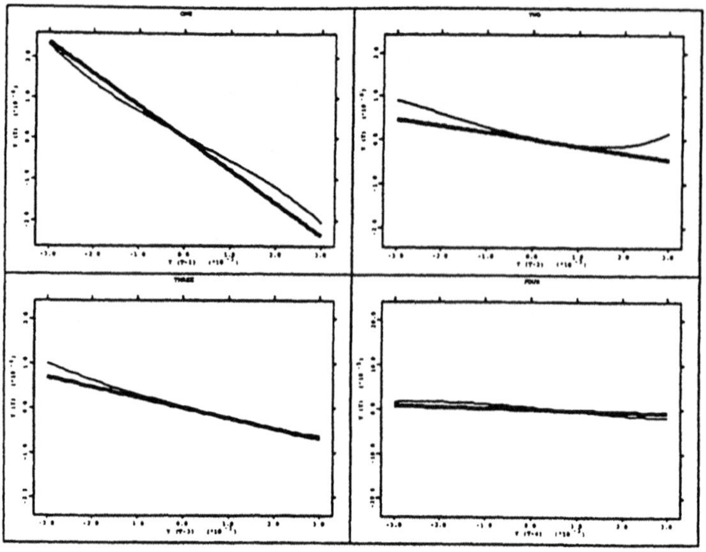

FIGURE 3.16. *Local linear estimates of $M_k(y_{t-k})$ for the DEM/USD returns using $h = 0.5$. First row: $k = 1, 2$, second row: $k = 3, 4$. The straight line represents the best linear predictor $\rho_k x$. In all panels the abscissa ranges from -0.003 to 0.003 and the ordinate from -0.00025 to 0.00025.*

the signal variance. Thus, the quality of prediction strongly depends on the type of nonlinear model, the time horizon, and the noise variance.

Nonlinear forecasting can be based on either parametric models or purely nonparametric approaches.

3.6.1 Parametric Approaches

There are basically two parametric approaches in nonlinear time series forecasting, namely, the numerical integration and simulation methods.

3.6.1.1 Numerical Integration

The basic idea of this method is to use a recursive integral equation to evaluate the conditional density of y_{t+k} given y_t for $k \geq 1$. Once an estimate of the conditional density is obtained, the conditional expectation $\mathrm{E}[y_{t+k} \mid y_t]$ can be calculated, which is the optimal forecast in a quadratic distance sense.

Consider for example the simple nonlinear AR(1) model

$$y_{t+1} = \phi(y_t) + \varepsilon_{t+1},$$

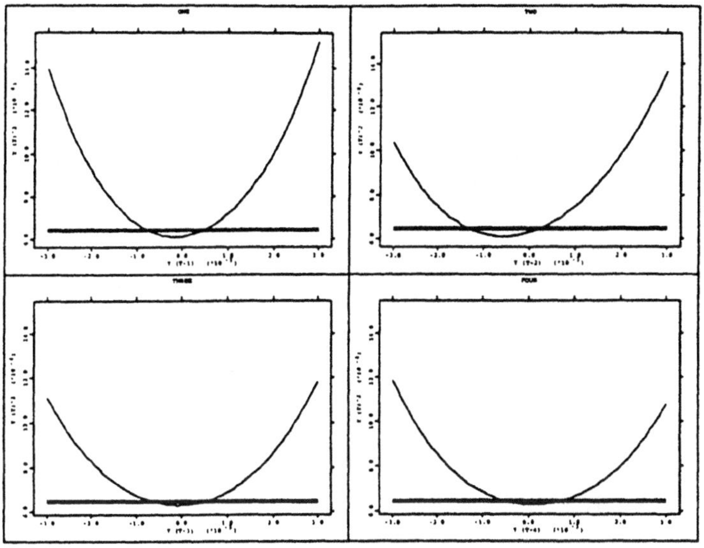

FIGURE 3.17. *Local linear estimates of $V_k(y_{t-k})$ for the DEM/USD returns using $h = 0.5$. First row: $k = 1, 2$, second row: $k = 3, 4$. The straight line represents the estimate of σ_ξ^2. In all panels the abscissa ranges from -0.003 to 0.003 and the ordinate from 0.0006 to 0.0014.*

with some parametric nonlinear function $\phi(\cdot)$. One–step prediction is the simplest case, because $E[y_{t+1} \mid y_t] = \phi(y_t)$. For $k > 1$, however, it is in general not optimal to set the noise terms $\varepsilon_{t+1}, \ldots, \varepsilon_{t+k-1}$ equal to zero when calculating the intermediate conditional expectations.

To obtain an estimate of the conditional density $g_k(y_{t+k} \mid y_t)$, Jones (1978) uses the integral equation

$$g_k(x \mid y_t) = \int_{-\infty}^{\infty} f\{x - \hat{\phi}(y)\} g_{k-1}(y \mid y_t) dy,$$

where $\hat{\phi}$ denotes the estimated function ϕ, and $f(\cdot)$ is the density function of the noise ε_t.

The method can be easily extended to the general nonlinear AR(p) case. Note that this method can provide exact forecasts, but the computation is intensive. Also, the result heavily depends on the parameter estimation.

3.6.1.2 Simulation

Assume the nonlinear AR(p) model

$$y_{t+1} = \phi(y_t, \ldots, y_{t-p+1}) + \varepsilon_{t+1},$$

where the distribution of ε_t is known and the nonlinear function $\phi(\cdot)$ is estimated by $\hat{\phi}(\cdot)$. We can get recursively

$$\hat{y}_{i,t}(k) = \hat{\phi}\left(\hat{y}_{i,t}(k-1), \ldots, \hat{y}_{i,t}(k-p)\right) + \varepsilon_{i,t+k}, \quad i = 1, \ldots, N,$$

for $k = 1, 2, \ldots$ where $\varepsilon_{i,t+k}$ is drawn from the distribution of ε_t and $\hat{y}_{i,t}(m) = y_{t+m}$, for $m \leq 0$. The kth step ahead prediction is then defined as

$$\hat{y}_t(k) = \frac{1}{N} \sum_{i=1}^{N} \hat{y}_{i,t}(k).$$

When there is no assumption about the distribution of ε_t, the bootstrap method can be used.

3.6.2 Nonparametric Approaches

3.6.2.1 Direct Kernel Smoother

Consider the nonlinear AR(1) model $y_t = \phi(y_{t-1}) + \varepsilon_t$. Since the conditional mean $\mathrm{E}[y_{t+k} \mid y_t = x]$ is the least squares predictor for k-step ahead prediction, Auestad and Tjøstheim (1990) and Härdle and Vieu (1992) proposed to use the ordinary Nadaraya–Watson estimator

$$\hat{m}_{h,k}(x) = \frac{\sum\limits_{t=1}^{n-k} K_h(x - y_t) y_{t+k}}{\sum\limits_{t=1}^{n-k} K_h(x - y_t)} \tag{3.47}$$

to estimate $\mathrm{E}[y_{t+k} \mid y_t = x]$ directly. An analogous k–step local linear predictor was in fact used by Härdle and Hafner (1996) in the prediction competition in Breckling and Hillmer (1996), where the DEM ten–year interest rate plotted in Section 2.3 was supposed to be predicted $k = 60$ days ahead for the period 93/12/23 to 94/12/23, using the sample period 87/07/01 to 93/12/22. As performance criteria, the mean standard deviation (MSD), mean absolute deviation (MAD) and corresponding information ratios (IR_1 and IR_2) indicating the performance relative to naive prediction were used. Denoting r_t and $\hat{r}_t$ the actual and predicted interest rate at time t, respectively, the criteria are defined as

$$MSD = \left[T^{-1} \sum_{t=1}^{T} (r_{t+60} - \hat{r}_{t+60})^2 \right]^{1/2} \tag{3.48}$$

$$IR_1 = \frac{\sum_{t=1}^{T} (r_{t+60} - \hat{r}_{t+60})^2}{\sum_{t=1}^{T} (r_{t+60} - r_t)^2} \tag{3.49}$$

h	MSD	IR_1	MAD	IR_2	$Bias$
0.04	0.546057	0.9945	0.483374	0.9969	0.3887
0.045	0.545846	0.9937	0.483248	0.9966	0.3882
0.05	0.545769	0.9935	0.483120	0.9964	0.3881
0.055	0.546078	0.9946	0.483367	0.9969	0.3885
0.06	0.545941	0.9941	0.483255	0.9966	0.3884
0.07	0.546249	0.9952	0.483497	0.9971	0.3889
0.1	0.546776	0.9972	0.484013	0.9982	0.3898

TABLE 3.3. *Prediction results of the local linear predictor of Härdle and Hafner (1996) for the DEM ten-year interest rates for selected bandwidths.*

$$MAD = T^{-1}\sum_{t=1}^{T} | r_{t+60} - \hat{r}_{t+60} | \tag{3.50}$$

$$IR_2 = \frac{\sum_{t=1}^{T} | r_{t+60} - \hat{r}_{t+60} |}{\sum_{t=1}^{T} | r_{t+60} - r_t |} \tag{3.51}$$

$$Bias = T^{-1}\sum_{t=1}^{T}(r_{t+60} - \hat{r}_{t+60}), \tag{3.52}$$

where $T = 262$ predictions had to be calculated. The results of Härdle and Hafner (1996) are given in Table 3.3. Although the model had some explanatory power as indicated by the variance ratio $\mathrm{Var}(\hat{\varepsilon}_t)/\mathrm{Var}(y_t) = 0.9396$, the predictions using the above criteria obviously do not substantially improve naive forecasts. Similar conclusions were drawn for most other approaches in Breckling and Hillmer (1996), where for example econometric simultaneous equation models and neural networks were used. The trend switch of the prediction period, visible in Figure 2.5, caused problems for all methods. This is reflected by the positive bias in Table 3.3.

3.6.2.2 Multistage Smoother

In the preceding section, predictions of y_{t+k} based on information at time t were obtained by directly estimating the k–step conditional expectation nonparametrically. Note, however, that the variables $y_{t+1}, \ldots, y_{t+k-1}$ contain substantial information about the conditional mean function $\mathrm{E}[y_{t+k} \mid y_t]$. Chen (1995) proposed a multistage kernel smoother, which utilizes this information. For example, consider two-step ahead forecasting. Due to the Markov property, we have

$$\begin{aligned} m_{h,2}(x) &= \mathrm{E}[y_{t+2} \mid y_t = x] \\ &= \mathrm{E}(\mathrm{E}[y_{t+2} \mid y_{t+1}, y_t] \mid y_t = x) \end{aligned}$$

$$= \quad \mathrm{E}(\mathrm{E}[y_{t+2} \mid y_{t+1}] \mid y_t = x).$$

Define $f(y) = \mathrm{E}[y_{t+2} \mid y_{t+1} = y]$. Ideally, if we knew $f(\cdot)$, we would use the pairs $\{f(y_{t+1}), y_t\}$, $t = 1, \ldots, (n-1)$ to estimate $\mathrm{E}[y_{t+2} \mid y_t]$, instead of using the pairs $\{y_{t+2}, y_t\}$ as the estimator in (3.47). The error $\varepsilon_{t+2} = y_{t+2} - f(y_{t+1})$ is $O(1)$, i.e. it does not disappear for $n \longrightarrow \infty$. Hence, if we can estimate the function $f(\cdot)$ with an estimator $\hat{f}(\cdot)$ that has a smaller error rate and use the pairs $\left\{\hat{f}(y_{t+1}), y_t\right\}$ to estimate $\mathrm{E}[y_{t+2} \mid y_t]$, we should achieve a smaller error. This observation motivated the following estimator, which is called "multistage smoother". It is defined as

$$\hat{m}_{h_1,h_2}(x) = \frac{\sum_{t=1}^{n-1} K\{(x - y_t)/h_2\}\hat{f}_{h_1}(y_{t+1})}{\sum_{t=1}^{n-1} K\{(x - y_t)/h_2\}} \tag{3.53}$$

where

$$\hat{f}_{h_1}(x) = \frac{\sum_{j=1}^{n-1} K\{(x - y_j)/h_1\}y_{j+1}}{\sum_{j=1}^{n-1} K\{(x - y_j)/h_1\}}.$$

The new smoother was shown to have a smaller mean square error.

Example 3.7 (Gold Prices) *The estimators in (3.47) and (3.53) are applied to the gold price example. A 10–step prediction is computed with both estimators. For the multistage smoother a recursive algorithm is needed that computes at the* k^{th} *step a smoother of the* $(k-1)^{th}$ *smoother, beginning with the simple one–step predictor. The estimates are shown in Figure 3.18 and 3.19, respectively. Looking at the scales of the ordinates, the difference becomes obvious: The multistage smoother is much closer to the unconditional mean of* y_t *than the direct smoother.*

3.7 Directionality and Reversibility

The concept of reversibility refers to the property of a stochastic process under reversion of time. Intuitively, if the stochastic properties are the same for either direction of time, the process is called *reversible*. If, on the other hand, the stochastic properties depend on the direction of time, the process is called *irreversible* or *directional*. This is formalized in the following definition.

Definition 3.1 (Reversibility) *A stationary time series* $\{y_t\}$, $t = 0, \pm1, \pm2, \ldots$ *is said to be reversible, if for every positive integer* r *and every*

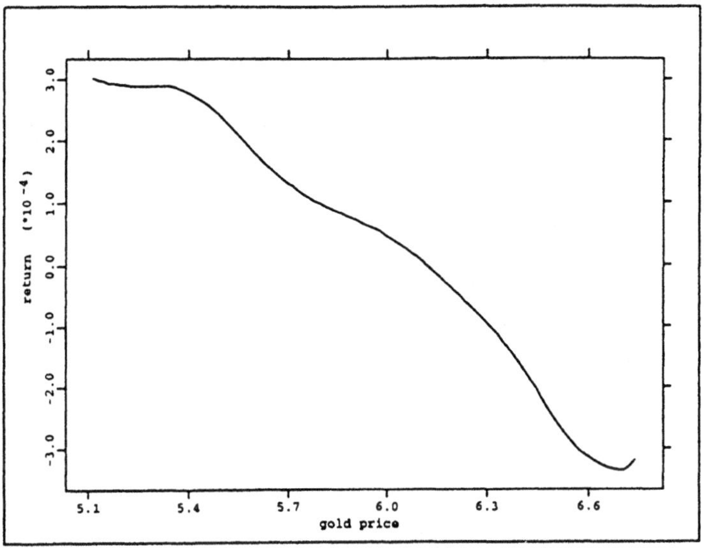

FIGURE 3.18. *10-step prediction for the gold price example using the direct Nadaraya-Watson estimator,* $h = 0.5$.

$t_1, t_2, \ldots, t_r \in \mathbb{Z}$ *the vectors* $(y_{t_1}, \ldots, y_{t_r})$ *and* $(y_{-t_1}, \ldots, y_{-t_r})$ *have the same joint probability distribution. If the series is not reversible, it is said to be irreversible or* directional.

Obviously, reversibility is a very strong property because, for instance, it implies strict stationarity. In practice, the importance of the reversibility issue is twofold. First, finding that an observed time series is directional (e.g. by looking at the reversed time plots or testing with the *TR test* of Ramsey and Rothman (1991)), the practical researcher is advised to choose a model which is directional, too. Second, in certain cases, for example when generating starting values, the back-forecasting technique of Box and Jenkins (1976) can be applied if the process is reversible. For this procedure, reversibility is not necessary, but sufficient.

It is well known that Gaussian linear ARMA models are reversible. The verification of (ir)reversibility for the most common nonlinear time series models described in this chapter is not completely solved. Even for linear ARMA processes with non–Gaussian innovations (ir)reversibility depends on the type of the distribution, e.g. the skewness. Lawrance (1991) gives an example of a (degenerated) nonlinear reversible process. However, as Tong (1990) notes, "time irreversibility is the rule rather than the exception when it comes to nonlinearity" (Tong (1990, p.197)). Indeed, it is known that the

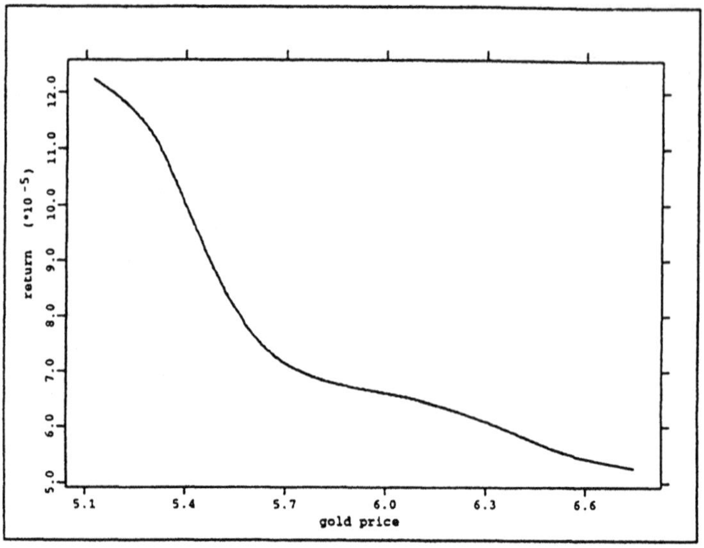

FIGURE 3.19. *10-step prediction for the gold price example using the multistage smoother,* $h = 0.5$.

general forms of the bilinear, EXPAR, and threshold AR models discussed in this chapter are directional. However, a remark on (ir)reversibility of ARCH processes was not found in the literature. The proof that ARCH processes are directional is postponed to Section 4.11.

The above mentioned TR test of Ramsey and Rothman (1991) is based on the fact that for a reversible time series $\{y_t\}_{t\in\mathbb{Z}}$

$$\mathrm{E}[y_t^i y_{t+r}^j] = \mathrm{E}[y_t^j y_{t+r}^i] \tag{3.54}$$

for all $i, j, r \in \mathbb{N}$. Therefore, one can construct a test based on the difference of the estimates of the expectations in (3.54). Ramsey and Rothman (1991) only consider the case $i = 1, j = 2$ (or vice versa), for which they derive asymptotic normality of the test statistic under mixing conditions and the null hypothesis of reversibility. As will be seen in Section 4.11, however, this test statistic has no power against ARCH processes. To reject reversibility of ARCH processes, higher orders i or j are required.

Rothman (1994) rejects reversibility of a stock return series with the TR test for $i = 1, j = 2$, and thus also rejects (G)ARCH models, for which this test should have passed. Instead, he finds a bilinear model to be better able to reflect the directional behavior of the series.

3.8 Conclusions

This chapter provided a survey of the most important nonlinear time series models. After a brief digression on deterministic chaos, which revealed the non-ability to estimate a 'dimension' of FX rates due to the high noise level, stochastic models were introduced. We have seen that various parametric or nonparametric models are able to produce conditional heteroskedasticity, the most prominent and powerful being the ARCH model class, which will therefore be studied separately in the following chapter. Typical realizations of the discussed parametric models were shown in order to facilitate visual comparison of their stochastic properties. A general nonparametric autoregressive model of order one was presented and some estimation techniques sketched. For higher autoregressive orders, restricted models such as additive models (NAAR) or functional coefficent AR (FCAR) models were discussed with empirical examples. Tests for linearity were presented especially with respect to conditional heteroskedasticity. In two different ways, the high frequency FX return series were shown to have highly significant ARCH–effects. The first was the ARCH–LM test of Engle (1982), the second an informal nonparametric test suggested by Hjellvik and Tjøstheim (1995). Parametric and nonparametric approaches to prediction with nonlinear models were outlined. For ten–step prediction of a gold price series, a multistage smoother was shown to be much closer to the unconditional mean than the direct kernel smoother. Finally, the topic of (ir)reversibility of nonlinear time series models was sketched and noted that for the strict Definition 3.1, most nonlinear models will be irreversible. For ARCH models, this will be shown in Section 4.11.

Conclusions

4 ARCH Models and Extensions

4.1 Introduction

Since the introduction of autoregressive conditional heteroskedastic models (ARCH) by Engle (1982), an enormous boom has evolved in both theory and applications. It became obvious that a powerful model class was developed that copes with the most important feature of financial time series, namely conditional heteroskedasticity. Especially after the fall of Bretton Woods and the subsequent free–floating period of exchange rates in the seventies, such a model was demanded by practitioners and researchers. The stylized fact was the observation that volatilities tend to cluster: large and small price changes of either sign both tend to persist. Correct estimation and prediction of volatility is most important for major financial institutes, because volatility is directly related to usual risk measures, as it was seen in Section 2.1. In theory and practice, the return of financial assets is equal to the riskfree rate (provided it exists), plus some individual risk premium. Models to estimate the risk premium have been developed in the ARCH framework since Domowitz and Hakkio (1985) used a function of the conditional variance as a proxy for risk premium in the FX market. Therefore, ARCH models soon were used by financial analysts. In the meantime, however, a growing literature detected anomalies of the standard models and various extensions were considered. Today it is clear that standard ARCH models can only be the starting point of model specification and extensive use of specification tests has to be made. Recently, several surveys appeared in the literature, e.g. Bollerslev et al. (1992), Bera and Higgins (1993), and the monograph by Gouriéroux (1992).

After building the theoretical framework of ARCH models, the emphasis shall lay on more flexible ARCH models. The main benchmark will be the high frequency foreign exchange rate data set HFDF93 described in Section 2.4. The models discussed in this chapter are purely parametric. For non-parametric and semiparametric approaches see the next chapter. For tests against conditional heteroskedasticity, see Section 3.5.2.

4.2 Standard ARCH and GARCH

4.2.1 ARCH: Definition, Moments and Stationarity

An ARCH model can be formulated for the original series or for an error term. In most financial applications, the error ε_t of a regression or time series model is conditionally heteroskedastic. In a time series context, an autoregression model of order P with ARCH error term of order q can be written as

$$
\begin{aligned}
y_t &= \mu + \phi_1 y_{t-1} + \ldots + \phi_P y_{t-P} + \varepsilon_t && (4.1)\\
\mathrm{E}[\varepsilon_t \mid \psi_{t-1}] &= 0 && (4.2)\\
\mathrm{Var}[\varepsilon_t \mid \psi_{t-1}] &= \sigma_t^2 && (4.3)\\
\sigma_t^2 &= \omega + \alpha_1 \varepsilon_{t-1}^2 + \ldots + \alpha_q \varepsilon_{t-q}^2, && (4.4)
\end{aligned}
$$

with $\omega > 0$, $\alpha_i \geq 0$, $i = 1, \ldots, q$. As in previous chapters, ψ_t denotes the information set available at time t. A more restrictive and very often used definition is

$$\varepsilon_t | \psi_{t-1} \sim N(0, \sigma_t^2). \tag{4.5}$$

However, as will be seen later the normality assumption of the conditional distribution of ε_t is not always appropriate *a priori*. Drost and Nijman (1993) call the definition given in (4.2) and (4.3) *semi-strong ARCH*, whereas *strong* ARCH is defined as the model

$$\varepsilon_t = \sigma_t \xi_t, \tag{4.6}$$

where ξ_t is *i.i.d.* with mean zero and variance one. It is easy to see that (4.6) is equivalent to (4.5), if ξ_t is normally distributed. The notion of strong ARCH is mostly used in the literature and will also be used in this chapter unless otherwise stated. Note, however, that strong ARCH excludes the dependence of higher order conditional moments besides the conditional variance. A model to deal with such higher order dependencies will be discussed in Section 5.3 in a nonparametric framework. Weak ARCH in the definition of Drost and Nijman (1993) refers to a model where σ_t^2 is the best linear prediction of ε_t^2 given the information set at time $t-1$. This general notion, however, is rarely used in the literature.

Turning back to (4.1), observe that conditional heteroskedasticity does not affect the stationarity conditions for y_t if ε_t is stationary, so y_t is stationary if all the roots of the characteristic polynomial $(1 - \phi_1 z - \ldots - \phi_P z^P)$ lie outside the unit circle. For estimation of (4.1), it is inefficient to neglect conditional heteroskedastic effects in ε_t. In general, estimation of the conditional variance parameters affects the estimation of the mean parameters, and vice versa.

Because $\text{Cov}[\varepsilon_t, \varepsilon_{t-k} \mid \psi_{t-k-1}] = 0$ and $\text{E}[\varepsilon_t \mid \psi_{t-1}] = 0$, ε_t is white noise in the sense of Definition 2.3. However, as can be seen from (4.3), ε_t is not an independent sequence and therefore not strict white noise.

Engle (1982) established moment conditions for the ARCH(1) process by assuming conditional normality. If the conditional distribution is symmetric, say normal, then all odd moments are zero. $\text{E}[\varepsilon_t^2]$ exists if $\alpha_1 < 1$. In this case, $\text{Var}(\varepsilon_t) = \text{E}[\varepsilon_t^2] = \omega/(1-\alpha_1)$. $\text{E}[\varepsilon_t^4]$ exists, if $3\alpha_1^2 < 1$, and

$$\text{E}[\varepsilon_t^4] = \frac{3\omega^2}{(1-\alpha_1)^2} \frac{1-\alpha_1^2}{1-3\alpha_1^2}.$$

It follows immediately that ε_t has a leptokurtic unconditional distribution, i.e. the kurtosis $\text{Kurt}(\varepsilon_t)$ is

$$\text{Kurt}(\varepsilon_t) \equiv \frac{\text{E}[\varepsilon_t^4]}{\text{E}[\varepsilon_t^2]^2} = 3\frac{1-\alpha_1^2}{1-3\alpha_1^2},$$

so for conditional homoskedasticity ($\alpha_1 = 0$), $\text{Kurt}(\varepsilon_t) = 3$, and for conditional heteroskedasticity ($\alpha_1 > 0$), $\text{Kurt}(\varepsilon_t) > 3$. Because of this 'fat tails' property, ARCH models are particularly suited for financial series, which often exhibit such behavior, see Chapter 2 for examples.

Following Theorem 2 of Engle (1982), the ARCH(q) process is covariance stationary if and only if all the roots of the associated characteristic equation lie outside the unit circle. Because the ARCH parameters are restricted to be nonnegative, this is equivalent to the condition $\alpha_1 + \cdots + \alpha_q < 1$. Then the unconditional variance of ε_t exists and is equal to $\omega/(1-\alpha_1-\ldots-\alpha_q)$. If $\alpha_1 + \cdots + \alpha_q \geq 1$, the unconditional variance is infinite, but the process may still be strictly stationary. More details on this issue will be given in Section 4.4, where we consider persistence of shocks in the generalized ARCH model.

4.2.2 ARCH: Estimation

As shown by Weiss (1986b) and Pantula (1988), least squares estimators for ARCH models are consistent and asymptotically normal, but less efficient than generalized method of moments (GMM) and maximum likelihood estimators (MLE). As Hamilton (1994) notes, MLE can be interpreted as a GMM estimation with orthogonality condition that the score is zero. The standard estimation tool is MLE. Suppose a time series $y_t, t = 1, \ldots, n$, is observed. Starting point is the specification of the conditional density of the residuals ε_t. In most applications, the normal distribution was assumed, so that the conditional density assumes the form

$$f(\varepsilon_t|\psi_{t-1}) = \frac{1}{\sqrt{2\pi}\sigma_t} \exp\left\{-\frac{1}{2}\frac{\varepsilon_t^2}{\sigma_t^2}\right\}. \tag{4.7}$$

Consider again the general AR(P)-ARCH(q) model in (4.4). Writing $\theta = (\theta_1, \theta_2)$ with $\theta_1 = (\mu, \phi_1, \ldots, \phi_P)$ and $\theta_2 = (\omega, \alpha_1, \ldots, \alpha_q)$, the log likelihood becomes

$$\begin{aligned} \log L(\theta) &= \sum_{t=1}^{n} l_t(\theta) \equiv \sum_{t=1}^{n} \log f(\varepsilon_t|\psi_{t-1};\theta) \\ &= -n/2\log(2\pi) - 1/2\sum_{t=1}^{n}\log\sigma_t^2 - 1/2\sum_{t=1}^{n}\frac{\varepsilon_t^2}{\sigma_t^2}. \qquad (4.8) \end{aligned}$$

The object of MLE is to maximize (4.8) with respect to the conditional mean parameters θ_1 and the conditional variance parameters θ_2. For ease of notation, let $x_t \equiv (y_{t-1}, \ldots, y_{t-P})$. Then the first order conditions for the tth observation are

$$\frac{\partial l_t}{\partial \theta_1} = \frac{\varepsilon_t x_t'}{\sigma_t^2} + \frac{1}{2\sigma_t^2}\frac{\partial \sigma_t^2}{\partial \theta_1}\left(\frac{\varepsilon_t^2}{\sigma_t^2} - 1\right), \qquad (4.9)$$

or, using $\partial\sigma_t^2/\partial\theta_1 = -2\sum_{i=1}^{q}\alpha_i\varepsilon_{t-i}x_{t-i}'$,

$$\frac{\partial l_t}{\partial \theta_1} = \frac{\varepsilon_t x_t'}{\sigma_t^2} - \frac{1}{\sigma_t^2}\left(\frac{\varepsilon_t^2}{\sigma_t^2} - 1\right)\sum_{i=1}^{q}\alpha_i\varepsilon_{t-i}x_{t-i}', \qquad (4.10)$$

and

$$\frac{\partial l_t}{\partial \theta_2} = \frac{1}{2\sigma_t^2}\frac{\partial \sigma_t^2}{\partial \theta_2}\left(\frac{\varepsilon_t^2}{\sigma_t^2} - 1\right) = \frac{1}{2\sigma_t^2}Z_t\left(\frac{\varepsilon_t^2}{\sigma_t^2} - 1\right), \qquad (4.11)$$

with $Z_t \equiv (1, \varepsilon_{t-1}^2, \ldots, \varepsilon_{t-q}^2)$.

The likelihood can be maximized using the scores in (4.9) and (4.11). Any optimization routine can be used, but the algorithm of Berndt, Hall, Hall and Hausman (1974, BHHH) has proved to be suitable for this situation. In the iterative procedure, the parameters of the $(i+1)^{th}$ iteration are obtained by

$$\theta^{(i+1)} = \theta^{(i)} + \lambda_i\left(\sum_{t=1}^{n}\frac{\partial l_t}{\partial \theta}\frac{\partial l_t}{\partial \theta'}\right)^{-1}\sum_{t=1}^{n}\frac{\partial l_t}{\partial \theta}, \qquad (4.12)$$

where λ_i denotes a variable step length, and $\partial l_t/\partial\theta$ is calculated at $\theta^{(i)}$.

Under certain regularity conditions, see White (1982), Gouriéroux, Monfort and Trognon (1984) and Gouriéroux and Monfort (1995), the maximum likelihood estimates are strongly consistent and asymptotically normal. If the conditional distribution is correctly specified, i.e. if ε_t is indeed conditionally normal, then the asymptotic covariance matrix of the ML estimates is given as usual by the inverse of the information matrix J, i.e. the negative expectation of the Hessian:

$$J = -E\left(\frac{\partial^2 l_t(\theta)}{\partial\theta\partial\theta'}\right).$$

If the true conditional distribution is not normal, then it has been shown by Weiss (1986b) that Quasi MLE is still consistent, but the asymptotic covariance matrix becomes

$$\mathrm{Var}_{as}\left(\sqrt{n}(\hat{\theta}-\theta)\right) = J^{-1}IJ^{-1}, \tag{4.13}$$

with I equal to the expected outer product of the scores

$$I = E\left(\frac{\partial l_t(\theta)}{\partial \theta}\frac{\partial l_t(\theta)}{\partial \theta'}\right).$$

Estimates of I and J are obtained by replacing the expecatation operator by the arithmetic mean. If the true conditional distribution is normal, then $I = J$, and the outer product can be used from the last step of the BHHH algorithm. Explicit expressions for I and J are given by Gouriéroux (1992, pp.79). If the form of the conditional variance equation is symmetric and regular in the sense of Engle (1982), then the asymptotic covariance matrix is block-diagonal and mean and variance parameters can be estimated separately. This important result does not hold for 'asymmetric' ARCH models such as ARCH-M and EGARCH models, which are to be discussed later.

Although QMLE in the case of misspecification is still consistent, it is less efficient than MLE of a correct specified conditional variance. Engle and Gonzalez-Rivera (1991) found that the relative efficiency of QMLE, defined as

$$RE_\theta = \frac{\mathrm{Var}(\hat{\theta}_{MLE})}{\mathrm{Var}(\hat{\theta}_{QMLE})}, \tag{4.14}$$

can be considerably low. For example, if the true conditional distribution is a Student's t with 5 degrees of freedom, the relative efficiency of the parameter estimates of a GARCH(1,1) model is around 0.41 for different parameter values. This indicates the importance of a correct specification of the conditional distribution. For relaxations of the conditional normality assumption, see Section 4.3.

A problem of ARCH(q) models is that for some applications large lag orders are required such that many parameters have to be estimated under inequality restrictions. Thus, it was proposed by Engle (1982) to use a linearly declining lag structure such as

$$\sigma_t^2 = \omega + \alpha_1 \sum_{i=1}^{q} w_i \varepsilon_{t-i}^2,$$

with

$$w_i = \frac{2(q+1-i)}{q(q+1)},$$

so that only two parameters are to be estimated. The following section deals with a generalization of the ARCH(q) model that allows for both parsimonious parametrization and flexible lag structures.

4.2.3 Generalized ARCH

Bollerslev (1986) generalized Engle's ARCH model by introducing autoregressive terms into the conditional variance equation:

$$\varepsilon_t|\psi_{t-1} \sim N(0,\sigma_t^2) \tag{4.15}$$

$$\sigma_t^2 = \omega + \sum_{i=1}^{q} \alpha_i \varepsilon_{t-i}^2 + \sum_{j=1}^{p} \beta_j \sigma_{t-j}^2 . \tag{4.16}$$

Sufficient, but not necessary conditions for the nonnegativity of σ_t^2 for all t are $\omega > 0$, $\alpha_i \geq 0$, $i = 1,\ldots,q$ and $\beta_j \geq 0$, $j = 1,\ldots,p$. Again, ψ_t denotes the information set available at t, and ε_t can be the error term of a regression or time series model.

If all the roots of the polynomial $(1-\beta_1 z - \ldots - \beta_p z^p)$ lie outside the unit circle, the GARCH(p,q) model can be written as an ARCH(∞) model. More importantly, define $v_t \equiv \varepsilon_t^2 - \sigma_t^2$, which has mean zero and is serially uncorrelated. Then GARCH(p,q) can be interpreted as an ARMA model in terms of ε_t^2, i.e.

$$\varepsilon_t^2 = \omega + \sum_{i=1}^{m} \gamma_i \varepsilon_{t-i}^2 - \sum_{j=1}^{p} \beta_j v_{t-j} + v_t, \tag{4.17}$$

where $m = \max(p,q)$, $\gamma_i = \alpha_i + \beta_i$, $\alpha_i = 0$, if $i > q$, and $\beta_i = 0$, if $i > p$. This is an ARMA(m,p) model with conditionally heteroskedastic error terms v_t. Thus, many analogous conclusions may be drawn.

From Theorem 1 in Bollerslev (1986), ε_t is covariance stationary, which is equivalent to the existence of the unconditional variance, if and only if $\sum_{i=1}^{q} \alpha_i + \sum_{j=1}^{p} \beta_j < 1$. Then it follows for the unconditional variance of ε_t

$$\mathrm{Var}(\varepsilon_t) = \frac{\omega}{1-\sum_{i=1}^{q}\alpha_i - \sum_{j=1}^{p}\beta_j}, \tag{4.18}$$

which is constant for given parameters.

Moment conditions for the general GARCH(p,q) process are unknown. Only for low–order models these have been derived. For example, the fourth moment of a GARCH(1,1) process exists if and only if $3\alpha_1^2 + 2\alpha_1\beta_1 + \beta_1^2 < 1$. The kurtosis Kurt($\varepsilon_t$) is then given by

$$\mathrm{Kurt}[\varepsilon_t] = \frac{\mathrm{E}[\varepsilon_t^4]}{(\mathrm{E}[\varepsilon_t^2])^2} = 3 + 6\alpha_1^2/(1-\beta_1^2 - 2\alpha_1\beta_1 - 3\alpha_1^2),$$

which is larger than 3, so that ε_t is leptokurtic.

Estimation of the GARCH(p,q) model is similar to the estimation of an ARCH(q) model, except that the additional autoregressive terms need to be considered when calculating the derivatives of σ_t^2 with respect to the mean parameters θ_1 and variance parameters θ_2. Denote $z_t = (1, \varepsilon_{t-1}^2, \dots, \varepsilon_{t-q}^2, \sigma_{t-1}^2, \dots, \sigma_{t-p}^2)$. Then in (4.9), $\partial\sigma_t^2/\partial\theta_1$ is replaced by

$$\frac{\partial\sigma_t^2}{\partial\theta_1} = -2\sum_{i=1}^{q}\alpha_i\varepsilon_{t-i}x'_{t-i} + \sum_{j=1}^{p}\beta_j\frac{\partial\sigma_{t-j}^2}{\partial\theta_1}, \tag{4.19}$$

and in (4.11), $\partial\sigma_t^2/\partial\theta_2$ is replaced by

$$\frac{\partial\sigma_t^2}{\partial\theta_2} = z_t + \sum_{j=1}^{p}\beta_j\frac{\partial\sigma_{t-j}^2}{\partial\theta_2}. \tag{4.20}$$

Note that unlike Z_t in ARCH models, z_t also contains lagged values of conditional variances. In the next section, the assumption of conditional normality in (4.15) will be relaxed.

4.3 Specification of the Conditional Distribution

If the conditional distribution of ε_t is assumed to be normal as in (4.15), then the unconditional distribution is not normal with heavier tails than the normal distribution. Equivalently, the unconditional kurtosis, Kurt$[\varepsilon_t]$, is not smaller than the conditional kurtosis, Kurt$[\varepsilon_t|\psi_{t-1}]$, because

$$\text{Kurt}[\varepsilon_t] = \frac{\text{E}[\varepsilon_t^4]}{\left(\text{E}[\varepsilon_t^2]\right)^2} = \frac{\text{E}\left(\text{E}[\varepsilon_t^4|\psi_{t-1}]\right)}{\left(\text{E}[\sigma_t^2]\right)^2} = \text{Kurt}[\varepsilon_t|\psi_{t-1}]\frac{\text{E}[\sigma_t^4]}{\left(\text{E}[\sigma_t^2]\right)^2},$$

and $\text{E}[\sigma_t^4] \geq \left(\text{E}[\sigma_t^2]\right)^2$ for $\sigma_t^2 > 0, t = 1, \dots, n$ (Jensen's inequality). Gouriéroux (1992, pp.46) has pointed out an interesting relationship between the kurtosis and conditional heteroskedasticity under conditional normality. Define the *excess kurtosis* as $k_e[\cdot] \equiv \text{Kurt}[\cdot] - 3$. Then

$$k_e[\varepsilon_t] = 3\frac{\text{Var}\left(\text{E}[\varepsilon_t^2|\psi_{t-1}]\right)}{\left(\text{E}[\varepsilon_t^2]\right)^2}. \tag{4.21}$$

The right hand side of (4.21) can be interpreted as a measure of conditional heteroskedasticity, because it relates the fluctuation of the conditional variance, measured by its variance, to the square of the unconditional variance.

Therefore, conditional heteroskedasticity can explain at least partially the leptokurtosis of ε_t. In practice it may be important to find out whether it is the only reason. The question is whether the conditional distribution is leptokurtic as well. The results would be an even higher unconditional kurtosis and a misspecified likelihood function. In fact, many recent financial applications of ARCH models suggested a conditionally fat tailed distribution. MLE can of course be applied for various fat–tailed or skewed distributions as well as for the Gaussian, once this distribution is specified. For example, Nelson (1991) worked with the generalized error distribution (GED) and Engle and Gonzalez-Rivera (1991) used the Student's t and the Gamma distributions. The latter we will not consider here, because the evidence of conditionally skewed distributions has in general been rather weak for most financial series compared with the fat tails property. The next paragraph deals with the assumption of conditionally Student's t distributed errors and is followed by a nonparametric density estimation procedure, suggested by Engle and Gonzalez-Rivera (1991).

4.3.1 Conditionally Student's t Distributed Errors

A Student's t distribution with the same mean and variance as a normal distribution has more probability mass in the centre and in the tails of the distribution. The limiting distribution for increasing degrees of freedom is the normal distribution. For one degree of freedom, the Cauchy distribution is obtained, which does not possess any finite moments.

Consider the conditional Student's t distribution with $\nu > 2$ degrees of freedom, i.e.

$$\begin{aligned} f(\varepsilon_t|\psi_{t-1}) &= 1/\sqrt{\pi}\Gamma\left(\frac{\nu+1}{2}\right)\left(\Gamma\left(\frac{\nu}{2}\right)\right)^{-1} \\ &\times \; ((\nu-2)\sigma_t^2)^{-1/2}\left(1+\frac{\varepsilon_t^2}{\sigma_t^2(\nu-2)}\right)^{-(\nu+1)/2} . \end{aligned} \tag{4.22}$$

Then the scores of the likelihood function are given by

$$\begin{aligned} \frac{\partial l_t}{\partial \theta_1} = -\frac{1}{2\sigma_t^2}\frac{\partial \sigma_t^2}{\partial \theta_1} &+ (\nu+1)\left(1+\frac{\varepsilon_t^2}{\sigma_t^2(\nu-2)}\right)^{-1} \\ &\times \frac{\varepsilon_t x_t \sigma_t^2 - \varepsilon_t^2 \frac{\partial \sigma_t^2}{\partial \theta_1}}{\sigma_t^4(\nu-2)} \end{aligned} \tag{4.23}$$

and

$$\frac{\partial l_t}{\partial \theta_2} = -\frac{1}{2\sigma_t^2}\frac{\partial \sigma_t^2}{\partial \theta_2}\left(1-\frac{(\nu+1)\varepsilon_t^2}{\varepsilon_t^2+\sigma_t^2(\nu-2)}\right). \tag{4.24}$$

Obviously, $\partial\sigma_t^2/\partial\theta_1$ and $\partial\sigma_t^2/\partial\theta_2$ are not affected by the distributional assumption, so only depend on whether an ARCH or GARCH model (or any of the following extensions) is estimated.

If the model is correctly specified, the asymptotic covariance matrix is again given by the inverse of the information matrix or, equivalently, by the inverse of the outer product of the scores. In general, the degrees of freedom ν will not be known, so the likelihood has to be maximized also with respect to ν.

4.3.2 Nonparametric Estimation of the Conditional Error Density

Engle and Gonzalez-Rivera (1991) have proposed a nonparametric estimation of the conditional density of the error terms ε_t. Because of this nonparametric element of model specification they call this 'Semiparametric ARCH', but note that this is another type of semiparametric estimation than combining parametric and nonparametric functional forms of the explanatory variables. This type of semiparametric models will be discussed in Section 5.5. Here, the functional form is still parametric.

The conditional density of ε_t is given by

$$\varepsilon_t|\psi_{t-1} \sim f(0, \sigma_t^2), \tag{4.25}$$

with some unknown density function $f(\cdot)$, which will be estimated nonparametrically. The standardized residuals $\xi_t \equiv \varepsilon_t/\sigma_t$ are *i.i.d.* with mean zero and variance one, provided that higher order moments of $f(\cdot)$ are not time-varying.

The log-likelihood function is

$$\log L(\theta) = \sum_{t=1}^{n} \log f(\varepsilon_t|\psi_{t-1}),$$

where again $\theta = (\theta_1, \theta_2)$ contains mean and variance parameters. Denoting the density of the standardized residuals by $g(\xi_t)$ and using the equivalence $f(\varepsilon_t|\psi_{t-1}) = \sigma_t^{-1} g(\xi_t)$, the likelihood can be written in terms of ξ_t as

$$\log L(\theta) = \sum_{t=1}^{n} l_t(\theta) = -\sum_{t=1}^{n} \log \sigma_t + \sum_{t=1}^{n} \log g(\xi_t). \tag{4.26}$$

The following procedure has been proposed by Engle and Gonzalez-Rivera (1991) to maximize (4.26) with respect to θ and $g(\cdot)$:

1. Estimate θ consistently, for example by QMLE.
2. Construct the estimated residuals by $\hat{\xi}_t = \hat{\varepsilon}_t/\hat{\sigma}_t$ and standardize them.
3. Estimate the density of $\hat{\xi}_t$ nonparametrically. Call this density estimate $\hat{g}(\cdot)$.

4. Maximize (4.26) with respect to θ, keeping $\hat{g}(\cdot)$ fixed.

In step 3, Engle and Gonzalez-Rivera (1991) used the discrete maximum penalized likelihood estimation (DMPLE) technique of Tapia and Thompson (1978), but any other nonparametric density estimate, such as kernel estimates, can be used as well. In step 4, the scores are needed for an iterative algorithm as BHHH. In this case, they have the form

$$\frac{\partial l_t}{\partial \theta} = -\frac{1}{2\sigma_t^2}\frac{\partial \sigma_t^2}{\partial \theta} + \sigma_t^{-1}\left(\frac{\partial \varepsilon_t}{\partial \theta} - \frac{\varepsilon_t}{2\sigma_t^2}\frac{\partial \sigma_t^2}{\partial \theta}\right)\frac{\hat{g}_t'}{\hat{g}_t}.$$

A crucial part of this score function is $\hat{g}_t'/\hat{g}_t$, which is very sensitive to biased density estimates in low–density areas. Härdle (1990) provides efficient estimates for the case of kernel density estimation. The reason why Engle and Gonzalez-Rivera (1991) used the DMPLE technique is that $\hat{g}_t'/\hat{g}_t$ then takes a simple form.

The simulation results of Engle and Gonzalez-Rivera (1991) show that the estimation procedure does not provide adaptive estimates in the sense of Bickel (1982), because in this case not knowing the conditional distribution implies a loss of efficiency compared to the case where it is known. Linton (1993) achieved adaptive estimation of semiparametric ARCH models via a reparametrization of the conditional variance.

4.4 Persistence of Volatility

Recall from (4.17) that a GARCH(p,q) model can be written in terms of squared errors as an ARMA(m,p) model with $m = \max(p,q)$. Introducing the lag operator $L\,y_t \equiv y_{t-1}$, and the lag–polynomials $\alpha(L) = \alpha_1 L + \cdots + \alpha_q L^q$, and $\beta(L) = \beta_1 L + \cdots + \beta_p L^p$, the GARCH$(p,q)$ model can be written as

$$\sigma_t^2 = \omega + \alpha(L)\varepsilon_t^2 + \beta(L)\sigma_t^2,$$

and in the ARMA(m,q) representation as

$$[1 - \alpha(L) - \beta(L)]\varepsilon_t^2 = \omega + [1 - \beta(L)]v_t \tag{4.27}$$

with $v_t \equiv \varepsilon_t^2 - \sigma_t^2$.

An important empirical question is whether shocks have a short term, long term or permanent impact on volatility forecasts. Recall from Section 2.4 that one feature of high frequency FX rates is a slow hyberbolic decay of the ACF of squared (or absolute) returns. For financial time series in general GARCH parameter estimates resulted which either just met the covariance stationarity condition $\alpha(1) + \beta(1) < 1$ very closely, or implied persistence if $\alpha(1) + \beta(1) \geq 1$. Engle and Bollerslev (1986) defined shocks to be persistent in volatility if shocks have a permanent impact on the optimal forecasts of future volatility. If the GARCH process is persistent, then the unconditional variance is infinite and, hence, the model is not covariance stationary. However, it may still be strictly stationary. Indeed, Nelson (1990b) showed that the GARCH(1,1) process is strictly stationary if $E[\log(\alpha\xi_t^2 + \beta)] < 0$. If, for instance, ξ_t is standard normal, then this condition is weaker then the condition for covariance stationarity, $\alpha + \beta < 1$.

The empirical observations motivated new classes of models: the integrated GARCH (IGARCH) model and the fractionally integrated GARCH (FIGARCH) model. IGARCH implies persistence, permanent memory and infinite variance, FIGARCH implies non–persistence, long memory and infinite variance. In practice, it is important but also difficult to distinguish between the short memory GARCH, long memory FIGARCH and permanent memory IGARCH model. In the following, we want to take a closer look at these models.

4.4.1 Integrated GARCH

Engle and Bollerslev (1986) defined ARCH models to be *integrated in variance of order d* [IGARCH(p, d, q)], if in (4.27) the autoregressive polynomial $[1 - \alpha(z) - \beta(z)]$ contains $d > 0$ unit roots, and $m - d$ roots outside the unit circle. For the IGARCH$(p, 1, q)$ model with one unit root, the autoregressive polynomial can be factorized as $\Phi(z)(1 - z)$, and the model can be written as

$$\Phi(L)(1 - L)\varepsilon_t^2 = \omega + [1 - \beta(L)]v_t. \tag{4.28}$$

An IGARCH model of order one is given by

$$\sigma_t^2 = \omega + \alpha\varepsilon_{t-1}^2 + (1 - \alpha)\sigma_{t-1}^2. \tag{4.29}$$

The integration in variance implies that shocks will have a permanent impact on volatility forecasts and, hence, volatility is persistent. If the process starts infinitely far in the past, the unconditional variance is not finite.

The relationship between models that are integrated in mean and integrated in variance is not completely analogous. For example, if $\omega = 0$ in (4.28), then σ_t^2 collapses to zero almost surely. If $\omega > 0$, then σ_t^2 is strictly stationary and ergodic, see Geweke (1986) and Nelson (1990b). Thus, standard IGARCH models with $\omega > 0$ are strictly stationary, but not covariance stationary since the unconditional variance does not exist. For this property of IGARCH, it cannot be compared with random walks. An unappealing economic feature is that shocks to volatility will shift the whole term structure of risk premia and not only the short end. This is clearly against the empirical observation that long term risk premia are much less sensitive to shocks than at the short term.

4.4.2 Fractionally Integrated GARCH

A linear ARMA model can be written as

$$\phi(L)y_t = \theta(L)\varepsilon_t \tag{4.30}$$

with autoregressive polynomial $\phi(L)$ and moving average polynomial $\theta(L)$, where L denotes the usual lag operator. This model is stationary if all the roots of the autoregressive polynomial lie outside the unit circle. If $\phi(L)$ can be factorized into $\Phi(L)(1-L)$, the model is called integrated of order one, or I(1). It is well-known that the autocorrelation function (ACF) of a stationary ARMA process declines geometrically. Because of the fast decay, these models are also called short memory processes. For many real time series, especially in hydrology and financial economics, a long-term dependence can be observed in the ACF. Recall from Section 2.4 that the high frequency FX rates have this property. Such phenomena demand more flexible models that allow a slow hyperbolic decay of the ACF. It is possible to generalize standard ARIMA models by allowing a fractional differencing operator, $(1-L)^d$ with $d \in \mathbb{R}$. A *fractionally integrated ARMA model* (ARFIMA) is then defined as

$$\Phi(L)(1-L)^d y_t = \theta(L)\varepsilon_t. \tag{4.31}$$

An ARFIMA process with $d > 0$ is characterized by a not summable absolute covariance function. The model is stationary for $-0.5 < d < 0.5$. Applications to foreign exchange rates are provided by Mills (1993). Tschernig (1995) combines this model with a GARCH error term. Now the notion of long-term dependence in ARFIMA models directly conveys to the conditional variance, based on the ARMA representation of a GARCH process in (4.17) and (4.27).

Recall that if the autoregressive polynomial $[1-\alpha(z)-\beta(z)]$ contains a unit root, the process is integrated in variance as the IGARCH model of Engle and Bollerslev (1986) and can be written as in (4.28).

Now it is straightforward to adopt the long memory definition of the ARFIMA model class and write

$$\Phi(L)(1-L)^d\varepsilon_t^2 = \omega + [1-\beta(L)]v_t, \tag{4.32}$$

with $0 < d < 1$. This fractionally integrated GARCH model (FIGARCH) has recently been proposed by Baillie et al. (1996). As IGARCH models,

FIGARCH models with $d > 0$ are not covariance stationary because the unconditional variance of ε_t does not exist. However, the process is strictly stationary and ergodic. Unlike IGARCH, shocks are not persistent in volatility (recall the definition of persistence given above), but they have a long term impact.

Simulations and applications to daily stock returns and option pricing are provided by Bollerslev and Mikkelsen (1995).

4.5 Asymmetry of Volatility

The original idea of models of the ARCH type was that the *size* of recent innovations determined today's volatility. The standard ARCH models, however, are symmetric in the sense that the *signs* of the innovations are not relevant. In other words, 'good news' have the same impact on volatility as 'bad news', if they imply the same absolute return. As noted in Section 2.2, this basic property is not fulfilled for many financial series. Especially stock returns usually have a higher impact on volatility when ε_{t-1} is negative. This so-called leverage effect demands for more flexible, asymmetric models of volatility. Among the various extensions of ARCH models, many tried to overcome the symmetry restriction of conventional ARCH models, see the survey of Engle and Ng (1993). The most important parametric models in this context, exponential and threshold ARCH models, shall be discussed in the following. For nonparametric models, which are the most flexible asymmetric models, it is referred to Chapter 5.

4.5.1 Exponential GARCH

Denote by ξ_t a sequence of *i.i.d.* random variables with mean zero and variance one. Then the general exponential GARCH model, introduced by Nelson (1991), is given by

$$\log \sigma_t^2 = \omega_t + \sum_{k=1}^{\infty} \beta_k g(\xi_{t-k}), \tag{4.33}$$

where ω_t, β_k are deterministic coefficients, and

$$g(\xi_t) = \theta \xi_t + \gamma(|\xi_t| - E|\xi_t|). \tag{4.34}$$

Obviously, $E\left[g(\xi_t)\right] = 0$.

The EGARCH model in (4.33) has some substantial differences from original ARCH models:

- Volatility, as measured by the conditional variance σ_t^2, is an explicit multiplicative function of lagged innovations.

- Volatility is driven by the *i.i.d.* sequence ξ_t, rather than by the conditionally heteroskedastic sequence ε_t. Observe, however, that for given starting values a GARCH model can be written as a function of lagged ξ_t's as well, see the representation in (4.42).

- Volatility can react asymmetrically to 'good news' and 'bad news'.

- The parameter conditions for strict and covariance stationarity coincide for general distributions of ξ_t.

- The parameters in (4.33) and (4.34) need not be restricted to be positive.

The function $g(\cdot)$ in (4.34) is piecewise linear. It contains two parameters that determine what can be termed the 'size impact' and 'sign impact' of news on volatility, the former being the usual ARCH effect, and the latter the asymmetry, for example the leverage effect. The term $\gamma(|\xi_t| - E|\xi_t|)$ drives the size impact of news to volatility, whereas the term $\theta\xi_t$ allows for the sign impact. Thus, γ is expected to be positive, θ to be negative.

For estimation of EGARCH models, the infinite moving average model in (4.33) has to be represented by a finite autoregressive moving average model such as

$$\Delta(L)\log\sigma_t^2 = \omega + \Psi(L)g(\xi_t), \tag{4.35}$$

with lag polynomials $\Delta(L)$ and $\Psi(L)$ of order p and q, respectively.

A general advantage of exponential models over additive models is that no parameter restrictions have to be imposed. Thus, possible instabilities of standard optimization routines are avoided. On the other hand, consistency and the asymptotic distribution of the maximum likelihood estimators are still open issues.

Assume that $\omega_t = \omega = 0$ and $\sum_{k=1}^{\infty}\beta_k^2 < \infty$. Then σ_t^2 is strictly stationary and ergodic (Nelson (1991), Theorem 2.1). Furthermore, under these assumptions the unconditional variance exists if ξ_t has a generalized error distribution (GED) with 'tail thickness parameter' $\zeta > 1$ (Nelson (1991, Theorem 2.2); the GED is 'fat-tailed' for $\zeta < 2$). The Gaussian distribution is a special case of the GED ($\zeta = 2$). Nelson also gives rather complicated formulae for the unconditional moments. The problem is that some other fat-tailed distributions such as the Student's t distribution do not yield existence of any higher unconditional moments. The reason for this is the exponential increase of the conditional variance, which of course can cause the unconditional variance to explode if the probability mass at the tails is sufficiently large. So the existence of the unconditional variance crucially depends on the distribution of ξ_t, which is a rather unappealing property of EGARCH.

4.5.2 Threshold ARCH Models

The idea of threshold ARCH (TARCH) models is to divide the support of the innovations in disjoint intervals and to fit a piecewise linear function to the conditional standard deviation. This was done by Zakoian (1994). If there is just one threshold, this will usually be the zero line. In this case a threshold ARCH model of order q can be written as

$$\sigma_t = \omega + \sum_{i=1}^{q} \alpha_i^+ \varepsilon_{t-i}^+ + \sum_{t=1}^{q} \alpha_i^- \varepsilon_{t-i}^-, \tag{4.36}$$

with $\varepsilon_t^+ = \max(\varepsilon_t, 0)$ and $\varepsilon_t^- = \min(\varepsilon_t, 0)$. Note that the conditional standard deviation is modelled rather than the conditional variance.

Rabemananjara and Zakoian (1993) extended this model to a TGARCH by adding an autoregressive conditional standard deviation term as in the classical GARCH model. They also provide conditions for covariance stationarity. However, the properties of quasi maximum likelihood estimates (QMLE) are not obvious, because σ_t is not differentiable. In particular, asymptotic normality remains an open issue.

Instead of fitting a piecewise linear function, Gouriéroux and Monfort (1992) used a piecewise constant function over a partition of the support of the innovations. Let $A_j, j = 1, \ldots, J$ denote this partition. Then the qualitative threshold ARCH model (QTARCH) of order one can be written as

$$y_t = \sum_{j=1}^{J} m_j I(y_{t-1} \in A_j) + \sum_{j=1}^{J} s_j I(y_{t-1} \in A_j)\xi_t, \tag{4.37}$$

where $I(\cdot)$ denotes the indicator function, and m_j and s_j are scalars. As before, ξ_t is an *i.i.d.* sequence with mean zero and variance one. In (4.37), both conditional mean and conditional variance are modelled as piecewise constant functions. Note also that (4.37) is a homogeneous Markov chain of order one. Models of higher order can easily be established. Gouriéroux and Monfort (1992) provide an extensive discussion of the statistical properties of (4.37) and also show asymptotic normality of QMLE.

4.6 Risk and Return

In finance theory, the relationship beween risk and return plays a predominant role. As described in more detail in the second chapter, the main measure of risk has been the standard deviation. Many well-known financial models such as the capital asset pricing model (CAPM) imply a linear relationship between the return of an asset and a risk measure. It was seen in Section 2.1.1 that in the CAPM the risk factor β is dependent on the covariance with the market portfolio, where in an intertemporal version the covariance can assumed to be time-varying. The development of ARCH models and the possibility to explicitly model volatility arose the demand for econometric models with risk/volatility as a regressor. Among other approaches, the paper by Engle et al. (1987) had the most influence on subsequent literature. The idea of their ARCH in mean (ARCH–M) model shall be sketched briefly.

Let y_t be a covariance stationary excess return series of some financial asset, and σ_t^2 its conditional variance, specified as an ARCH(1) model. Then the ARCH-M model is written as

$$\begin{aligned} y_t &= \delta g(\sigma_t^2) + \varepsilon_t \\ \sigma_t^2 &= \omega + \alpha\varepsilon_{t-1}^2, \end{aligned} \tag{4.38}$$

where $g(\cdot)$ is some parametric function. In most applications, the square root (i.e. linearity in the standard deviation) or logarithmic functions were used, and this is still controversial. The term $\delta g(\sigma_t^2)$ is the specification of a risk premium. Thus, if $g(x) = \sqrt{x}$, one would expect δ to be positive, so that y_t depends positively on the risk premium. Obviously, not significant estimates of δ do not imply that there is no risk premium, because a nonlinear risk premium might be apparent. Therefore, the correct specification of (4.38) is important. Nonparametric pre–estimates of the risk premium are able to give information about the functional form. This was done with considerable success e.g. by Pagan and Hong (1991) and Linton (1992).

4.7 Asymmetry and Persistence of the FX Rates

In this section, estimation results of parametric ARCH models of the foreign exchange rate series described in Section 2.4 are presented. We focus on two main issues: persistence and asymmetry of the estimated volatility equation.

Recall from Section 2.4 that the Dollar rates are negatively autocorrelated at the first lags. To overcome this, an AR(3) and AR(2) model was fitted to the returns of the DEM/USD and JPY/USD returns, respectively. A constant was not included, because the unconditional means of the series are

FX rate	DEM/USD	JPY/USD
ϕ_1	-0.0811	-0.1031
	(0.006)	(0.0063)
ϕ_2	-0.0236	-0.0219
	(0.007)	(0.0063)
ϕ_3	-0.0265	
	(0.006)	
log$L$	145,403.6	141,346.8

TABLE 4.1. *MLE results for the AR(2) and AR(3) model fitted to the non-standardized returns of DEM/USD and JPY/USD, respectively.*

very small, see Section 2.4. Low-order moving average models could have been estimated as well, but due to the small - though highly significant - absolute values of the autocorrelations, no substantially different results are to be expected. The orders of the AR(P) models were chosen by the Schwarz information criterion, see Schwarz (1978). Maximum likelihood estimation results are given in Table 4.1.

The residuals of the estimated AR(3) model were now used for the estimation of ARCH models. As can be seen from (4.9), the estimation of the conditional variance parameters affects the parameter estimates of the conditional mean, so the estimation should be performed simultaneously. This was also done, but no remarkable differences were detected. This can be explained by the large data set, because neglection of conditional heteroskedasticity in the error term still allows consistent - though not efficient - estimation of the autoregressive parameters. So the residual series ε_t with mean zero will serve as the basic series for subsequent models.

To start with, the results of a GARCH(1,1) model are given in Table 4.2. The estimation was performed by QMLE and the BHHH optimization algorithm of Berndt et al. (1974, BHHH). The standard errors are heteroskedasticity-consistent, see White (1980). Because the original series has a very small unconditional variance, numerical problems arose with the use of the BHHH algorithm. Therefore, the residuals were divided by the standard deviation, so that the unconditional variance of the transformed series is equal to one. This only affects the value of ω, but not the parameters of interest, namely α and β. If the value of ω of the original series was of interest, this could be obtained by using $\hat{\omega} = (1 - \hat{\alpha} - \hat{\beta})\hat{\sigma}^2$. For example $\hat{\omega} = 3.88\text{E}{-08}$ and the value of the log likelihood function becomes 146,893.4 for DEM/USD. Thus, an improvement over the conditionally homoskedastic

	GARCH			IGARCH		
FX rate	DM/US	JP/US	JP/DM	DM/US	JP/US	JP/DM
ω	.063	.035	.032	.020	.026	.010
	(.006)	(.003)	(.004)	(.002)	(.002)	(.001)
α	.102	.141	.085	.107	.152	.076
	(.007)	(.008)	(.006)	(.005)	(.007)	(.004)
β	.838	.840	.886			
	(.011)	(.008)	(.007)			
log L	-34,639	-30,550	-31,672	-34,819	-32,650	-31,744
$m(\hat{\xi}_t)$	.005	−.009	−.017	.005	−.008	−.017
Var$(\hat{\xi}_t)$	.999	1.0	1.0	.93	.97	.954
$s(\hat{\xi}_t)$	.22	.04	−.15	.24	.04	−.17
$k(\hat{\xi}_t)$	9.73	12.04	6.71	11.43	12.04	6.70

TABLE 4.2. *QMLE results for the GARCH(1,1) and IGARCH models. Heteroskedasticity–consistent standard errors are given in parentheses. log L denotes the log likelihood value, m, s and k the mean, skewness and kurtosis, respectively.*

AR(3) model is achieved.

Observe that $\alpha + \beta = 0.94$, 0.98 and 0.97 respectively, so the parameter estimates imply a conditional variance close to the unit root. However, the corresponding likelihood–ratio test statistics are 360.6, 4199.8 and 143.0, so that the null hypothesis of a unit root is rejected in all cases.

The distribution of the estimated residuals $\hat{\xi}_t$ still is highly leptokurtic for all rates, as indicated by the values of the kurtosis. The standard deviation of $\sqrt{24/n}$ of the estimated kurtosis indicates significant deviation of the estimated residuals from normality, i.e. misspecification of the conditional distribution for all rates. The leptokurtosis implied by conditional heteroskedasticity is not strong enough to account for the leptokurtosis observed for the *unconditional* returns if ξ_t is assumed to be normally distributed. Plausible alternative assumptions will not be pursued in this context, because we know that the normality assumption yields consistent parameter estimates, whereas in general this does not hold for other likelihoods in the case of misspecification. Therefore we also apply QMLE to the following models.

Turning to the persistence issue, the IGARCH(1,1) model

$$\sigma_t^2 = \omega + \alpha\varepsilon_t^2 + (1-\alpha)\sigma_{t-1}^2. \tag{4.39}$$

is estimated and the results are also reported in Table 4.2. Obviously, the fit is outperformed by the GARCH model. Note that the kurtosis of the residuals

FX rate	DEM/USD	JPY/USD	JPY/DEM
ω	0.0055	0.0127	0.0047
	(0.0012)	(0.0038)	(0.0032)
θ	-0.0022	-0.0118	-0.0160
	(0.0048)	(0.0119)	(0.0102)
γ	0.1426	0.2454	0.2140
	(0.0096)	(0.0210)	(0.0157)
β	0.9426	0.8754	0.8440
	(0.0044)	(0.0115)	(0.0157)
$\log L$	-34,652.3	-32,864.8	-31,877.4
$m(\hat{\xi})$	0.0062	-0.0079	-0.0149
$\text{Var}(\hat{\xi})$	1.0144	0.9416	0.9791
$s(\hat{\xi})$	0.25	0.0588	-0.1159
$k(\hat{\xi}_t)$	9.51	12.01	7.30

TABLE 4.3. *QMLE results for the EGARCH(1,1) model. Notes as in Table 4.2.*

has even increased for DEM/USD. Also, the variance of the residuals is 0.93 for DEM/USD, i.e. the fit overestimates the unconditional variance. These facts indicate misspecification of the IGARCH model. The degree of persistence in the data does not seem to be large enough to justify a permanent impact of shocks on volatility forecasts.

The second topic is asymmetry. For this, the EGARCH(1,1) model is estimated as

$$\log\sigma_t^2 = \omega + \theta\xi_{t-1} + \gamma\left(|\xi_{t-1}| - \sqrt{2/\pi}\right) + \beta\log\sigma_{t-1}^2 \qquad (4.40)$$

with $\xi_t \sim N(0,1)$. Results are reported in Table 4.3. The likelihood value is slightly smaller than the GARCH likelihood. Most important is the nonsignificance of the asymmetry parameter θ. Based on this result one would argue that shocks to the DEM/USD rate to either side have the same impact on volatility. However, that this conclusion is misleading will be demonstrated in the next chapter. Note also that except for the JPY/DEM returns, the estimate of β is larger than the corresponding β of the GARCH estimation. An explanation for this is provided in Section 4.8 in the context of news impact functions.

The first 500 estimated conditional variances (this covers approximately one week) for the different models are depicted in Figure 4.1, 4.2 and 4.3. Each top panel shows the corresponding residuals of the fitted AR models to the Dollar rates and the original JPY/DEM series, respectively. After the EMS crisis in September 1992, this subsample is still dominated by large volatilities. Two major jumps occur during this first week. Recall from Section 2.4.9 that the first jump is actually a turbulent period consisting of two jumps at $t = 144$ and $t = 148$ in ϑ–time, which corresponds to 92/10/02, 11:50 - 12:30 in GMT. The news identified were "Germany lowers yield on 5–years notes", and "BUBA rates to stay steady for 'time being' ". The latter headline refers to a statement of the German Bundesbank. It can be observed that first adjustments occur in the DEM/USD rate, whereas the less liquid JPY/USD and JPY/DEM follow after for arbitrage reasons. The second jump in DEM/USD was related to "Georgia accuses Russia shooting helicopter", which occurred on 92/10/05 at 16:42 GMT. However, this was merely a representative among others in a very turbulent market. Interestingly, in this case volatility seems to spill over from the JPY/DEM rate, where a jump occurs around $t = 230$, to JPY/USD (around $t = 260$) and DEM/USD ($t = 281$). This indicates that news affecting volatility of minor rates may indirectly affect volatility of major rates as well.

Although the GARCH and IGARCH estimated volatilities appear to react similarly to news, it can be seen that IGARCH overweighs outliers relative to GARCH (note that the same scales are used). This holds even stronger for EGARCH if the shock is very large, as for the second jump in the subsample. Thus, the conclusion of Engle and Ng (1993) that EGARCH tends to overweigh outliers is confirmed.

Summary statistics of the estimated volatilities are given in Table 4.4 together with residual diagnostics. $Q_2(m)$ denotes the Box–Ljung portmanteau statistic of squared residuals, i.e.

$$Q_2(m) = n(n+2)\sum_{i=1}^{m}(n-i)^{-1}\rho_i^2,$$

where $\rho_i = \text{Corr}(\xi_t^2, \xi_{t-i}^2)$, which is asymptotically χ^2 distributed with degrees of freedom equal to m minus the number of estimated parameters, cf. McLeod and Li (1983) and Section 3.5.

4.8 News Impact Functions

Consider an ARCH(1) model as in (4.4) with $q = 1$. It is easy to regard σ_t^2 as a function of ε_{t-1}, in this case a parabolic function. Now consider the GARCH(1,1) model as in (4.16), where σ_t^2 is a function of infinitely many lagged ε_t's. In other words, the ARCH(1) model has the Markov property, whereas the GARCH(1,1) model does not because the conditional variance

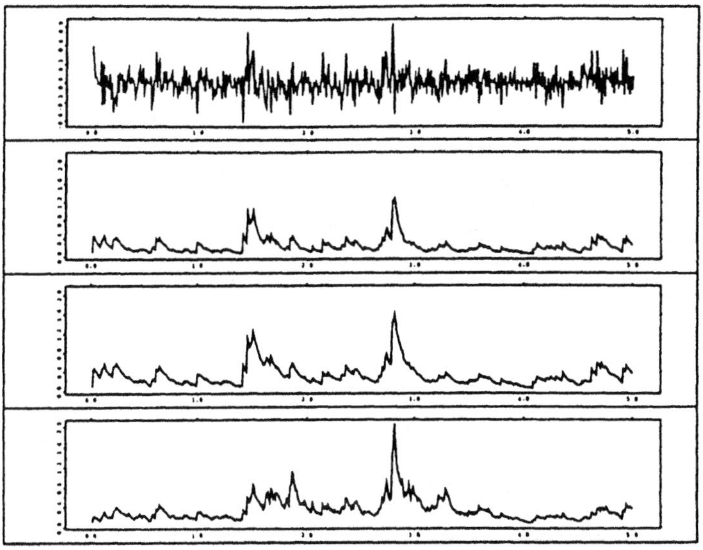

FIGURE 4.1. *The first 500 residuals of the fitted AR(3) model to DEM/USD and estimated GARCH, IGARCH and EGARCH volatilities (from top to bottom). The ordinates of all volatility panels range from 0 to 20.*

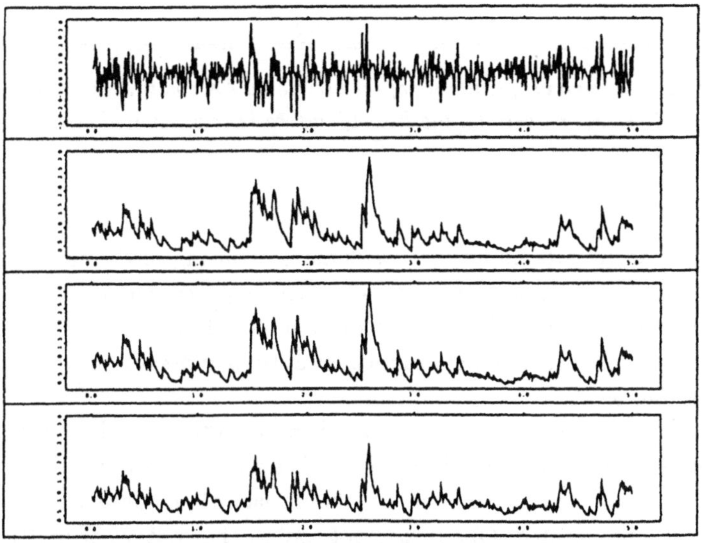

FIGURE 4.2. *The first 500 residuals of the fitted AR(2) model to JPY/USD and estimated GARCH, IGARCH and EGARCH volatilities (from top to bottom). The ordinates of all volatility panels range from 0 to 20.*

	Model	GARCH	IGARCH	EGARCH
	Min(σ_t^2)	0.42	0.27	0.35
DEM/USD	Max(σ_t^2)	20.81	23.15	20.51
	Mean(σ_t^2)	1.02	1.19	1.03
	Var(σ_t^2)	0.56	1.06	0.51
	$Q_2(10)$	10.84	20.47	63.94
	$Q_2(100)$	97.32	94.34	121.88
	$Q_2(1000)$	1197.43	1258.26	1166.17
	Min(σ_t^2)	0.23	0.19	0.33
JPY/USD	Max(σ_t^2)	41.48	45.14	25.95
	Mean(σ_t^2)	1.09	1.17	0.97
	Var(σ_t^2)	1.96	2.44	0.40
	$Q_2(10)$	39.67	43.87	90.94
	$Q_2(100)$	218.75	204.23	529.59
	$Q_2(1000)$	1307.03	1182.87	2770.36
	Min(σ_t^2)	0.32	0.20	0.43
JPY/DEM	Max(σ_t^2)	14.21	13.34	12.61
	Mean(σ_t^2)	1.03	1.13	0.98
	Var(σ_t^2)	0.49	0.69	0.14
	$Q_2(10)$	32.43	46.29	103.95
	$Q_2(100)$	197.96	215.11	770.61
	$Q_2(1000)$	1359.6	1152.2	3189.9

TABLE 4.4. *Summary statistics of the estimated FX volatilities and residual diagnostics. $Q_2(m)$ denotes the Box–Ljung statistic of squared residuals, ξ_t^2, with m lags.*

depends on an infinite number of residuals. According to the rational expectations paradigm economic agents build their expectations of future volatility on all available and relevant information including prices. Therefore, the GARCH(1,1) model is in most practical situations more appropriate than the ARCH(1) model.

It is now of interest to ask how economic news influence subsequent volatility. In other words, how fast does the market adjust to an exogenous shock? This question can only be answered if the impact of one news announcement or shock can be isolated. One important tool in the context of multiple time series analysis is the *impulse response* analysis as introduced by Sims (1980). It examines the influence of an isolated unit shock in one variable on the variable itself and all other variables. For a critical discussion of the impulse

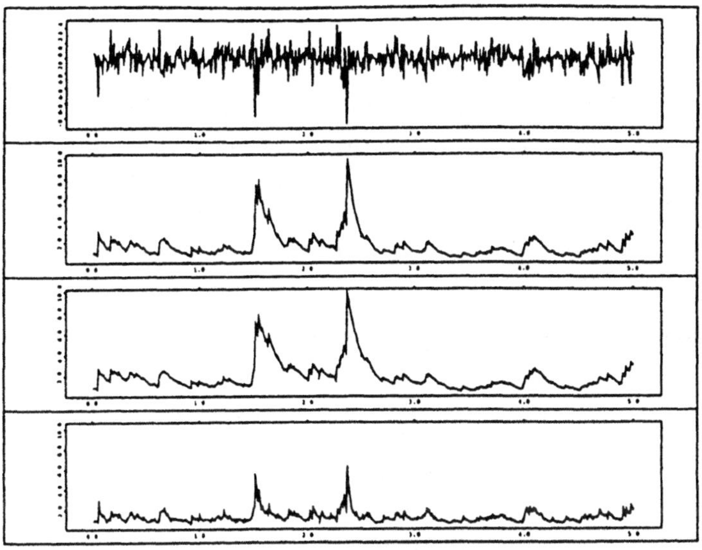

FIGURE 4.3. *The first 500 returns of JPY/DEM and estimated GARCH, IGARCH and EGARCH volatilities (from top to bottom). The ordinates of all volatility panels range from 0 to 20.*

response analysis, see e.g. Lütkepohl (1991). Conventionally, the response was measured by the level of a stationary series, but the ideas convey to the volatility issue.

Consider the general conditionally heteroskedastic model

$$\varepsilon_t = \sigma_t \xi_t, \tag{4.41}$$

where ε_t could be either the original series or a residual term, ξ_t is *i.i.d.* with mean zero and variance one, and σ_t depends on the information set at time $t-1$.

First, we define *news* or, equivalently, *shock* to be an independent innovation to the system, i.e. the *i.i.d.* distributed ξ_t. Note that this is not equivalent to the definition of *news* by Engle and Ng (1993).

Now we need to ask how the conditional variance σ_t^2 depends on past innovations. For the EGARCH model (4.33) this is immediately clear, and the GARCH(1,1) model can be rewritten as

$$\begin{aligned}\sigma_t^2 &= \omega + \alpha\varepsilon_{t-1}^2 + \beta\sigma_{t-1}^2 \\ &= \omega\left(1 + \sum_{j=1}^{t-1}\prod_{i=1}^{j}(\alpha\xi_{t-i}^2 + \beta)\right) + \sigma_0^2\prod_{i=1}^{t}(\alpha\xi_{t-i}^2 + \beta),\end{aligned} \tag{4.42}$$

which follows by iterative substitution. Thus, the GARCH model is additive in the ε_t's, but multiplicative in the innovations.

Definition 4.1 (News Impact Function) *Assume that the volatility of a series ε_t has arrived at the unconditional variance of the series at $t = 0$, $\sigma_0^2 = \sigma^2$. Let a shock occur at $t = 0$, i.e. ξ_0, of arbitrary size, and let all subsequent innovations up to time $t-1$ be zero: $\xi_i = 0,\ i = 1, \ldots, t-1$. Then the news impact function of volatility is defined as the variance of ε_t conditional on this information.*

Proposition 4.1 *The news impact function of a GARCH(1,1) model is given by*

$$\sigma_t^2 = \omega \frac{1-\beta^t}{1-\beta} + \sigma^2(\beta^t + \alpha\beta^{t-1}\xi_0^2), \tag{4.43}$$

and for an EGARCH(1,1) model by

$$\sigma_t^2 = C \exp\left(\beta^{t-1} g(\xi_0)\right) \tag{4.44}$$

with

$$C = \exp\left(\omega \frac{1-\beta^t}{1-\beta} + g(0)\frac{1-\beta^{t-1}}{1-\beta} + \beta^t \log \sigma^2\right).$$

The proof follows immediately by using (4.42) for the GARCH(1,1) model, (4.40) for the EGARCH(1,1) model, and Definition 4.1.

Remark 4.1 *Instead of setting all subsequent innovations to zero, an alternative definition is to set the terms ξ_{t-i}^2, $i = 1, \ldots, t-1$ in (4.42) for the GARCH model and $g(\xi_{t-i})$, $i = 1, \ldots, t-1$ in (4.33) for the EGARCH model to their expectations, i.e. one and zero, respectively. In this case the news impact functions would be*

$$\sigma_t^2 = \omega \frac{1-(\alpha+\beta)^t}{1-(\alpha+\beta)} + \sigma^2(\alpha\xi_0^2 + \beta)(\alpha+\beta)^{t-1},$$

for the GARCH model and

$$\sigma_t^2 = C \exp\left(\beta^{t-1} g(\xi_0)\right)$$

with

$$C = \exp\left(\omega \frac{1-\beta^t}{1-\beta} + \beta^t \log \sigma^2\right).$$

for the EGARCH model. It is obvious that the alternative definitions only affect the level of volatility against which the news impact function converges.

Engle and Ng (1993) introduced the *news impact curve* as the plot of σ_t^2 against ε_{t-1} for various models, so news are defined differently. This is just a matter of standardization if an isolated impulse is analyzed and all the other innovations are set to zero. Definition 4.1, however, is more general than the definition of Engle and Ng (1993), because it allows for an isolated shock k lags, not only one lag ago. The news impact function used here is not only a function of the shock, but also of the time lag of the shock. On the other hand, Definition 4.1 is more general than the usual methodology of impulse response functions to set the shock equal to one standard deviation. Here, arbitrary shocks are considered. Strictly speaking this comparison in a univariate framework is not appropriate because impulse response functions are designed for multiple time series analysis. The idea to consider a shock of arbitrary size in volatility, however, can also be used in a multivariate GARCH framework, cf. Hafner and Herwartz (1997). Thus, Definition 4.1 can be regarded as an attempt to unify the two concepts of *news impact curves* and *impulse response functions* in their usual sense.

Obviously, the impact of one shock, measured by the defined news impact functions, is decreasing faster in the EGARCH model than in the GARCH model, if the β's are equal. Thus, when fitting both models to a given series, the β of the EGARCH model should be larger than the β of the GARCH model. For the FX estimation results in Tables 4.2 and 4.3, this holds for DEM/USD and JPY/USD, but not for DEM/JPY.

For illustration, the estimated GARCH and EGARCH news impact functions for the standardized DEM/USD series are plotted in Figure 4.4 and 4.5. Equations (4.43) and (4.44) were used with $t = 1, \ldots, 15$ and amplitude of the shock ξ_0 restricted to the interval [-10, 10].

Note that the news impact function of the EGARCH model declines faster, even though the estimated β is larger than the estimated β in the GARCH model. For $t = 1$ and $|\xi_0|$ close to zero (large), the impact is larger for the EGARCH (GARCH) model, given the estimated parameters.

4.9 Temporal (Dis–)Aggregation

The choice of the frequency at which the underlying process is observed affects in general the properties of the observed process and consequently the estimation of a model for the observed process. If the process remains in the same class under temporal aggregation, it is called to be closed. For example, ARIMA processes are known to be closed, i.e. low frequency ARIMA processes can be obtained by aggregating high frequency ARIMA processes. Recently, Drost and Nijman (1993) have derived conditions for

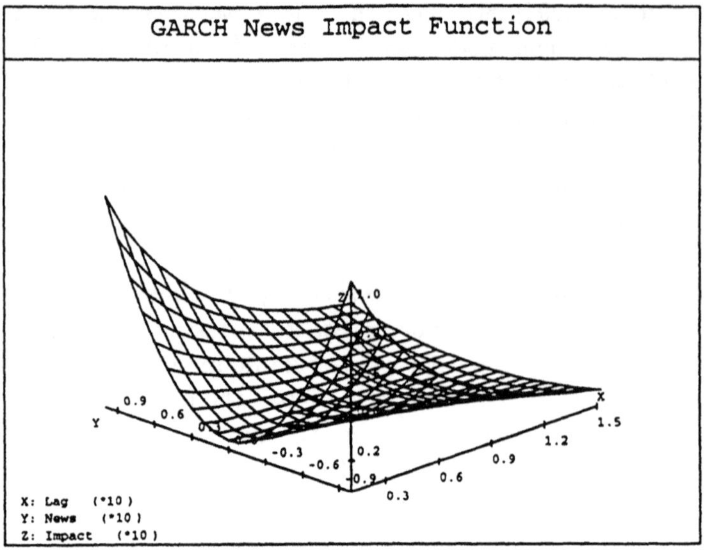

FIGURE 4.4. *The estimated GARCH news impact function for the standardized 20 minute DEM/USD returns.*

weak GARCH processes to be closed. If $y_t, t = 1, 2, \ldots$ is a stock variable, then the aggregated process is $y_{mt}, t = 1, 2, \ldots$, with positive integer m. If, on the other hand, y_t is a flow variable, then the low frequency process is $\sum_{i=0}^{m-1} y_{mt-i}, t = 1, 2, \cdots$.

For stock and flow variables, Drost and Nijman (1993) show that a weak GARCH(1,1) process is closed, and

$$(\alpha + \beta)^m = \alpha_{(m)} + \beta_{(m)}, \tag{4.45}$$

where α and β are the parameters of the original process, and $\alpha_{(m)}$ and $\beta_{(m)}$ the parameters of the aggregated process. For instance, if $\{\varepsilon_t\}$ is the residual series of a stock variable, then the aggregated GARCH process is

$$\sigma_{mt}^2 = \omega_{(m)} + \alpha_{(m)}\varepsilon_{m(t-1)}^2 + \beta_{(m)}\sigma_{m(t-1)}^2$$

with $t = 1, 2, \cdots$ and aggregation parameter m. As a consequence of (4.45), conditional heteroskedasticity disappears for highly aggregated processes. Note, however, that the conditions are derived for weak GARCH processes. Semi–strong and strong GARCH models are not closed under temporal aggregation.

The empirical evidence is in accordance to this theory for medium and low frequencies. The 'degree' of conditional heteroskedasticity, indicated by

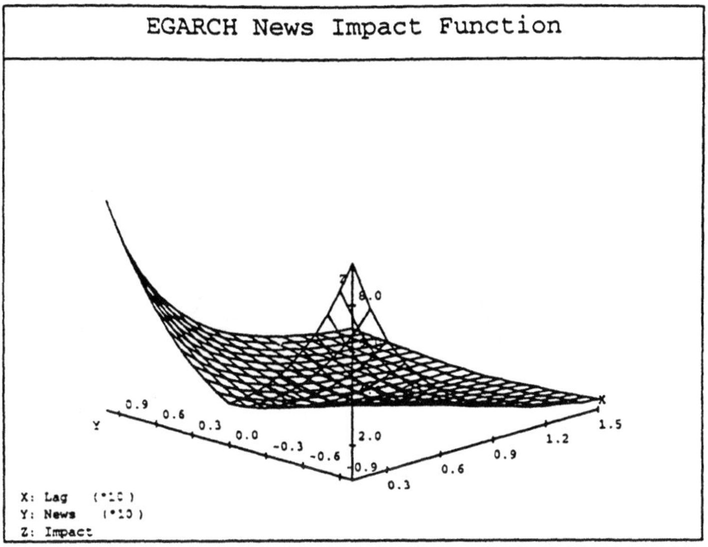

FIGURE 4.5. *The estimated EGARCH news impact function for the standardized 20 minute DEM/USD returns.*

$\alpha_{(m)} + \beta_{(m)}$, decreases monotonically for daily, weekly, and monthly data. For even longer time intervals, it is mostly found to be insignificant. As the empirical contributions of Andersen and Bollerslev (1995) and Schnidrig and Würtz (1995) with the same HFDF93 data set show, however, this theory does not hold for high-frequency data, in particular for 30 minute to two hour time intervals. The parameter estimates obtained for these frequencies implied less persistence than what would be expected under the aggregation theory. Andersen and Bollerslev (1995) use a de–seasonalization technique based on the Flexible Fourier Form (FFF), Schnidrig and Würtz (1995) a time scale similar to our ϑ–scale.

Nelson (1990a) showed that GARCH processes may serve as diffusion approximations when the frequency is high. In his setup, $\omega_{(m)}$ and $\alpha_{(m)}$ approach zero and $\beta_{(m)}$ approaches one as the sampling interval is decreased. Moreover, he derives the limit distributions for the conditional variances. For GARCH this is the inverse Gamma (Theorem 2.3), for EGARCH the lognormal distribution (Theorem 3.4). The following procedure was applied in order to see how well the estimated 20 minute DEM/USD volatilities (see Section 4.7) approximate these limit distributions. For the GARCH case, the inverse of the estimated conditional variance, σ_t^{-2}, was constructed and the density estimated by a kernel density estimator. For the limit distribution, the pa-

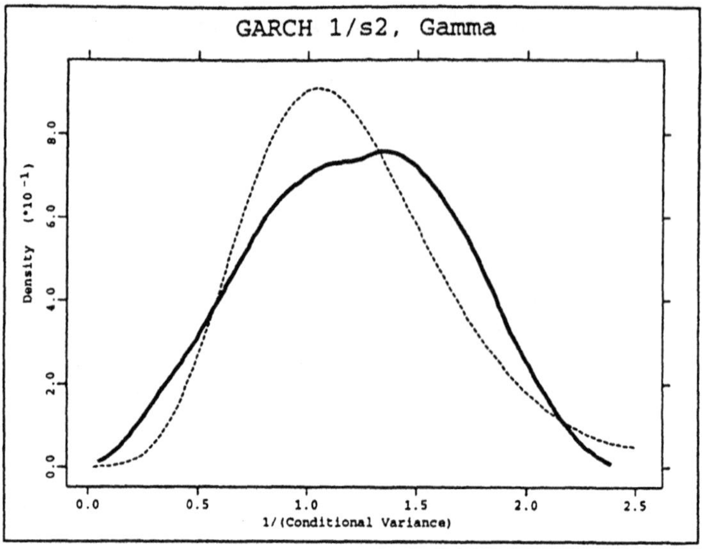

FIGURE 4.6. *Kernel density estimate of DEM/USD GARCH inverse volatilities (thick line) and a smoothed limiting Gamma distribution (broken line).*

rameters are not known. They could be estimated if the process parameters and the aggregation parameter m were available for different frequencies. Gouriéroux (1992, pp.87) suggests an estimation procedure based on the estimation of an ARCH(1) model, but this does not convey to the GARCH case and ARCH(1) models clearly are misspecified for the FX rates. Therefore, the density parameters of the Gamma distribution $\Gamma(x;\kappa,\theta)$ are chosen such that the first two moments of the limit and empirical distribution are equal. Thus, the expectation $\mathrm{E}[X]=\kappa\theta$ was set equal to $n^{-1}\sum_{t=1}^{n}\sigma_t^{-2}=1.23$, and $\mathrm{Var}(X)=\kappa\theta^2$ equal to $(n-1)^{-1}\sum_{t=1}^{n}(\sigma_t^{-2}-1.23)^2=0.211$. The resulting parameter estimates are $\kappa=7.172$ and $\theta=0.1715$. In order to compare the obtained limit distribution with the smoothed empirical distribution, the density was plotted on fixed equidistant design with equal number of knots n, and smoothed with a kernel regression smoother. The resulting plot is shown in Figure 4.6.

For the EGARCH case, the limit distribution of σ_t^2 is log-normal, as shown in Nelson (1990a, Theorem 3.4). Figure 4.7 shows the kernel density estimate of $\log\sigma_t^2$ together with a smoothed normal density.

The empirical GARCH distribution of σ_t^{-2} appears to be skewed to the left rather than to the right as the limiting Gamma density. Very small values of

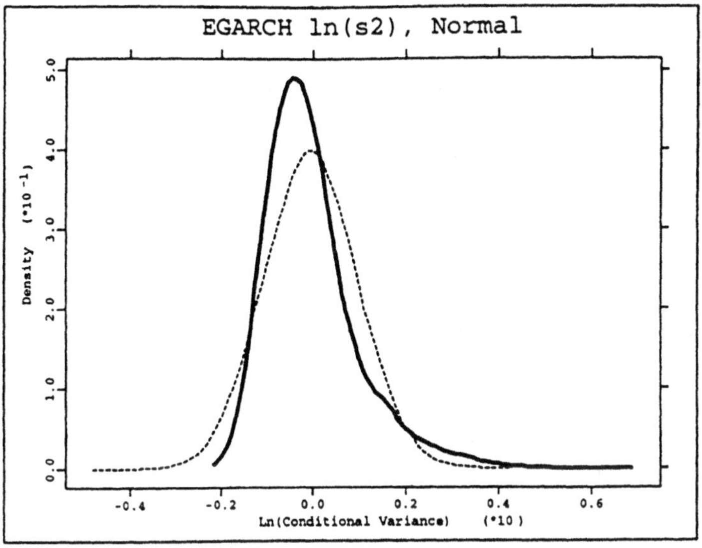

FIGURE 4.7. *Kernel density estimate of DEM/USD EGARCH log volatilities (thick line) and a smoothed limiting Normal distribution (broken line).*

σ_t^{-2}, i.e. large volatilities, have more probability mass than under the limit distribution. The same holds for the EGARCH case, where the empirical distribution of $\log \sigma_t^2$ is skewed to the right. Very small (large) volatilities occur less (more) often than under the limiting log-normal distribution.

Although this is a rather informal and empirical investigation, it reveals that the 20 minute volatilities do not approximate their limiting distributions well under the hypothesis that the GARCH/EGARCH models are correctly specified. This, however, is in accordance with the results of Andersen and Bollerslev (1995) and Schnidrig and Würtz (1995) that GARCH models do not fit high frequency FX volatilities as good as medium and low frequency volatilities.

4.10 Market Components and Heterogeneous ARCH

In the light of the previous section one might ask which time resolution is appropriate for an analysis of FX rate volatility. For example, if all market participants held open positions at least ten minutes, but not longer than 20 minutes, it would not be feasible to analyze daily series, because this information would not be relevant. However, market participants on FX markets are heterogeneous by means of profession. There are market makers (banks) who permanently observe the short–run movements of the rates in order to exploit arbitrage opportunities. On the other hand, there are institutions such as central banks which rather observe the market on a day–to–day scale, say. Price changes on a fine scale are relevant for the investment decisions of the short–term trader, but if they cancel on a coarse scale they are irrelevant for the long–term trader. Thus, both traders observe different price processes and thus react differently, although the underlying process is the same.

The idea for the econometric analysis is to divide the market into several components, correponding to the different typical market observation intervals, and construct models that reflect the behavior of the market components. Müller, Dacorogna, Davé, Olsen, Pictet and Weizsäcker (1995) have proposed a heterogeneous ARCH (HARCH) model that is supposed to cope with heterogeneous volatility, i.e. volatility of different time resolutions. The HARCH(q) model has the form

$$\sigma_t^2 = \omega + \sum_{j=1}^{q} \alpha_j \left(\sum_{i=1}^{j} \varepsilon_{t-i} \right)^2 , \tag{4.46}$$

where $\omega > 0$ and $\alpha_j \geq 0$.

The idea of this formulation becomes obvious when looking at an alternative representation of the HARCH(2) process

$$\sigma_t^2 = \omega + (\alpha_1 + \alpha_2)\varepsilon_{t-1}^2 + \alpha_2 \varepsilon_{t-2}^2 + 2\alpha_2 \varepsilon_{t-1}\varepsilon_{t-2}. \tag{4.47}$$

The cross–term in (4.47) obviously decreases the conditional variance if the subsequent terms ε_{t-1} and ε_{t-2} have opposite signs. This represents the market component of the traders who observe the market at $t, t+2, t+4, \cdots$. The HARCH(q) model can be viewed as an ARCH(q) model with additional cross terms that reflect each market component. This economically appealing idea, however, is met by econometric difficulties. First, the model in its general form is far from being parsimonious. Müller, Dacorogna, Davé, Olsen, Pictet and Weizsäcker (1995) use for the estimation of a HARCH(1024) model six components with parameters restricted to be the same for each component. The categorization is of course arbitrary. Second, the model is in spirit an ARCH(q) model, and practice has shown that GARCH(1,1) fit most FX series (medium frequency) better than ARCH models of high order.

A HARCH model as in (4.46) and a nonparametric generalization were also checked for our 20 minute DEM/USD rate series. HARCH models of order up to 20 where estimated without restricting the coefficients and without a priori categories of market components. Thus, the last lag of a HARCH(20) model corresponds to approximately seven hours in ϑ–time. Some residual diagnostics are reported in Table 4.5, where $\rho_1(\xi_t^2)$ denotes the first order

q	2	3	4	5	7	10	20
$\rho_1(\xi_t^2)$	0.178	0.187	0.190	0.203	0.218	0.220	0.240
Kurt(ξ_t)	10.29	9.94	9.94	9.72	9.48	9.79	9.89

TABLE 4.5. *Residual statistics of the estimated HARCH(q) models for the 20 minute DEM/USD returns.*

autocorrelation of squared residuals, and Kurt(ξ_t) the unconditional kurtosis of the residuals. Surprisingly, first order autocorrelation of squared residuals even increased for higher orders.

The nonparametric HARCH (NHARCH) model takes the form

$$\sigma_t^2 = \omega + \sum_{j=1}^{q} g_j \left(\sum_{i=1}^{j} \varepsilon_{t-i} \right), \tag{4.48}$$

with smooth nonlinear functions $g_j(\cdot)$, $j = 1, \ldots, q$. These functions were estimated by smoothing splines, see Section 5.4 for details. Models up to order $q = 20$ were estimated in the general, unrestricted form. Results for the NHARCH model are not reported but available on request. The fitted volatilities were compared with the corresponding estimates of the multiplicative nonparametric ARCH model (MNARCH) introduced in Section 5.4. Now less surprisingly, for each q the NHARCH model was outperformed by the MNARCH model, as various residual diagnostics revealed.

These unfavorable results are explained by the predominance of short–term traders and their impact on market volatility. Qualitatively, Müller, Dacorogna, Davé, Olsen, Pictet and Weizsäcker (1995) also obtain a higher impact of intra–day components on volatility, but they do not report residual diagnostics. The cancellation of short–run price changes in the HARCH model diminishes the short–term impact. Speculation money in the FX market seems to determine volatility stronger than central bank intervention money. Of course this deserves a separate study. However, the HARCH model, although of some theoretical value, does not seem to cope with the features of FX rate volatility and will not be considered in the next chapter, where nonparametric ARCH and GARCH models are discussed.

4.11 Directionality of ARCH Processes

In Section 3.7, *reversibility* of a time series was defined and noticed that except for degenerated cases nonlinear processes in general are irreversible, or *directional.* In this section, directionality of the simple ARCH(1) process is shown. This result implies the directionality of more general GARCH processes.

Recall from (4.17) and (4.27) that (G)ARCH processes can be written as linear ARMA processes in terms of the squares of the series. However, the innovation in this representation is not Gaussian (and in fact not even *i.i.d.*), so that the reversibility property of Gaussian ARMA processes does not apply. Consider the ARCH(1) process

$$\varepsilon_t = \sqrt{\omega + \alpha\varepsilon_{t-1}^2}\,\xi_t, \tag{4.49}$$

with $\xi_t \sim N.i.d.(0,1)$, $\omega > 0$ and $\alpha > 0$. To ensure stationarity and the existence of the first six moments of ε_t, also assume that $\alpha < 15^{-1/3} \approx 0.405$ by Theorem 1 of Engle (1982).

Also recall from Section 3.7 that reversibility implies the equality of the expectations $\mathrm{E}[\varepsilon_t^i \varepsilon_{t+r}^j]$ and $\mathrm{E}[\varepsilon_t^j \varepsilon_{t+r}^i]$ for every positive integer i, j, and r. Because of the symmetry of the innovation in (4.49), all such expectations are zero for odd integers i or j. In particular,

$$\mathrm{E}[\varepsilon_t \varepsilon_{t-1}^2] = \mathrm{E}[\varepsilon_{t-1}\varepsilon_t^2] = 0, \tag{4.50}$$

so that the TR test statistic of Ramsey and Rothman (1991) is zero for ARCH processes, giving no evidence against reversibility. To detect directionality, higher orders have to be considered. For instance,

$$\mathrm{E}[\varepsilon_t^2 \varepsilon_{t-1}^4] = \omega m_4 + \alpha m_6, \tag{4.51}$$

whereas

$$\mathrm{E}[\varepsilon_{t-1}^2 \varepsilon_t^4] = 3\frac{\omega^3}{1-\alpha} + 6\alpha\omega m_4 + 3\alpha^2 m_6, \tag{4.52}$$

where $m_4 = \mathrm{E}[\varepsilon_t^4]$, and $m_6 = \mathrm{E}[\varepsilon_t^6]$.

When calculating m_4 and m_6 by the formulae given in Engle (1982), it is straightforward to show that (4.51) and (4.52) are in general not equal. This counterexample shows that ARCH processes are indeed directional.

However, from a second order point of view ARCH processes can be considered as 'reversible' not in the strict definition as in Section 3.7, but regarding the linearity of $\{\varepsilon_t^2\}$. To see this, rewrite (4.49) as

$$\varepsilon_t^2 = \omega + \alpha\varepsilon_{t-1}^2 + v_t \tag{4.53}$$

with $v_t \equiv \varepsilon_t^2 - \mathrm{E}[\varepsilon_t^2 \mid \varepsilon_{t-1}]$. v_t has mean zero, constant variance and zero serial correlation. Also, v_t is uncorrelated with ε_{t-1}^2. Now ε_{t-1}^2 can be written as

$$\varepsilon_{t-1}^2 = \omega + \alpha\varepsilon_t^2 + \eta_t, \tag{4.54}$$

with η_t being uncorrelated with ε_t^2. Thus, the best linear projection $\mathcal{P}$ of ε_{t-1}^2 on a constant, ε_t and ε_t^2 is

$$\mathcal{P}(\varepsilon_{t-1}^2 \mid \varepsilon_t) = \omega + \alpha\varepsilon_t^2. \tag{4.55}$$

This is just the reversed weak ARCH process, where *weak* ARCH is defined by Drost and Nijman (1993).

Considering linear functions in the squares of ε_t, backward and forward prediction yield the same results, so we will restrict the following derivations to the case of forward prediction. Because we assumed $\alpha < 1$, ε_t and ε_t^2 are stationary and for larger lags the projection in (4.55) approaches the unconditional variance of ε_t. Formally,

$$\operatorname{plim} \mathcal{P}(\varepsilon_{t-k}^2 \mid \varepsilon_t) = \operatorname{plim} \mathcal{P}(\varepsilon_{t+k}^2 \mid \varepsilon_t) = \mathrm{E}[\varepsilon_t^2] = \frac{\omega}{1-\alpha} \equiv \sigma^2, \tag{4.56}$$

for $k \longrightarrow \infty$. Defining the centered impact function $g(x) \equiv \alpha(x^2 - \sigma^2)$, we obtain

$$\operatorname{plim} \mathcal{P}[g(\varepsilon_{t+k}) \mid \varepsilon_t] = 0 \tag{4.57}$$

for $k \longrightarrow \infty$. For example, in the ARCH(1) case we have

$$\begin{aligned}
\mathcal{P}[g(\varepsilon_{t+1}) \mid \varepsilon_t] &= -\frac{\alpha^2\omega}{1-\alpha} + \alpha^2\varepsilon_t^2, \\
\mathcal{P}[g(\varepsilon_{t+2}) \mid \varepsilon_t] &= \alpha\left(-\frac{\alpha^2\omega}{1-\alpha} + \alpha^2\varepsilon_t^2\right),
\end{aligned}$$

and in general

$$\mathcal{P}[g(\varepsilon_{t+k}) \mid \varepsilon_t] = \alpha^{k-1}\left(-\frac{\alpha^2\omega}{1-\alpha} + \alpha^2\varepsilon_t^2\right). \tag{4.58}$$

Thus, we obtain that

$$|\mathcal{P}[g(\varepsilon_{t+k_1}) \mid \varepsilon_t]| \geq |\mathcal{P}[g(\varepsilon_{t+k_2}) \mid \varepsilon_t]|, \tag{4.59}$$

for $0 < k_1 < k_2$. This result can be extended to the case of ARCH(q) and GARCH(p,q) models and will be used in Section 5.5 when assessing the model bias of a truncated additive model.

Concluding, it was seen that ARCH models are not reversible, but using the ARMA representation and the definition of weak ARCH it is possible to obtain the same linear projection for backward prediction as for forward prediction.

4.12 Conclusions

In this chapter, parametric ARCH and GARCH models were discussed with respect to their theoretical properties and estimation methods. Various extensions of the standard models were introduced, including relaxations of the conditional normality assumption, integrated and fractionally integrated GARCH models, asymmetric ARCH models, and ARCH–M models. Applied to the high frequency FX rates, the GARCH model outperformed the IGARCH model, and the asymmetry parameter of the EGARCH model was insignificant for all rates. It was concluded that the GARCH(1,1) model fits the FX return series reasonably well. A general definition of *news impact function* was given, allowing the analysis of the impact of an isolated shock of arbitrary size on volatility over time. For the estimated DEM/USD volatility, the news impact function was given for the GARCH and EGARCH estimates. Also, the estimated volatility distribution was compared with the limiting distribution under temporal disaggregation and remarkable differences were detected. The new heterogeneous ARCH (HARCH) model was motivated economically, but estimation results did not improve the GARCH fit. Finally, it was shown that (G)ARCH models are irreversible, where the reversibility definition of Lawrance (1991) was adopted. However, considering the ARMA representation of ARCH it was argued that from a second order point of view the projection of the news impact function can be reversed.

5

Nonparametric and Semiparametric Models

5.1 Introduction

In the previous chapter we have seen that parametric ARCH models have to a large extent the capability to explain the features of FX rate volatility. The GARCH model fit outperformed the IGARCH and EGARCH model fits. Based on this analysis one might conclude that the conditional variance of FX returns is neither integrated (permanent memory), nor asymmetric. To show that this conclusion would be rash is the objective of this chapter.

Recall from Section 3.4 that nonparametric time series analysis provides an important and powerful tool if certain conditions are satisfied. The price for obtaining high flexibility is in general a slower convergence rate than in the parametric case. For more general aspects of nonparametric time series analysis, see Section 3.4. This chapter deals with a closer description of nonparametric kernel estimation methods and the application to foreign exchange rate volatility. Here, the high frequency data set HFDF93 described in Section 2.4.4 will again serve as the benchmark series.

The outline is as follows. After the conditionally heteroskedastic autoregressive nonlinear model (CHARN) has been introduced in Section 5.2, kernel estimates such as the Nadaraya–Watson and local polynomial estimate and their properties will be described in Section 5.2.1. Model selection – in this framework bandwidth selection – and inference tools will be discussed in Sections 5.2.2 and 5.2.3. A Markovian model allowing for heterogeneous conditional skewness and kurtosis will be proposed in Section 5.3. A multiplicative nonparametric ARCH model will be introduced in Section 5.4, for which spline estimation techniques are applied. Lastly, a parsimonious nonparametric GARCH model will be proposed in Section 5.5, for which a simulation study gives information about the behavior of the estimates. The models shall be compared with respect to their ability to model the FX returns.

5.2 The CHARN Model

Consider a general nonlinear autoregressive model of order p:

$$y_t = f(y_{t-1}, \ldots, y_{t-p}) + \sigma(y_{t-1}, \ldots, y_{t-p})\xi_t, \tag{5.1}$$

where ξ_t is an *i.i.d.* sequence with mean zero and variance one. $\mathrm{E}[y_t|\psi_{t-1}] = f(\cdot)$ is the conditional mean, or *mean function*, and $\mathrm{Var}(y_t|\psi_{t-1}) = \sigma^2(\cdot)$ is the conditional variance, or *variance function*, where ψ_t denotes the information set available at t. Thus, model (5.1) allows for both nonlinear mean and variance functions and incorporates conditional heteroskedasticity. Due to the 'curse of dimensionality', the model (5.1) can be estimated only for small orders p. The amount of data required for smoothing in higher dimensions increases exponentially and is beyond the sample sizes one usually deals with in economics. To fit higher models nevertheless, restrictions have to be imposed on the nonlinear functions $f(\cdot)$ and $\sigma(\cdot)$. For instance, a natural restriction is to assume an additive structure for the mean function and a multiplicative structure for the volatility function. Additive models have been proposed in the time series context by Chen and Tsay (1993b).

By defining $Y_{t-1} = (y_{t-1}, \ldots, y_{t-p})'$, (5.1) can be written as a Markovian model with respect to Y_{t-1}, i.e. $y_t = f(Y_{t-1}) + \sigma(Y_{t-1})\xi_t$.

The model (5.1) with $p = 1$,

$$y_t = f(y_{t-1}) + \sigma(y_{t-1})\xi_t, \tag{5.2}$$

was termed *conditionally heteroskedastic autoregressive nonlinear* (CHARN) model, according to Bossaerts, Härdle and Hafner (1996). This section deals with the CHARN model, whereas higher order models will be discussed in Section 5.4 and 5.5.

The conditional expectation of the model (5.2) $\mathrm{E}[y_t|y_{t-1} = x] = f(x)$ can be written as

$$\begin{aligned} f(x) &= \int yp(y \mid x)dy \\ &= \frac{1}{p(x)} \int yp(x, y)dy, \end{aligned} \tag{5.3}$$

where $p(x, y)$ denotes the joint density of y_{t-1}, y_t, $p(y|x)$ the conditional density of y_t given y_{t-1} at x, and $p(x)$ the marginal density of y_{t-1} at x.

Analogously, the conditional variance function $\mathrm{Var}(y_t \mid y_{t-1} = x) = \sigma^2(x)$ is expressed as

$$\sigma^2(x) = \mathrm{E}\left[(y_t - \mathrm{E}[y_t \mid x])^2 \mid x\right]$$

$$
\begin{aligned}
&= \mathrm{E}[y_t^2 \mid x] - \{\mathrm{E}[y_t \mid x]\}^2 \\
&= \frac{1}{p(x)} \int y^2 p(x,y)dy - \{f(x)\}^2 . \qquad (5.4)
\end{aligned}
$$

In the following, kernel estimates of the mean and variance functions will be discussed.

5.2.1 *Kernel Estimates*

5.2.1.1 Kernel Functions

Nonparametric estimates of $f(x)$ and $\sigma^2(x)$ can be obtained by locally averaging the data, weighted by a *kernel function*. Kernel functions are continuous, bounded and symmetric functions satisfying $\int K(u)du = 1$. A kernel $K(u)$ is defined to be of order q if

$$
\int u^j K(u)du \begin{cases} = 0, & j = 1, \ldots, q-1 \\ \neq 0, & j = q. \end{cases} \qquad (5.5)
$$

For example, usual kernels of order two with bounded support are the Epanechnikov kernel

$$
K(u) = \frac{3}{4}(1-u^2)I(|u| \leq 1)
$$

and the quartic kernel

$$
K(u) = \frac{15}{16}(1-u^2)^2 I(|u| \leq 1),
$$

where $I(\cdot)$ denotes the indicator function. A popular example of a kernel with infinite support is the Gaussian kernel

$$
K(u) = \frac{1}{\sqrt{2\pi}} \exp\left(-\frac{1}{2}u^2\right).
$$

Higher order kernels allow for a smaller bias but require higher order differentiability of the functions. For the following assume that kernels are of order two.

For nonparametric estimation methods kernels can be used as weighting functions. Density estimation or scatterplot smoothing is based on a weighted local average of the data. A positive bandwidth h determines the degree of smoothing. For example, consider the estimation of a function at x given data $y_1, \ldots, y_n$. Then for a certain bandwidth the weights for each observation take the form

$$
K\left(\frac{x - y_i}{h}\right), \quad i = 1, \ldots, n
$$

and the indicator function of kernels with bounded support becomes $I(|x - y_i| < h)_{i=1}^n$. In other words, for local averages only data with distance from x less than h are involved.

5.2.1.2 Nadaraya–Watson Estimator

Nonparametric regression in the *i.i.d.* case has a long tradition since Nadaraya (1964) and Watson (1964) introduced the kernel–weighted local constant estimator, now known as the *Nadaraya–Watson estimator*. Natural estimates of $f(x)$ and $\sigma^2(x)$ have been derived by replacing the unknown densities in (5.3) and (5.4) by kernel density estimates. For the estimation of $p(x,y)$, the product kernel density estimate is used, i.e.

$$\hat{p}_h(x,y) = \frac{1}{n-1}\sum_{t=2}^{n} K_h\left(x - y_{t-1}\right) K_h\left(y - y_t\right). \tag{5.6}$$

with the definition $K_h(\cdot) \equiv h^{-1}K(\cdot/h)$.

The kernel density estimate of the marginal density $p(x)$ is simply

$$\hat{p}_h(x) = \frac{1}{n-1}\sum_{t=2}^{n} K_h\left(x - y_{t-1}\right). \tag{5.7}$$

Plugging (5.7) and (5.6) into (5.3) and (5.4), one obtains the Nadaraya–Watson estimators

$$\hat{f}_h(x) = \frac{\sum_{t=2}^{n} K_h(x - y_{t-1})y_t}{\sum_{t=2}^{n} K_h(x - y_{t-1})}, \tag{5.8}$$

and

$$\hat{\sigma}^2_h(x) = \frac{\sum_{t=2}^{n} K_h(x - y_{t-1})y_t^2}{\sum_{t=2}^{n} K_h(x - y_{t-1})} - \left\{\hat{f}_h(x)\right\}^2. \tag{5.9}$$

Unlike parametric estimates in the case of correct specification, nonparametric estimates are biased. Decreasing the bandwidth reduces the bias but increases the variance of the estimate. Thus, there is a trade-off between bias and variance. For a more formal treatment of the following statements see e.g. Härdle (1990, ch. 4).

Under mild conditions, the Nadaraya–Watson estimates of $f(x)$ and $\sigma^2(x)$ are consistent, if $h \to 0$ and $(nh) \to \infty$ as $n \to \infty$, and we obtain

$$\begin{aligned} \text{Bias}(\hat{f}_h(x)) &= \frac{h^2}{2}\left(f''(x) + 2\frac{f'(x)p'(x)}{p(x)}\right)\mu_2(K) + o(h^2), & (5.10)\\ \text{Var}(\hat{f}_h(x)) &= \frac{1}{nh}\frac{\sigma^2(x)}{p(x)}R(K) + o(\frac{1}{nh}), & (5.11)\end{aligned}$$

where $\mu_2(K) = \int u^2K(u)du$, and $R(K) = \int K^2(u)du$.

Bias and Variance expressions of $\hat{\sigma}^2_h(x)$ take analogous forms. Recall that the mean square error (MSE) is equal to squared bias plus variance. For the Nadaraya–Watson estimate and in fact for many other nonparametric estimates it follows that the MSE–optimal asymptotic rate of the bandwidth is $h \sim n^{-1/5}$, which gives an optimal rate of $n^{-4/5}$ for the MSE.

5.2.1.3 Local Polynomial Estimator

Recall from Section 3.4.3 that the Nadaraya–Watson estimate is a kernel weighted local constant estimate, a special case of kernel weighted local polynomial estimates (LPE). LPE with other than kernel weighting schemes, for example the LOWESS estimator of Cleveland (1979), are also common. However, the theoretical properties of the kernel-weighted LPE have been worked out thoroughly in recent years and shown that it has nice theoretical properties as, for instance, minimax efficency (Fan (1993)). For a recent treatise on LPE, see the monograph of Fan and Gijbels (1996).

Assume that the functions to be estimated are continuously differentiable up to order l. Then, local polynomials of degree l yield estimates of $f(x)$ and $\sigma^2(x)$ that are the solution of the following weighted least squares problems:

$$\hat{\beta}(x) = \arg \min_{\beta \in \mathbb{R}^{l+1}} \sum_{t=2}^{n} \left(y_t - \sum_{j=0}^{l} \beta_j (y_{t-1} - x)^j \right)^2 K_h(y_{t-1} - x) \qquad (5.12)$$

and

$$\hat{s}(x) = \arg \min_{s \in \mathbb{R}^{l+1}} \sum_{t=2}^{n} \left(y_t^2 - \sum_{j=0}^{l} s_j (y_{t-1} - x)^j \right)^2 K_h(y_{t-1} - x). \qquad (5.13)$$

The estimators $\hat{f}(x)$ and $\hat{\sigma}^2(x)$ are given by

$$\hat{f}(x) = \hat{\beta}_0(x) \quad \text{and} \quad \hat{\sigma}^2(x) = \hat{s}_0(x) - \{\hat{\beta}_0(x)\}^2.$$

Härdle and Tsybakov (1997) proved asymptotic normality of these estimators under conditions satisfying the assumptions of Tweedie (1975) and Diebolt and Guégan (1993).

Local polynomial estimates can easily be written in matrix form as well–known weighted least squares estimates for which fast and efficient algorithms exist. For example, consider the estimation of $f(x)$. Let $Y = (y_2, \ldots, y_n)'$, $W = \operatorname{diag}(K_h(y_{t-1} - x))_{t=2}^{n}$ and

$$X = \begin{pmatrix} 1 & y_1 - x & (y_1 - x)^2 & \cdots & (y_1 - x)^l \\ 1 & y_2 - x & (y_2 - x)^2 & \cdots & (y_2 - x)^l \\ \vdots & \vdots & \vdots & \ddots & \vdots \\ 1 & y_{n-1} - x & (y_{n-1} - x)^2 & \cdots & (y_{n-1} - x)^l \end{pmatrix}$$

with polynomial degree l. Then the local polynomial estimate of $f(x)$ is the first element of the $(l+1)$–vector $(\hat{\beta}_0 \cdots \hat{\beta}_l)'$,

$$\hat{\beta}(x) = (X'WX)^{-1}X'WY. \tag{5.14}$$

In practice, the polynomial degree l has to be chosen. The asymptotic behavior of local polynomial estimates is such that odd degrees should be preferred to even ones, i.e. local linear estimation outperforms Nadaraya–Watson, local cubic estimation outperforms local quadratic estimation, and so on. For local linear estimation ($l = 1$), the variance of $\hat{f}(x)$ is the same as for Nadaraya–Watson, but the bias is

$$\text{Bias}(\hat{f}_{l=1}(x)) = \frac{h^2}{2}\mu_2(K)f''(x) + o(h^2). \tag{5.15}$$

Comparing (5.15) with (5.10), the difference becomes obvious: The bias of the local linear estimate does not depend on the marginal density of y_t, which makes it less sensitive to low–density areas.

Important byproducts of local polynomial estimation are automatic estimates of the derivatives up to l^{th} order. For example, the jth derivative estimate of $f(x)$, $\hat{f}^{(j)}(x)$ is given by

$$\hat{f}^{(j)}(x) = j!\hat{\beta}_j(x).$$

5.2.2 *Bandwidth–Selection*

Generally, the choice of the bandwidth h is more crucial than the choice of the kernel. For local polynomial estimation in the case of independent, identically distributed observations, Fan and Gijbels (1995) provide a data-driven bandwidth selection rule that allows for bandwidth adaptation to the design density. Intuitively, the idea is to use larger bandwidths in low density areas in order to decrease the variance of the estimate. Of course, bandwidth adaptation requires much more computational power than the use of global bandwidths. Also, theoretical results for the more complicated case of dependent observations are rather sparse. Therefore, a global bandwidth is used for all subsequent estimations, and boundaries with very few observations are skipped in the pictures.

To balance the bias and variance of a kernel estimator locally, a distance measure in L^2 is predominantly used in practice. The mean square error (MSE) is calculated conditioning on a specified value of the explanatory variable. Thus, the MSE is a *local* goodness-of-fit criterion. However, *global* measures of discrepancy between the estimate and the true function are called for. This can be for example the integrated squared error (ISE)

$$ISE(h) = \int \{\hat{m}_h(x) - m(x)\}^2 w(x)dP(x) \tag{5.16}$$

or the average squared error (ASE)

$$ASE(h) = \frac{1}{n}\sum_{t=1}^{n} \{\hat{m}_h(y_t) - m(y_t)\}^2 w(y_t), \tag{5.17}$$

where $m(\cdot)$ is the unknown mean or variance function, $P(x)$ is the cumulative distribution function of x, and $w(\cdot)$ is a function that downweighs outliers. Both ISE and ASE are random variables, but the mean integrated squared error ($MISE$)

$$MISE(h) = E[ISE(h)] \tag{5.18}$$

is not. In the *i.i.d.* case it is known that under some mild conditions these measures are asymptotically equivalent in the sense that

$$sup_h|ASE(h) - MISE(h)|/MISE(h) \longrightarrow 0 \ a.s., \tag{5.19}$$

and

$$sup_h|ISE(h) - MISE(h)|/MISE(h) \longrightarrow 0 \ a.s., \tag{5.20}$$

where $h \in H_n$, with H_n denoting a compact set in $\mathbb{R}_+$, see Theorem 3.4 in Marron and Härdle (1986). As shown by Kim and Cox (1996, Lemma 4.2), this result still holds for the case of α-mixing time series. This important result justifies the use of ASE, which can be calculated without numerical integration. (5.17) cannot be minimized directly with respect to h, because $m(\cdot)$ is not known. Replacing $m(y_{t-1})$ by y_t and minimization yields undersmoothed estimates. One popular way to avoid undersmoothing is to use a *cross-validation* (CV) criterion. For example, if the mean function $f(x)$ is to be estimated by the Nadaraya–Watson estimate $\hat{f}_h(x)$, then the bandwidth $\hat{h}$ minimizing the following criterion is used:

$$CV(h) = \frac{1}{n-1}\sum_{t=2}^{n} \left(y_t - \hat{f}_{h,t}(y_{t-1})\right)^2 w(y_{t-1}), \tag{5.21}$$

with $\hat{f}_{h,t}(y_{t-1})$ the kernel estimate without using the tth observation.

Härdle and Vieu (1992) have shown for the Nadaraya–Watson estimator that minimizing (5.21) with respect to h yields asymptotic optimal estimates in the sense that

$$\frac{ASE(\hat{h})}{ASE(h_0)} \xrightarrow{P} 1, \tag{5.22}$$

where $h_0 = \arg\min_h ASE(h)$. Kim and Cox (1996) have extended this result to the multiple autoregression case.

No general results are available yet for the case of local polynomial estimation of time series models. However, it is conjectured that these results still hold for the more general local polynomial estimator. Therefore, in the applications in Section 5.2.4, the leave-one-out cross–validation criterion (5.21) will be used.

An alternative is to use the 'Time Series Cross–Validation' technique of Hart (1994), where the goal is to minimize mean–squared prediction error. A drawback of Hart's approach is the assumption of fixed design. Also, he uses the Gasser–Müller estimator, which is superior under fixed design, but has a larger variance than local polynomial estimation under the economically more relevant random design.

5.2.3 Uniform Confidence Bands

No closed form results are available for uniform confidence bands and confidence intervals in the general case of dependent observations. Bootstrap techniques are suggested, but they are computationally intensive. Therefore, it is assumed in the following that the results for the *i.i.d.* case can be applied also to weakly–dependent time series. The uniform confidence bands reported in the next sections are therefore to be treated carefully and only as an indication of how reliable the estimates are.

Uniform confidence bands of the kernel estimates are based on the asymptotic normality results for local polynomial estimates in the *i.i.d.* case. For this, $\sqrt{nh}\left(\hat{f}_h(x) - f(x)\right)$ is approximated by a Gaussian process in x, $G(x)$. Bickel and Rosenblatt (1973) derived the asymptotic distribution of the supremum of $|G(x)|$. Using this result, approximate 95% confidence bands can be constructed, see Härdle (1990, pp. 117) [1]. Let $\hat{f}_h(x)$ and $\hat{\sigma}_h^2(x)$ be the kernel estimates of the conditional mean and conditional variance, respectively. Then, under some regularity conditions the uniform confidence band for $\hat{f}_h(x)$, $[\underline{c}, \overline{c}]$, can be derived for the quartic kernel as

$$\underline{c}(x) = \hat{f}_h(x) - \{c_\alpha/a + d_n\}\sqrt{(5/7)\hat{\sigma}_h^2/(\hat{p}_h(x)nh)}, \tag{5.23}$$

with

$$d_n = a + 1/a \ln\sqrt{3/(4\pi^2)},$$

[1]Here, the formulae given in Algorithm 4.3.2. in Härdle (1990, p.117) were used in a corrected form.

and

$$a = \sqrt{2\ln(1/h)},$$

where $\bar{c}(x)$ is computed accordingly. For a confidence level of 95%, $c_\alpha = 3.66$. The confidence bands for $\hat{\sigma}^2_h(x)$ are of analogous form.

This does not involve a bias correction, so one could either use a bias-corrected estimate such as the Linton–Nielsen estimate (Linton and Nielsen (1994)) or assume that $h \sim n^{-\delta}$ with $\delta > 1/5$. For calculation of uniform confidence bands the XploRe macro `reguncb` was used in a corrected form.

5.2.4 FX Results

Local linear estimation of $f(x)$ and $\sigma^2(x)$ in (5.2) was applied to the FX rate series described in Section 2.4. Recalling the autocorrelation functions, a nonlinear autoregression of order one is plausible for both Dollar rates, whereas it is doubtful whether one lag in the variance function is sufficient to capture the linear long memory property of the squared and absolute returns. However, even though this model will turn out to have a misspecified variance function, it sheds light on the asymmetry issue. To see this, consider the case where the true conditional variance depends on more lags, i.e. $\sigma^2(\psi_{t-1}) = \text{Var}(y_t \mid \psi_{t-1})$ with $\psi_{t-1} = \{y_{t-1}, y_{t-2}, \ldots\}$, and

$$\sigma^2(\psi_{t-1}) = \omega + \sum_{i=1}^{q} g_i(y_{t-i})$$

with $q > 1$ and constant parameter ω. If all functions $g_i(\cdot)$ are symmetric, i.e. for all $u \in \mathbb{R}$ and $i = 1, \ldots, q$, $g_i(u) = g_i(-u)$, then $\text{Var}(y_t \mid y_{t-1})$ is symmetric with respect to y_{t-1}. Thus, if $\text{Var}(y_t \mid y_{t-1})$ is not found to be symmetric and the true conditional variance function is additively separable, then at least one of the functions $g_i(\cdot)$ is asymmetric. Therefore, estimation of the simple CHARN model gives information about the symmetry or asymmetry of volatility even when the model is misspecified.

Bandwidths were selected according to the cross–validation criterion described in Section 5.2.2. The conditional mean estimate only depends on one bandwidth h_1, whereas the conditional variance depends on h_1 and on the bandwidth for the estimate of $\text{E}[y_t^2 \mid y_{t-1}]$, h_2. In Table 5.1 the cross–validation–optimal bandwidths h_1 and h_2 are presented for the three FX rates. For calculation of $CV(h)$, the XploRe macro `lpregcvl` was used, see Härdle et al. (1995) for details. This macro bins the data into equally spaced intervals. The number of bins was chosen to be 200. Starting values for h_1 and h_2 were $50d$ for DEM/USD, $20d$ for JPY/USD and $25d$ for JPY/DEM, where d is the binwidth. Binning is also the reason why it is not always triv-

	DEM/USD	JPY/USD	JPY/DEM
h_1	0.00914	0.00317	0.00413
h_2	0.00756	0.00317	0.00212
pct	99.35	99.15	99.30

TABLE 5.1. *Cross–validation–optimal bandwidths for the FX rates and percentage (pct) of returns falling into the interval* $[-0.003; 0.003]$.

ial to find the minimum of $CV(h)$. Of course it is appropriate to increase the number of bins, but then computation becomes very intensive. Experiments with 500 and 1000 bins did not yield substantially different results. At least for the Dollar rates the local minima can also be assumed to be global minima.

For subsequent analyses the percentages (pct) of returns falling into the interval $[-0.003; 0.003]$ are given as well. Because of the high values, a truncation of the range in the plots of the nonparametric estimates is suggested. Thus, the plotted estimates do not suffer from sparseness of data and large variances at the boundaries.

Figure 5.1 and Figure 5.2 show the cross–validation functions for DEM/USD for the estimates of $\mathrm{E}[y_t \mid y_{t-1}]$ (minimum at $h_1 = .00914$) and $\mathrm{E}[y_t^2 \mid y_{t-1}]$ (minimum at $h_2 = .00756$), respectively. Note that these optimal bandwidths, especially h_1, are large relative to the range of the returns. Apart from the estimation at the boundaries, all of the observations are included in the weighted regression. Thus, a linear mean function estimate in the relevant part is determined.

Recall from Table 5.1 that the cross–validation optimal bandwidths for JPY/USD and JPY/DEM are smaller than for DEM/USD. The minimum of the CV function (not shown) was easy to find for JPY/USD, but not trivial for JPY/DEM, where some shifts and rescalings of the x-axis had to be performed in order to obtain reasonable bandwidths. They turned out to be of the same order as the optimal bandwidths for JPY/USD.

In Figure 5.3 the mean function of DEM/USD is plotted for a truncated range of the conditioning lagged return. The range is truncated to the interval $[-0.003; 0.003]$, covering about 99.35 % of the observations. As mentioned above, $f(y_{t-1})$ is forced to be linear because of the large optimal bandwidth. It has negative slope, which corresponds to the autocorrelation of the returns at the first lag reported in Section 2.4. Thus, a fit of a low–order linear AR (or MA) model seems to be appropriate.

Turning to the volatility functions, again the plot with truncated range is given for DEM/USD in Figure 5.4.

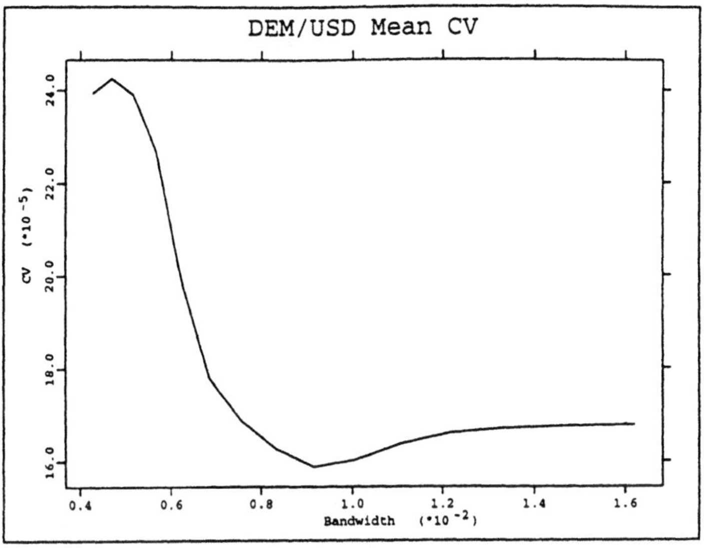

FIGURE 5.1. *The cross-validation function for the estimation of the conditional mean* $E[y_t \mid y_{t-1}]$ *of the DEM/USD returns.*

The volatility estimate is significantly skewed to the right. To see the significance, the following plot was generated: Denote by $\bar{c}(y_{t-1})$ the upper and by $\underline{c}(y_{t-1})$ the lower confidence limit. Now define the deviation function

$$d(x) \equiv \bar{c}(y_{t-1} = -x) - \underline{c}(y_{t-1} = x), \tag{5.24}$$

and plot $d(x)$ for $x > 0$. If $d(x) < 0$ for some $x > 0$, the corresponding confidence regions do not overlap and the asymmetry is significant in this part of the estimate. $d(x)$ is plotted in Figure 5.5 for DEM/USD.

It follows that the asymmetry is significant for $|y_{t-1}| > 0.0029$. Recall that this asymmetry was already reported in Section 2.4.9 for outliers. Thus, for large DEM/USD returns there is a leverage effect, but unlike the leverage effect in stock returns the one observed here is not easy to interpret. In the monetary literature, this would be related to *currency substitution*, see e.g. Visser (1991, pp.136). One approach is to compare the 'qualities' of different currencies, measured for example by the uncertainty about future inflation rates. Investors use the 'high quality' currency as a 'safe haven' for their capital. If the 'high quality' currency drops in value against other currencies by exogenous shocks, there is additional uncertainty in the FX market. Melvin (1985) found the DEM to be the most important substitute for other currencies, which is in line with our results that a depreciation of the DMark against the Dollar creates more uncertainty than an appreciation. However,

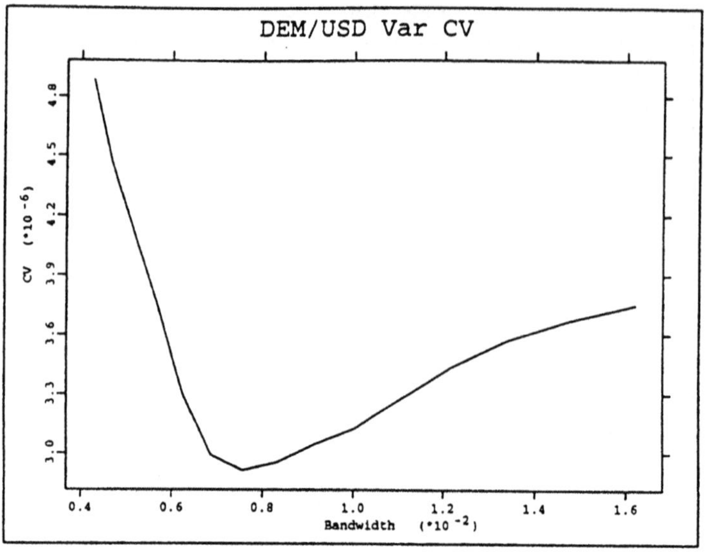

FIGURE 5.2. *The cross-validation function for the estimation of* $E[y_t^2 \mid y_{t-1}]$ *of the DEM/USD returns.*

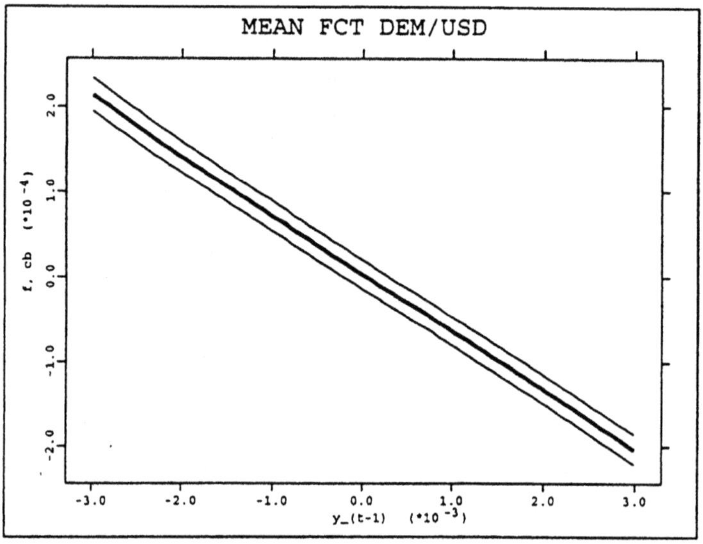

FIGURE 5.3. *The mean function for the DEM/USD returns together with approximate 95% confidence bands. The range is truncated to the interval* $[-0.003; 0.003]$, *covering 99.35% observations.*

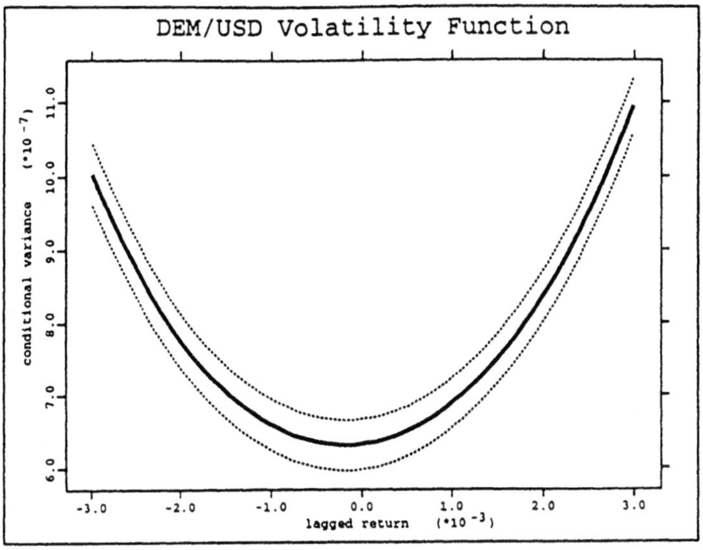

FIGURE 5.4. *The volatility function for the DEM/USD returns together with approximate 95% confidence bands. The range is truncated to the interval* $[-0.003; 0.003]$, *covering 99.35% observations.*

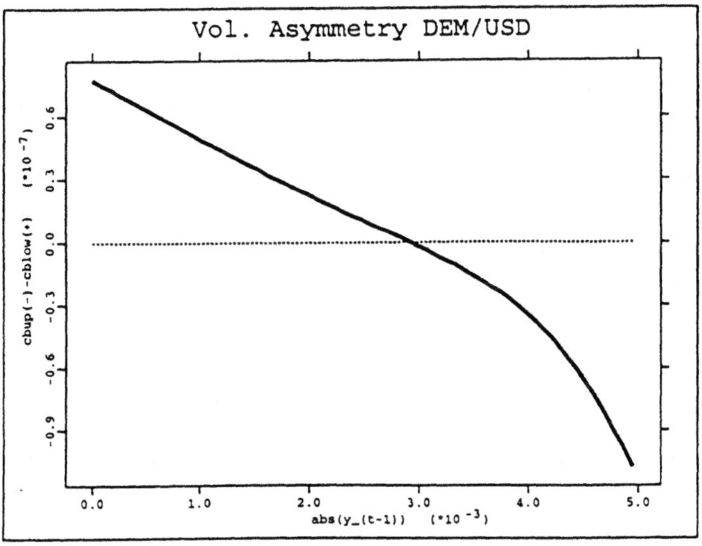

FIGURE 5.5. *DEM/USD volatility asymmetry. The thick line represents the difference between the upper confidence limit on the left side of Figure 5.4 and the lower confidence limit on the right side. Negative values indicate significant asymmetry.*

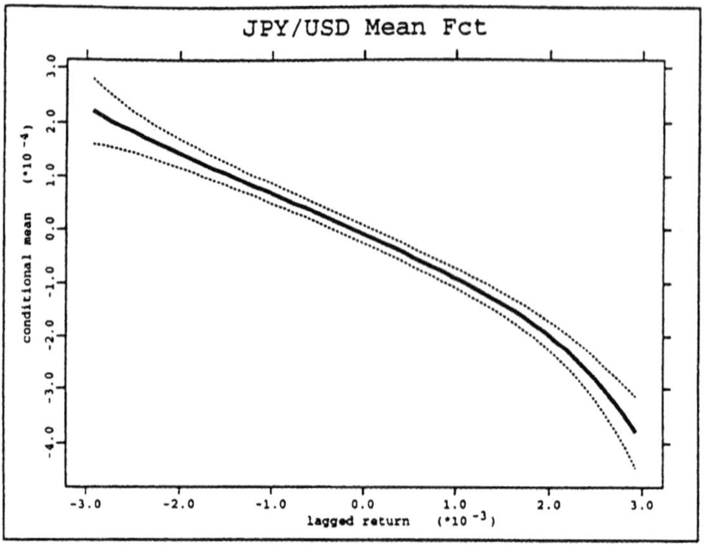

FIGURE 5.6. *The mean function for the JPY/USD returns together with approximate 95% confidence bands. The range is truncated to the interval* $[-0.003; 0.003]$, *covering 99.15% observations.*

the amount of pure speculation money in the 20 minute FX rates is too high to give precise explanations using macroeconomic arguments.

Figure 5.6 and 5.7 show the mean and volatility functions for JPY/USD. The results are very similar: the mean function is linear with negative slope, and the volatility function is skewed, but to a smaller extent. The impact on volatility is larger when the Yen drops against the Dollar (JPY/USD increases) than vice versa.

Figure 5.8 and Figure 5.9 show the corresponding plots for JPY/DEM. Because of the wide confidence bands, the mean function cannot be regarded as significant, which again corresponds to the non-significance of first-order JPY/DEM autocorrelation reported in Section 2.4. The shape of the JPY/DEM volatility function in Figure 5.9 is very similar to the previous ones, and the asymmetry is more distinct than for JPY/USD. The conclusion is that a large drop of the Yen against the two other major currencies causes more uncertainty than a large rise.

For the plots with non-truncated range (not shown), it could be observed for JPY/USD and JPY/DEM that for extreme outliers volatility does not appear to increase, but to settle on a high level or even to decrease, which is contradictory to standard ARCH models. Thus, in these cases there is a kind

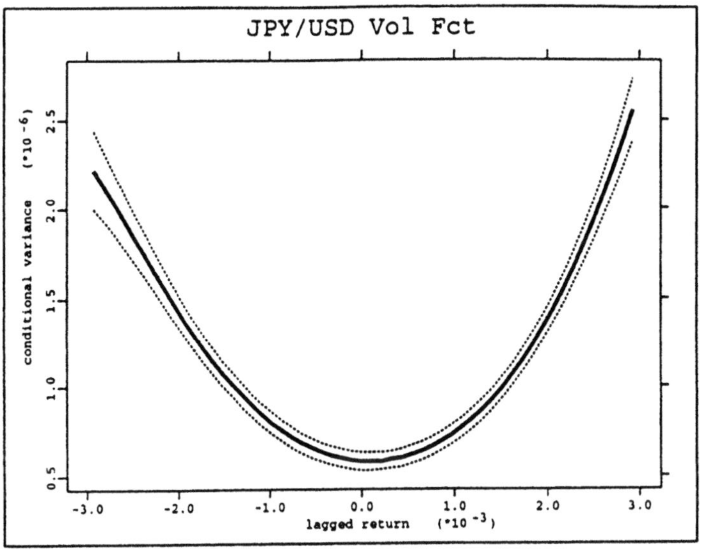

FIGURE 5.7. *The volatility function for the JPY/USD returns together with approximate 95% confidence bands. The range is truncated to the interval* $[-0.003; 0.003]$, *covering 99.15% observations.*

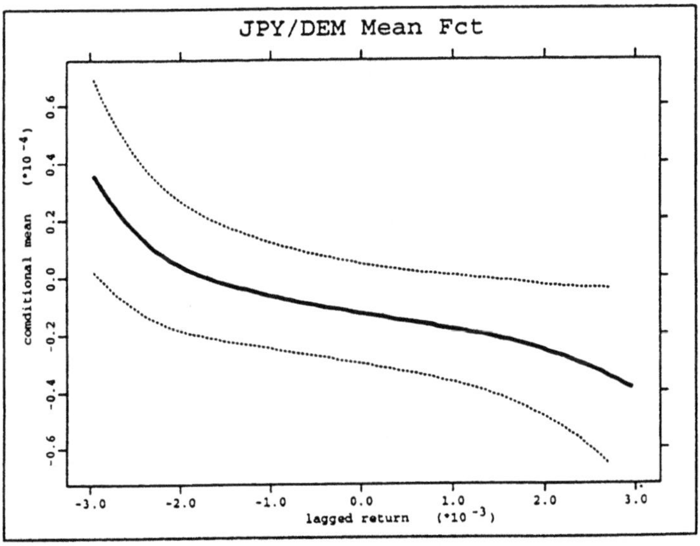

FIGURE 5.8. *The mean function for the JPY/DEM returns together with approximate 95% confidence bands. The range is truncated to the interval* $[-0.003; 0.003]$, *covering 99.3% observations.*

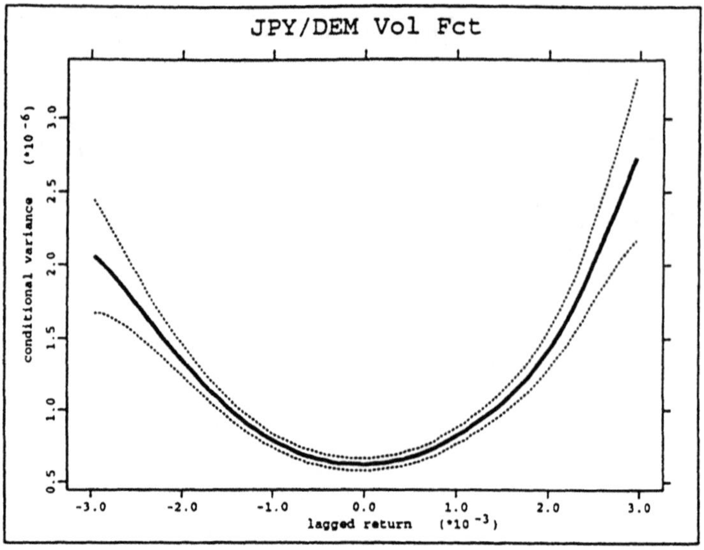

FIGURE 5.9. *The volatility function for the JPY/DEM returns together with approximate 95% confidence bands. The range is truncated to the interval* $[-0.003; 0.003]$, *covering 99.3% observations.*

of *saturation* level in volatility. Of course, inference in this part of the functions is less precise due to the sparseness of data and thus larger confidence bands. But since we observed this effect also for other financial time series, it seems to be a general rule rather than an artefact of boundary problems in nonparametric estimation. This implies that all standard parametric ARCH models, where volatility increases to infinity at the boundaries, overweigh the impact of large outliers on volatility.

Residual statistics are given in Table 5.2, and the first ten autocorrelations of the residuals, squared and absolute residuals in Table 5.3. Consider first the autocorrelations of the residuals and the corresponding Q_1 statistics. Although the Q_1 statistics of the Dollar rates are significant, the linear structure in the residuals is much weaker than in the returns. Now consider the autocorrelations of squared and absolute residuals and the Q_2–statistics. By comparing these values with the corresponding values for the returns in Table 2.10 it becomes obvious that the CHARN model of order one is not able to cope with the long–range dependence of squared and absolute returns. This result holds for all rates. As could be expected, only at the first lag the large positive autocorrelations were substantially reduced.

Concluding, the CHARN model indicates asymmetry of the FX rates but

FX rate	DEM/USD	JPY/USD	JPY/DEM
$m(\hat{\xi})$	-0.0098	-0.0012	0.0003
$\mathrm{Var}(\hat{\xi})$	0.9522	0.8943	0.9325
$s(\hat{\xi})$	0.2516	0.3079	-0.1853
$k(\hat{\xi}_t)$	8.8450	16.4050	8.4518
$Q_1(10)$	42.48*	21.58*	16.11
$Q_1(100)$	161.61*	130.51*	110.14
$Q_1(1000)$	1114.05	1244.63*	1098.62*
$Q_2(10)$	932.84*	368.14*	483.81*
$Q_2(100)$	2882.81*	1225.34*	1734.27*
$Q_2(1000)$	11551.10*	5032.68*	5044.25*

TABLE 5.2. *Residual statistics for the local linear estimation of a CHARN model: mean, variance, skewness and kurtosis. $Q_1(\cdot)$ and $Q_2(\cdot)$ denote the Portmanteau-statistics for the residuals and squared residuals, respectively. An asterisk marks significance at the 95% level.*

	DEM/USD			JPY/USD			JPY/DEM		
k	$\hat{\xi}_t$	$\hat{\xi}_t^2$	$\lvert\hat{\xi}_t\rvert$	$\hat{\xi}_t$	$\hat{\xi}_t^2$	$\lvert\hat{\xi}_t\rvert$	$\hat{\xi}_t$	$\hat{\xi}_t^2$	$\lvert\hat{\xi}_t\rvert$
1	.001	.058	.120	-.004	.015	.070	.001	.002	.026
2	-.020	.074	.120	-.018	.064	.126	-.010	.056	.097
3	-.021	.067	.119	-.004	.035	.112	.002	.061	.096
4	-.005	.082	.114	-.018	.032	.104	.014	.041	.078
5	.002	.065	.108	-.004	.025	.094	-.002	.034	.074
6	-.005	.063	.092	.005	.025	.087	-.011	.045	.079
7	.018	.043	.086	-.003	.041	.101	.002	.054	.077
8	.012	.038	.078	-.010	.050	.099	.015	.060	.081
9	.011	.059	.088	-.001	.042	.094	-.003	.046	.072
10	.013	.044	.080	.002	.034	.079	-.002	.020	.051

TABLE 5.3. *First ten autocorrelations of the CHARN residuals, squared and absolute residuals.*

is not able to cope with the long memory of volatility. Therefore, it only covers one aspect of the two issues, asymmetry and persistence. The following sections are devoted to refinements and improvements of the basic CHARN model.

5.3 Higher Order Conditional Moments and Stochastic Volatility

The standard CHARN model with *i.i.d.* error term ξ_t implies constant conditional third and higher moments, and thus, for instance, constant skewness and kurtosis of y_t conditional on y_{t-1}. This also holds for the strong ARCH model as defined in Section 4.2, but not necessarily for the semi-strong and weak ARCH models as defined by Drost and Nijman (1993). In practice, the standardized residuals of fitted ARCH models are mostly required to be *i.i.d.*, which corresponds to the strong ARCH definition, but only autocorrelation of standardized residuals and of their squares usually are checked for dependence. However, there may be dependencies in higher moments that are neglected.

As discussed in Chapter 2, economic agents may have utility functions that require higher order moments of returns, conditioned on the information set, for the evaluation of risk. Under such utility functions, the traditional $(\mu-\sigma)$ criterion is insufficient. To hedge risks, more complex strategies are required, see e.g. Mahieu (1995, ch.6) for a hedging model that uses the standard deviation and kurtosis of foreign exchange returns.

In this section a model is discussed that captures a rather complex form of conditional heterogeneity, consisting of time–varying second and higher conditional moments. By an additional error term, this model is in fact a nonlinear stochastic volatility model. It was proposed by Bossaerts, Härdle and Hafner (1996) in its rudimentary form, and extended by Yang and Hafner (1997).

Let ξ_t and δ_t be two independent mean zero, variance one *i.i.d.* error terms. Then, a nonlinear stochastic volatility model of order one can be specified as

$$y_t = f(y_{t-1}) + \sigma(y_{t-1})\eta_t\xi_t, \tag{5.25}$$

with

$$\eta_t = a(y_{t-1}) + \sqrt{1 - a^2(y_{t-1})}\delta_t, \tag{5.26}$$

where a is a nonlinear function satisfying $0 \leq a(y_t) \leq 1$ almost surely (a.s.). Non–negativity is imposed for identification. If η_t is interpreted as a stochastic scaling factor, then δ_t should have bounded support. This restriction is not necessary in general, i.e. η_t may take negative values.

By construction, $\mathrm{E}[y_t \mid y_{t-1}] = f(y_{t-1})$ and $\mathrm{Var}[y_t \mid y_{t-1}] = \sigma^2(y_{t-1})$. To see why the latter holds, note that $\mathrm{E}[\eta_t^2 \mid y_{t-1}] = 1$.

Consider two extreme cases for the function a: First, if $a(y_{t-1}) = 1$ a.s., then $\eta_t = 1$ a.s. and (5.25) reduces to the CHARN model (5.2). Second, if $a(y_{t-1}) = 0$ a.s., then $\eta_t = \delta_t$ a.s., and the scaling factor η_t is purely stochastic. Thus, the function a determines the trade-off between the ARCH-type CHARN model and a stochastic volatility model, depending on the lagged return.

The conditional skewness is given by

$$\begin{aligned}
\text{Skew}[y_t \mid y_{t-1}] &= \frac{\mathrm{E}\left[(y_t - f(y_{t-1}))^3 \mid y_{t-1}\right]}{\mathrm{E}\left[(y_t - f(y_{t-1}))^2 \mid y_{t-1}\right]^{3/2}} && (5.27)\\
&= \frac{\mathrm{E}\left[\sigma^3(y_{t-1})\eta_t^3\xi_t^3 \mid y_{t-1}\right]}{\sigma^3(y_{t-1})}\\
&= C_1\mathrm{E}[\eta_t^3 \mid y_{t-1}]\\
&= C_1[3a(y_{t-1}) - 2a^3(y_{t-1})], && (5.28)
\end{aligned}$$

with $C_1 = \mathrm{E}[\xi_t^3]$, and the conditional kurtosis by

$$\begin{aligned}
\text{Kurt}[y_t \mid y_{t-1}] &= \frac{\mathrm{E}\left[(y_t - f(y_{t-1}))^4 \mid y_{t-1}\right]}{\mathrm{E}\left[(y_t - f(y_{t-1}))^2 \mid y_{t-1}\right]^2} && (5.29)\\
&= \frac{\mathrm{E}\left[\sigma^4(y_{t-1})\eta_t^4\xi_t^4 \mid y_{t-1}\right]}{\sigma^4(y_{t-1})}\\
&= C_2\mathrm{E}[\eta_t^4 \mid y_{t-1}]\\
&= C_2[C_3 + (6 - 2C_3)a^2(y_{t-1}) +\\
&\quad +(C_3 - 5)a^4(y_{t-1})], && (5.30)
\end{aligned}$$

with $C_2 = \mathrm{E}[\xi_t^4]$ and $C_3 = \mathrm{E}[\delta_t^4]$. If, for example, δ_t and ξ_t are normally distributed, then (5.30) simplifies to

$$\text{Kurt}[y_t \mid y_{t-1}] = 9 - 6a^4(y_{t-1}).$$

If we want to specify a nontrivial conditional skewness, the distribution of ξ_t has to be asymmetric, i.e. $\mathrm{E}[\xi_t^3] \neq 0$.

To demonstrate nonparametric estimation of the functions, a small simulation study is provided. Suppose that the conditional skewness is zero, so that ξ_t can be N(0,1). Also, assume that the mean function f is zero. Let δ_t be mean zero, variance one uniformly distributed, i.e. with support $[-\sqrt{3}, \sqrt{3}]$,

$$a(x) = 1 - \frac{1 - \sqrt{3}/2}{x^2 + 1},$$

and

$$\sigma(x) = \frac{1}{2}\left(1 + \frac{x^2}{x^2 + 1}\right).$$

By construction, $\sqrt{3}/2 \leq a(x) < 1$ for $x \in \mathbb{R}$, such that $\eta_t > 0$ a.s., and $1/2 \leq \sigma(x) < 1$ for $x \in \mathbb{R}$. This prevents the process from degeneration

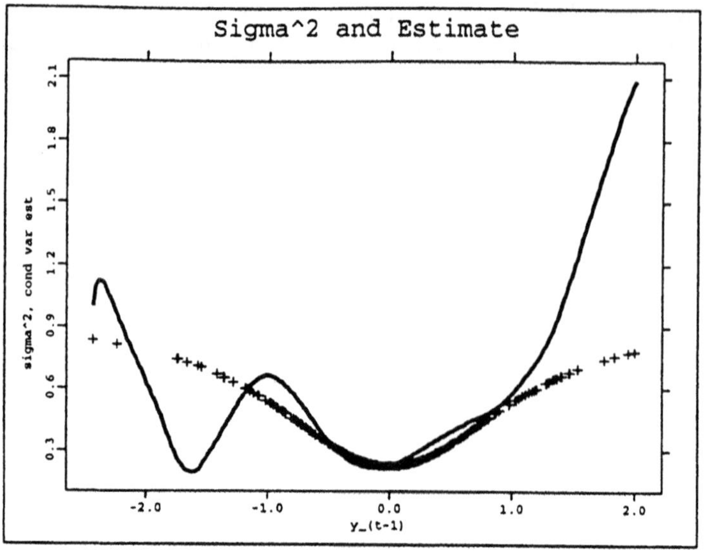

FIGURE 5.10. *True conditional variance $\sigma^2(x)$ (dotted) and local linear estimate with bandwidth 0.7 (solid).*

and explosion. The starting value y_0 is set to zero, and 500 values of y_t are generated.

The local linear estimation technique is applied. Figure 5.10 shows the true conditional variance $\sigma^2(x)$ and its kernel (quartic) weighted local linear estimate with bandwidth 0.7. Figure 5.11 shows the true conditional fourth moment

$$E[y_t^4 \mid y_{t-1}] = \sigma^4(y_{t-1})\mathrm{Kurt}[y_t \mid y_{t-1}]$$

as given above, and a local linear estimate with bandwidth 0.7. As can be seen the estimates are poor at the boundaries but fairly good elsewhere.

As in Bossaerts, Härdle and Hafner (1996), conditional higher order moments of the HFDF93 exchange rate returns are estimated, and results are shown for DEM/USD with ϑ–time transformation based on 10 minute time intervals, see Section 2.4. Recall from Section 2.4 that the unconditional distribution of exchange rate returns is highly leptokurtic. Thus, there are some extreme outliers which render nonparametric estimation with fixed bandwidth more difficult. Also, the asymptotic behavior of local linear estimation of (5.25) and (5.26) is not known. To avoid boundary effects, the following estimation procedure is used as in Bossaerts, Härdle and Hafner (1996). First, the pairs of returns (y_{t-1}, y_t) are sorted with respect to y_{t-1}. Second, the pairs are binned such that each bin contains 100 pairs of returns. Third, the

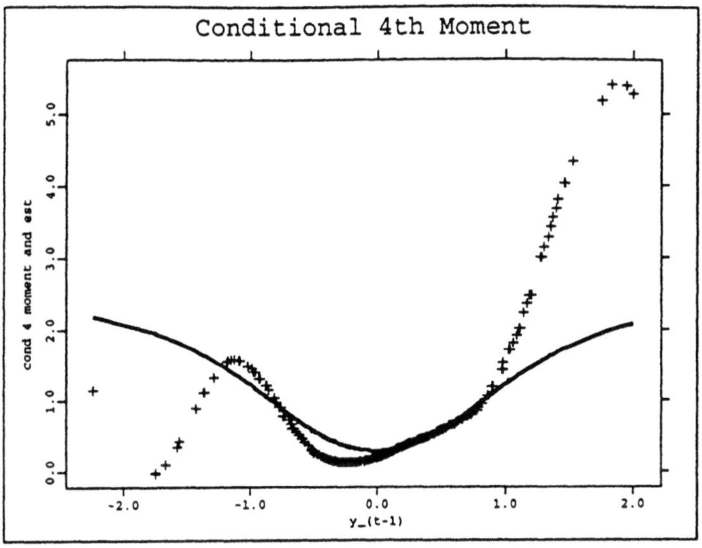

FIGURE 5.11. *True conditional fourth moment (solid) and local linear estimate with bandwidth 0.7 (dotted).*

conditional skewness and conditional kurtosis, i.e. the skewness and kurtosis of y_t, are computed for each bin. The resulting function is the skewness and kurtosis of y_t conditional on y_{t-1}. Finally, the functions are smoothed with a Nadaraya–Watson kernel smoother (quartic kernel, bandwidth $h = 0.005$). The results are shown in Figure 5.12 and 5.13.

Surprisingly, conditional skewness appears to be negative for large negative lagged returns, whereas the function increases for larger returns. Because the asymptotics of the estimation procedure are not known, only limited statistical inference is possible. However, it can be argued that the absolute value of conditional skewness for large positive or negative returns is relatively large compared to the unconditional skewness, which is of order 0.2. This holds even though the function was smoothed, i.e. the unsmoothed function has even larger peaks. Furthermore, the estimation procedure was applied to the following data sets: DEM/USD 20min, JPY/DEM 20min, JPY/USD 20min, and JPY/USD 10min. The estimated skewness and kurtosis functions are shown in Figures 5.14 to 5.21. For all rates the skewness function has a similar increasing shape. This is considered as evidence for the significance of this effect. Recall from Section 5.2.4 that the DEM/USD volatility function is asymmetric with higher volatility for positive returns than for negative ones of the same size. Interestingly, this excess increase in volatility is 'compen-

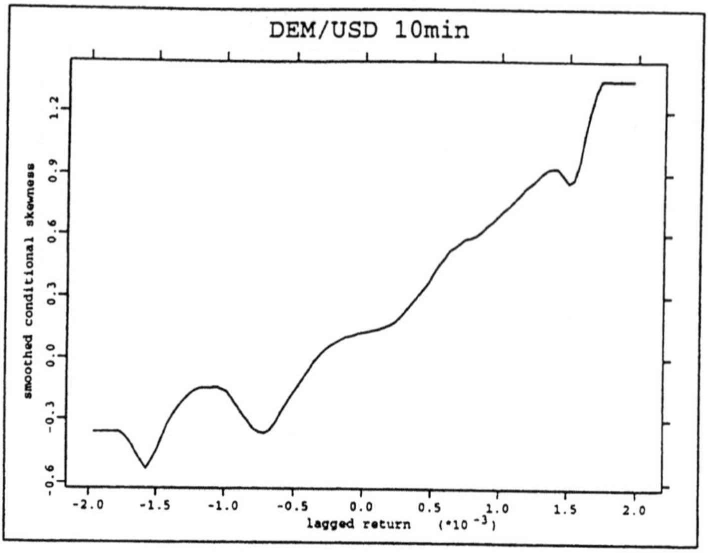

FIGURE 5.12. *Smoothed conditional skewness of the DEM/USD returns in ϑ-time based on 10 min time intervals. A Nadaraya–Watson kernel smoother with bandwidth* $h = 0.005$ *was used.*

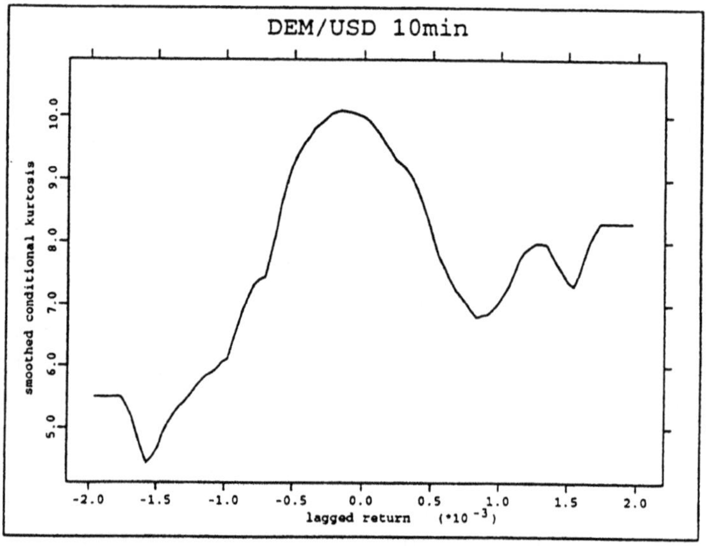

FIGURE 5.13. *Smoothed conditional kurtosis of the DEM/USD returns in ϑ-time based on 10 min time intervals. A Nadaraya–Watson kernel smoother with bandwidth* $h = 0.005$ *was used.*

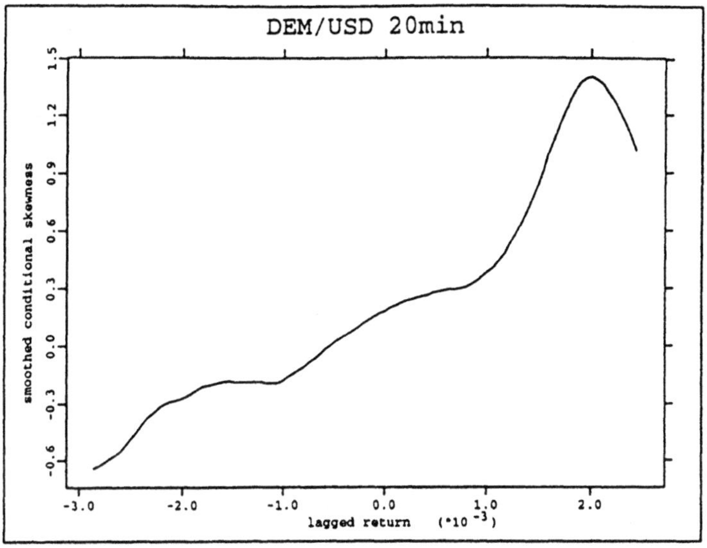

FIGURE 5.14. *Smoothed conditional skewness of the DEM/USD returns in ϑ-time based on 20 min time intervals. A Nadaraya-Watson kernel smoother with bandwidth* $h = 0.005$ *was used.*

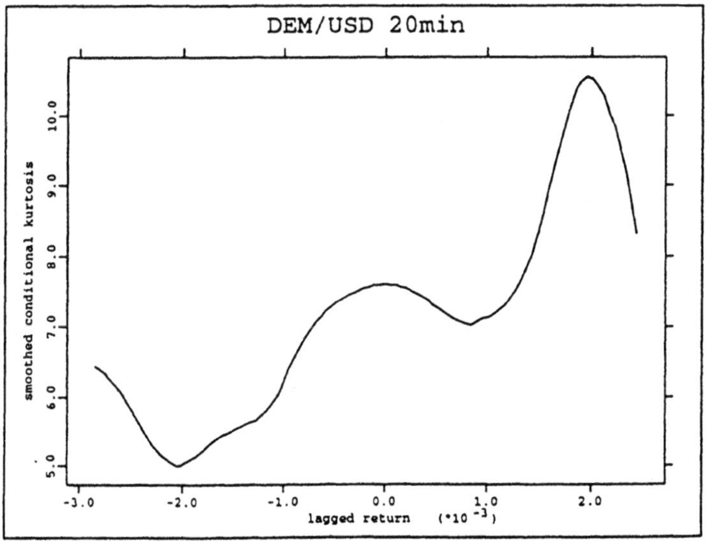

FIGURE 5.15. *Smoothed conditional kurtosis of the DEM/USD returns in ϑ-time based on 20 min time intervals. A Nadaraya-Watson kernel smoother with bandwidth* $h = 0.005$ *was used.*

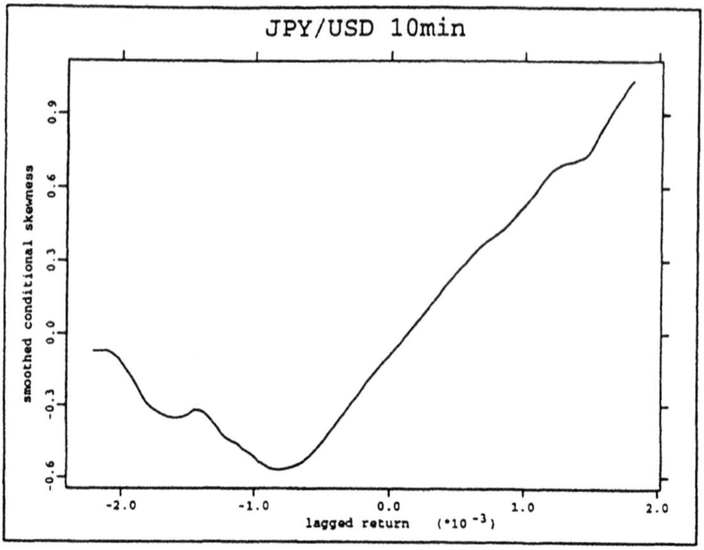

FIGURE 5.16. *Smoothed conditional skewness of the JPY/USD returns in ϑ–time based on 10 min time intervals. A Nadaraya–Watson kernel smoother with bandwidth* $h = 0.005$ *was used.*

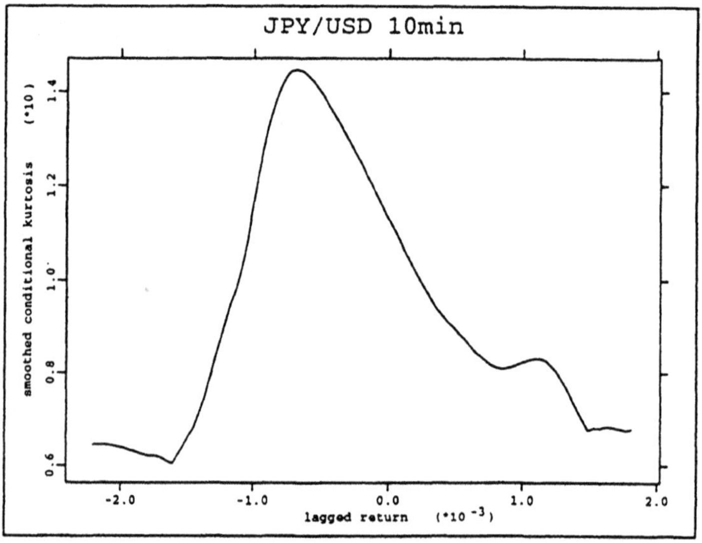

FIGURE 5.17. *Smoothed conditional kurtosis of the JPY/USD returns in ϑ–time based on 10 min time intervals. A Nadaraya–Watson kernel smoother with bandwidth* $h = 0.005$ *was used.*

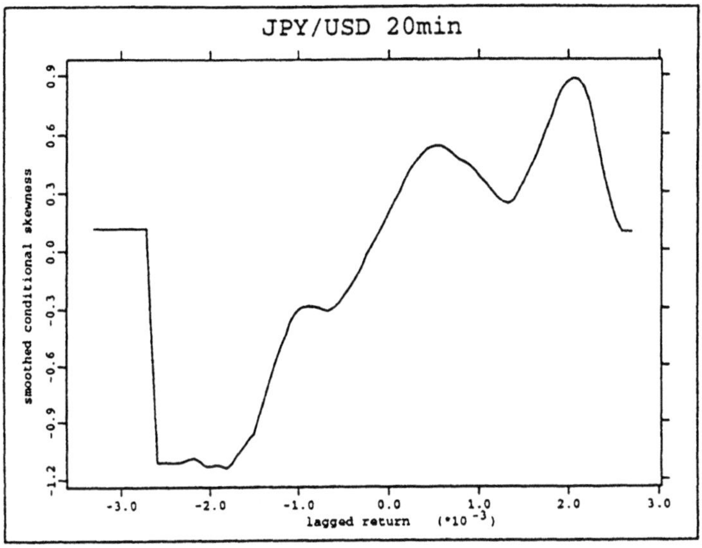

FIGURE 5.18. *Smoothed conditional skewness of the JPY/USD returns in* ϑ*-time based on 20 min time intervals. A Nadaraya–Watson kernel smoother with bandwidth* $h = 0.005$ *was used.*

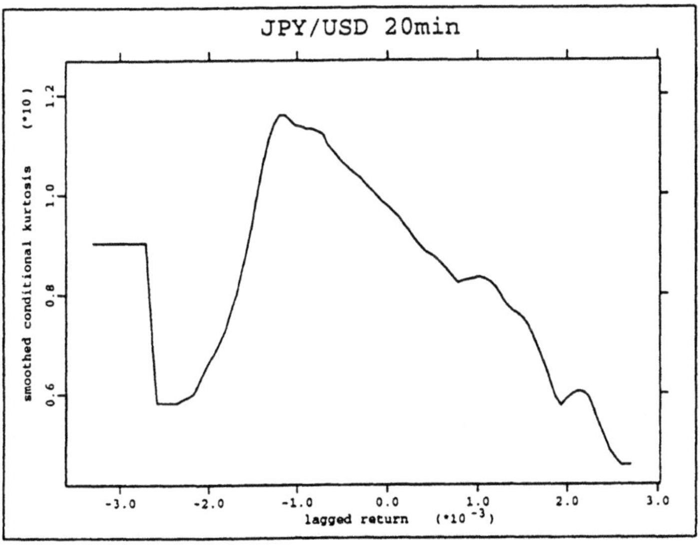

FIGURE 5.19. *Smoothed conditional kurtosis of the JPY/USD returns in* ϑ*-time based on 20 min time intervals. A Nadaraya–Watson kernel smoother with bandwidth* $h = 0.005$ *was used.*

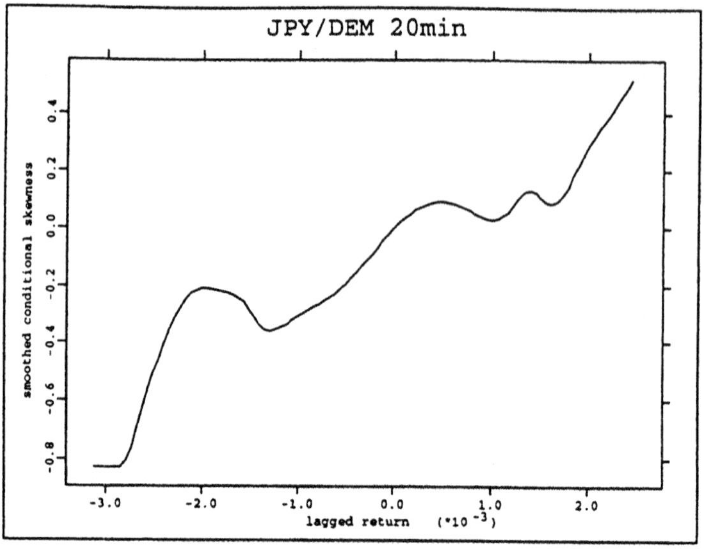

FIGURE 5.20. *Smoothed conditional skewness of the JPY/DEM returns in ϑ-time based on 20 min time intervals. A Nadaraya–Watson kernel smoother with bandwidth* $h = 0.005$ *was used.*

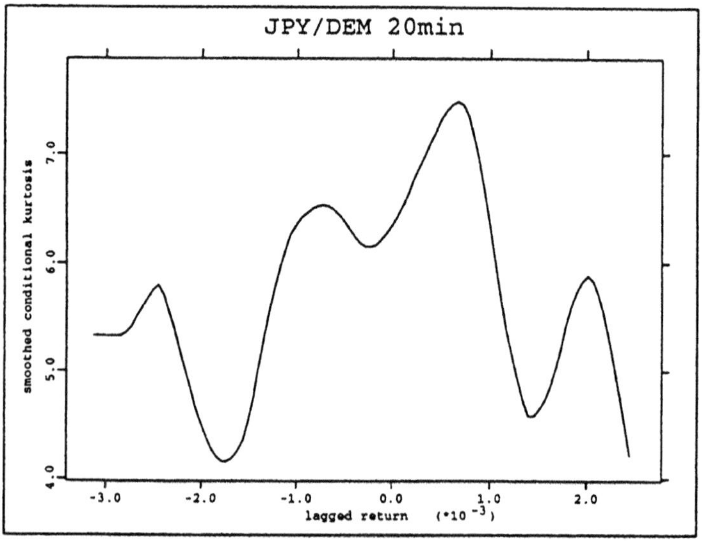

FIGURE 5.21. *Smoothed conditional kurtosis of the JPY/DEM returns in ϑ-time based on 20 min time intervals. A Nadaraya–Watson kernel smoother with bandwidth* $h = 0.005$ *was used.*

sated' by a positive skewness, which tends to decrease risk in most financial analysts' point of view. For large negative returns, on the other hand, volatility increases less, but the skewness is negative, which tends to increase risk. Thus, there is a trade-off between volatility and skewness.

Conditional kurtosis also reveals some remarkable features of exchange rate returns. For DEM/USD 10min returns, conditional kurtosis is highest for small negative lagged returns and decreases for larger absolute returns. It is lowest for large negative returns. Again the absolute values vary relatively large around the unconditional kurtosis of order 9, which indicates significance of this kurtosis effect. Thus, volatility and kurtosis effects are inverted: Increasing volatility is 'compensated' by decreasing kurtosis, and vice versa. There is also an asymmetry effect: The kurtosis function is higher for large positive lagged returns than for negative ones of the same size. Thus, although there is a *size* trade–off between volatility and kurtosis, there is no *sign* trade–off. The shapes of the kurtosis functions of JPY/USD 20min and JPY/USD 10min are very similar to DEM/USD 10min. The DEM/USD 20min kurtosis has an additional peak for very large positive lagged return, and JPY/DEM 20min tends to have lower conditional kurtosis for large returns of either sign.

Concluding, second order moments appear to be insufficient to fully describe the statistical properties of exchange rate returns. In particular, there is a partial trade–off between volatility and higher order conditional moments for most rates analysed.

5.4 Multiplicative Nonparametric ARCH Models

To capture the long memory in volatility it is necessary to generalize the nonparametric models described in the preceding sections. A direct nonparametric analogue to a GARCH model such as

$$\begin{aligned} \varepsilon_t &= \sigma_t \xi_t, \\ \sigma_t^2 &= g(\sigma_{t-1}^2, \varepsilon_{t-1}) \end{aligned}$$

with some unknown function $g(\cdot)$ is only possible to estimate iteratively and convergence is highly sensitive to the initialization of $g(\cdot)$ and to the starting value of the conditional variance.

However, a GARCH model can be approximated by an ARCH model of sufficiently high order, so it is natural to think of a purely nonparametric ARCH(q) model. Unfortunately, estimating a non–restricted model of high order raises the 'curse of dimensionality'. Recently, several authors have estimated additive models in a time series context, see e.g. Chen and Tsay

(1993b) for the mean function. This restriction conveys to the variance function, where it is more natural to specify a multiplicative model. Of course by taking logarithms this can be transformed to an additive model. Also, this is a suitable and well-known way to ensure that the variance function is always positive. For example, the EGARCH and Stochastic Volatility models have this specification. Recently, Yang and Härdle (1997) have derived theoretical results for a nonparametric model with additive mean and multiplicative volatility function. They propose to use marginal integration as in Linton and Nielsen (1995) to estimate the functions. Here, a different way of estimation was pursued.

As reported in Section 4.7, the conditional mean $E[y_t \mid \psi_{t-1}]$ of DEM/USD is specified as an AR(3) model. Because of the huge data set conditional heteroskedasticity did not affect the mean parameter estimates. The linear mean function is kept, and the mean zero residual series $\varepsilon_t = y_t - E[y_t \mid \psi_{t-1}]$ is used for volatility models. Now, write a multiplicative nonparametric ARCH model of order q as

$$\begin{aligned} \varepsilon_t &= \sigma_t \xi_t, \\ \sigma_t &= \prod_{j=1}^{q} g_j(\varepsilon_{t-j}), \end{aligned} \tag{5.31}$$

with $\xi_t \sim i.i.d.(0,1)$ and continuous, bounded and positive functions $g_j(\cdot)$. For estimation of σ_t one could use marginal integration as in Linton and Nielsen (1995), but for high orders this also runs into the 'curse of dimensionality'. Therefore, (5.31) is transformed to

$$\log|\varepsilon_t| = \sum_{j=1}^{q} \log g_j(\varepsilon_{t-j}) + \log|\xi_t|, \tag{5.32}$$

and standard estimation techniques for additive models are applied. In general, the error term $\log|\xi_t|$ does not have mean zero. If ξ_t is normally distributed, then $E[\log|\xi_t|] \approx -0.635$, as shown in Appendix A. The normality assumption is used to simplify this subject, knowing that in most financial applications the conditional distribution is leptokurtic. Simulations for various fat-tailed distributions showed that $E[\log|\xi_t|]$ is not much smaller than -0.635. Experiments with -0.9 did not substantially change the results. Note that if the response variable in (5.32) was formulated as $\log \varepsilon_t^2$, then the estimated functions would just be scaled by the factor two, so this does not matter.

The model can thus be estimated as

$$\varepsilon_t^* = \log \sigma_t + \xi_t^*, \tag{5.33}$$

with $\varepsilon_t^* \equiv \log|\varepsilon_t| + 0.635$, $\xi_t^* \equiv \log|\xi_t| + 0.635$, and $\mathrm{E}[\xi_t^*] = 0$.

For estimation of the nonparametric functions $g_j(\cdot)$, basically two methods are available: the backfitting procedure of Hastie and Tibshirani (1990), and the estimation based on marginal integration, as in Linton and Nielsen (1995). The integration estimator has the advantage of a closed form expression, which implies that it is non-iterative. Also, confidence intervals can be constructed. On the other hand, for large dimensions q and large data sets, the estimator at present is computationally expensive and the choice of bandwidths is a difficult problem as simulation studies show. Therefore, the backfitting procedure of Hastie and Tibshirani (1990) was used here, because efficient implementations in standard packages, S–Plus in this case, exist, see e.g. Venables and Ripley (1994). The backfitting procedure is iterative with the following steps:

1. Initialization: $\log g_j(\varepsilon_{t-j}) = 0, \; j = 1, \ldots, q$
2. Repeat for $j = 1, \ldots, q, \; 1, \ldots, q, \ldots$

$$\log g_j(\varepsilon_{t-j}) = S_j\left(\varepsilon_t^* - \sum_{k \neq j} \log g_k(\varepsilon_{t-k}) \;\middle|\; \varepsilon_{t-j}\right),$$

3. until the residual sum of squares

$$\sum_{t=q+1}^{n}\left\{\varepsilon_t^* - \sum_{j=1}^{q} \log g_j(\varepsilon_{t-j})\right\}^2$$

converges.

In step 2., $S_j(Y_t|X_t)$ denotes a scatterplot smoother of the response variable Y given X.

As Chen and Tsay (1993b) note, the backfitting procedure works in the time series context if the series is geometrically ergodic and α–mixing, that is, the dependence structure is not too strong. For the scatterplot smoother in step 2, a standard nonparametric estimator such as kernel or spline estimator can be applied under these conditions. Because no kernel weighted local linear estimate was available for the **gam** macro in S–Plus, the spline method was chosen here. The simplest case is the following: A response variable y_i and a univariate explanatory variable x_i are observed at $i = 1, \ldots, n$. Then a spline smoother minimizes

$$\sum_{i=1}^{n}\{y_i - m(x_i)\}^2 + \lambda \int \{m''(x)\}^2 \, dx \tag{5.34}$$

where $m(x)$ denotes the regression function in the class of cubic polynomials, and λ a positive smoothing parameter that determines the degree of penalty for a too wiggly function $m(x)$.

As kernel estimates, spline smoothers also can be written as linear functions of the response variable, i.e.

$$\mathbf{m}_\lambda = \mathbf{W}_\lambda \, \mathbf{y},$$

where $\mathbf{W}$ is a $[n \times n]$ weighting or smoother matrix depending on λ, and $\mathbf{y} = (y_1, \ldots, y_n)'$. Under technical conditions, Silverman (1984) derived the asymptotic equivalent kernel estimate, where the kernel is of higher order with adaptive bandwidth.

For the choice of the smoothing parameter, Chen and Tsay (1993b) suggest a generalized cross–validation criterion. For the model (5.33), this takes the form

$$GCV(\lambda) = \frac{\sum_{t=q+1}^{n} \left[\varepsilon_t^* - \sum_{j=1}^{q} \log g_j(\varepsilon_{t-j})\right]^2}{(n-q)\left\{1 - [1 + \sum_{j=1}^{q}(\mathrm{tr}\,\mathbf{W}_{\lambda,j} - 1)]/n\right\}^2}, \tag{5.35}$$

where $\mathrm{tr}\,\mathbf{W}_{\lambda,j}$ is the trace of the jth smoother matrix. (5.35) is minimized with respect to λ. More generally, a different smoothing parameter λ can be used for each lag.

An alternative way to determine the smoothing parameter is to fix the 'degrees of freedom', $1 + \sum_{j=1}^{q}(\mathrm{tr}\,\mathbf{W}_{\lambda,j} - 1)$. This is the case in the S–Plus macro **gam**, where the default number of degrees of freedom is four. This was accepted here. Experiments with smaller or larger degrees of freedom did not improve the results reported in the following.

Models up to order $q = 15$ were estimated. As an illustration, the resulting plots for MNARCH(5) are shown in Figure 5.22. Interestingly, the corresponding estimated functions of higher order models are very similar.

Recall from Chapter 4 that GARCH volatility depends additively on functions of the residuals ε_t, whereas EGARCH models are multiplicative in the standardized residuals $\xi_t = \varepsilon_t/\sigma_t$. Thus, these models cannot be compared directly with the model (5.31). However, if in the EGARCH model the residuals were standardized by the *unconditional* standard deviation, it is obvious from (4.33) and (4.34) that the functions $\log g_j(\cdot)$ would be piecewise linear and downscaled for higher lags. For the estimated MNARCH(5) model (see Figure 5.22) this seems to hold quite well for the first lag, whereas for lags two to five the impact of outliers, induced by important news, on volatility increases slower than linearly. However, this has to be treated carefully because the confidence intervals as obtained by the S–Plus output are only indicative.

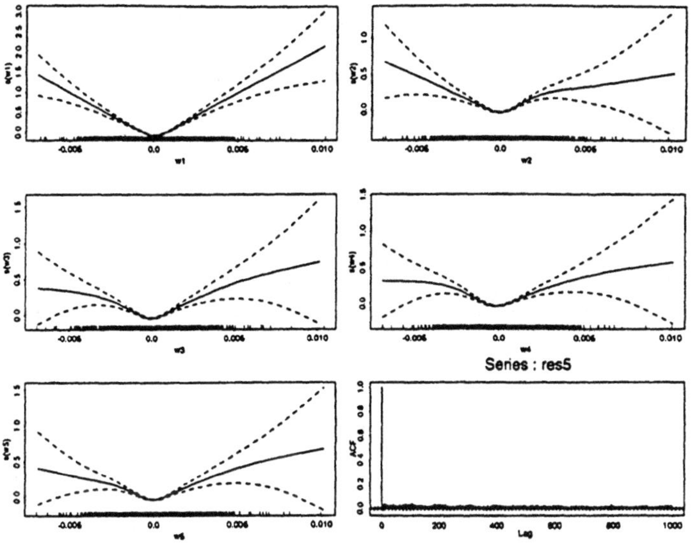

FIGURE 5.22. *Estimated nonparametric functions* $\log g_j(\cdot), j = 1, \ldots, 5$, *for the MNARCH(5) model. The functions are plotted together with indicative confidence intervals. The bottom right plot shows the ACF of absolute residuals up to lag 1000.*

Residual diagnostics for $q = 5, 10, 12, 15$ are reported in Table 5.4. As in Pagan and Schwert (1990), parameter estimates and coefficient of determination R^2 are given for the linear regression

$$\hat{\varepsilon}_t^2 = \alpha_0 + \alpha_1 \hat{\sigma}_t^2 + v_t,$$

with parameters α_0 and α_1, and error term v_t. OLS estimation is applied and reported standard errors are heteroskedasticity-consistent, see White (1980). Ideally, α_0 should be zero and α_1 one. Finally, the Box–Ljung statistics of the squared residuals are reported.

The results show that MNARCH(q) models with q sufficiently large yield serially uncorrelated squared residuals, which may be surprising when recalling the long memory of volatility. Considering the R^2 and the $Q_2(m)$ statistics, the MNARCH fits are similar to the parametric GARCH fits. The first 500 DEM/USD volatilities estimated by CHARN, MNARCH(5) and MNARCH(12) are plotted in Figure 5.23, where again the scales are adjusted for comparison. It becomes obvious that MNARCH models only of high order can reproduce some of the GARCH volatility behavior with large β. Low order models tend to estimate volatility with sudden bursts rather

Model	α_0	α_1	R^2 (%)	$Q_2(10)$	$Q_2(100)$
GARCH(1,1)	0.18 (0.03)	0.81 (0.02)	4.19	10.84	97.32
IGARCH(1,1)	0.32 (0.03)	0.57 (0.02)	4.02	20.47*	94.34
EGARCH(1,1)	0.21 (0.03)	0.76 (0.02)	3.41	63.94*	121.88
CHARN	0 (0)	2.38 (0.02)	1.66	932.84*	2882.81*
MNARCH(5)	0 (0)	0.58 (0.02)	3.87	37.38*	327.36*
MNARCH(10)	0 (0)	0.60 (0.02)	4.01	6.33	146.28*
MNARCH(12)	0 (0)	0.59 (0.02)	4.03	6.07	128.34
MNARCH(15)	0 (0)	0.58 (0.02)	3.88	5.57	113.35

TABLE 5.4. *Residual diagnostics for selected models; R^2: coefficient of determination of the regression $\hat{\varepsilon}_t^2 = \alpha_0 + \alpha_1 \hat{\sigma}_t^2 + v_t$; $Q_2(m)$: Box–Ljung statistic of squared residuals with m lags. An asterisk marks 95% significance.*

than a close to unit root behavior. The fits of MNARCH(q) with $q > 10$ can compete with the GARCH fit, and the additional flexibility allows to detect asymmetries at certain lags. In this case, the second lag has an impact on volatility that would not be captured by standard GARCH models.

To alleviate the immense computing power needed to estimate nonparametric models of high order, one may combine nonparametric flexibility and parametric autoregression in a semiparametric framework. This approach will be discussed in the next section.

5.5 Nonparametric Generalized ARCH Models

On the one hand the CHARN model introduced in Section 5.2 is able to deal with asymmetric volatility functions, on the other hand it is restricted due to its Markov property to short memory processes. The success of standard GARCH models, however, can be explained by their ability to sufficiently reflect the long memory property of high frequency financial time series, if the conditional variance process is close to being integrated. To capture both asymmetry and persistence, many parametric extensions of GARCH appeared in the literature, an overview of which is given by Engle and Ng (1993). The general problem is that the econometrician does not know beforehand which type of asymmetry the data reflect. Thus, he can either estimate a variety of parametric models, not knowing which one is correct, or estimate a nonparametric GARCH model which reveals the type of asymmetry, and subsequently, if necessary and possible, specify the functional form of the

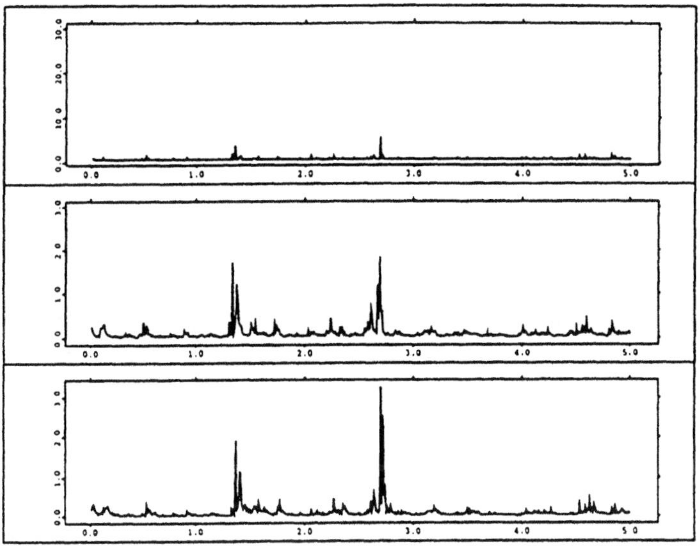

FIGURE 5.23. *The first 500 estimated DEM/USD volatilities of CHARN, MNARCH(5) and MNARCH(12) (from top to bottom). All ordinates range from 0 to 30.*

volatility function and estimate a parametric GARCH model based on this function.

The idea outlined in the following has been applied similarly in the framework of qualitative threshold ARCH (QTARCH) models by Gouriéroux and Monfort (1992), see Section 4.5.2. They test the restrictions of a GARCH model and estimate a generalized QTARCH model. In Hafner, Tjøstheim and Yang (1997) the idea was adopted for the more general case of nonparametric impact functions. Because we are not in a parametric framework, we cannot estimate a generalized ARCH model directly, but rather have to consider other estimation methods.

5.5.1 Estimates of the News Impact Curve and Autoregression Coefficient

As noted above in Section 5.4, a direct one–step estimation of nonparametric GARCH models is not possible due to the infinite information set. A simple idea for a two–step estimation arises when looking at the following respresentation of a GARCH(1,1) model:

$$\begin{aligned}\sigma_t^2 &= \omega + \alpha y_{t-1}^2 + \beta\sigma_{t-1}^2 \\ &= \phi(y_{t-1}) + \beta\phi(y_{t-2}) + \dots \\ &= \frac{\mathrm{E}[\phi(y)]}{1-\beta} + g(y_{t-1}) + \beta g(y_{t-2}) + \dots \end{aligned} \tag{5.36}$$

where y has the stationary distribution, $\phi(y) = \omega + \alpha y^2$, and $g(y) = \phi(y) - \mathrm{E}[\phi(y)]$, such that $g(\cdot)$ is a mean zero function. It should be emphasized that the function $\phi(y)$ can more generally be a nonlinear function that allows the process y_t to be ergodic with stationary distribution that has finite first and second moments. We assume covariance stationarity, i.e. $\alpha + \beta < 1$.

Let σ^2 denote the variance of the stationary distribution of y. Then

$$\sigma^2 = \frac{\mathrm{E}[\phi(y)]}{1-\beta},$$

so that $\mathrm{E}[\phi(y)]$ can be calculated for fixed parameter values. By definition, there is a one–to–one relationship between the functions $\phi(\cdot)$ and $g(\cdot)$, such that estimates of $\phi(\cdot)$ can directly be obtained from estimates of $g(\cdot)$. This is relevant for the estimation of additive models, where usually the univariate functions are restricted to have mean zero.

The idea is to estimate the general nonparametric additive ARCH model of order p

$$\sigma_t^2 = \sigma^2 + g_1(y_{t-1}) + g_2(y_{t-2}) + \dots + g_p(y_{t-p}) \tag{5.37}$$

with sufficiently large p. If the true model is GARCH(1,1), then an estimate of β can be obtained by the OLS estimate of β in the regression

$$g_2(x) = \beta_0 + \beta g_1(x), \tag{5.38}$$

that is

$$\hat{\beta} = \frac{\sum_{t=p+1}^{n} g_1(y_t) g_2(y_t)}{\sum_{t=p+1}^{n} g_1^2(y_t)}. \tag{5.39}$$

Note that this estimator is biased because of the truncation of the infinite information set in (5.37) at lag p. Let us call this the 'model bias'. Thus, there are two biases: the model bias due to model misspecification and the statistical bias due to nonparametric estimation. Since we assumed covariance stationarity, we have $\beta < 1$ and the model bias goes to zero if the truncation lag p is increased.

5.5.2 A Simulation Study

To evaluate the finite sample properties of this estimator, a simulation study is provided. Two GARCH(1,1) processes with typical parameter values are generated. The first process (*process A*) is

$$\sigma_t^2 = 0.1 + 0.2y_{t-1}^2 + 0.7\sigma_{t-1}^2,$$

and the second (*process B*) is

$$\sigma_t^2 = 0.1 + 0.4y_{t-1}^2 + 0.5\sigma_{t-1}^2,$$

both having an unconditional variance of one and the same 'degree' of persistence, $\alpha + \beta = 0.9$, which is close to typical parameter estimates of financial time series, see Section 4.7. To avoid boundary problems, outliers were trimmed to the five and 95 percentiles, respectively.

Three sets of simulations with sample sizes 100, 500 and 2000 were generated for each process and order $p = 2$ and $p = 3$ in (5.37). In order to evaluate the influence of the choice of the bandwidth on the estimator, a grid ranging from 'small' to 'large' bandwidths was used. Each simulated process started with the unconditional means, i.e. $y_0 = 0$ and $\sigma_0^2 = 1$. In Table 5.5, the means of the parameter estimate of 100 replications with sample size $n = 100$ and corresponding standard deviations are given. For additional information about the approximation of the true function $g(y_{t-1}) = \alpha(y_{t-1}^2 - \sigma^2)$, the OLS estimate of b of the regression

$$g(y_{t-1}) = a + b\hat{g}(y_{t-1})$$

was computed and the mean and standard deviation reported.

Obviously, the estimates for $n = 100$ are strongly biased with too large standard deviations. This does not change when the lag order p is increased. In general, the estimation results did not change significantly for increases of the lag orders p to three and four. This holds for all simulation sets.

Consider the simulation results with sample size $n = 500$ in Table 5.6. For estimates of b close to the 'true' value one, which is the case for $h \approx 0.75$ and $h < 0.25$ for the processes A and B, respectively, the corresponding estimates of β are biased downward. On the other hand, for the choice of h that yields unbiased estimates of β, the estimate of b has a positive bias. This is explained by the model misspecification of (5.37): Suppose the true model is weak GARCH in the definition of Drost and Nijman (1993), so that $g(x) = \alpha(x^2 - \sigma^2)$. Then

$$\mathcal{P}(y_t^2 | y_{t-1}, y_{t-2}) = \sigma^2 + g(y_{t-1}) + \beta g(y_{t-2}) + \beta^2 \mathcal{P}[g(y_{t-3}) \mid y_{t-1}, y_{t-2}] + \cdots$$

		Process A ($\beta = 0.7$)		Process B ($\beta = 0.5$)	
p	h	$\hat{b}$	$\hat{\beta}$	$\hat{b}$	$\hat{\beta}$
2	0.5	0.348 (0.263)	0.200 (0.354)	0.800 (0.556)	0.187 (0.329)
2	0.75	0.445 (0.345)	0.262 (0.445)	0.916 (0.729)	0.218 (0.434)
2	1.0	0.504 (0.429)	0.279 (0.532)	1.004 (0.945)	0.229 (0.550)
2	1.25	0.614 (0.523)	0.312 (0.557)	1.109 (1.149)	0.248 (0.633)
2	1.5	0.687 (0.599)	0.336 (0.602)	1.245 (1.325)	0.261 (0.680)
3	0.5	0.338 (0.271)	0.185 (0.373)	0.740 (0.551)	0.177 (0.323)
3	1.0	0.493 (0.469)	0.287 (0.576)	0.791 (1.106)	0.268 (0.607)

TABLE 5.5. *Results of the simulation study: Parameter estimates of β and standard errors in parentheses for the processes A and B with bandwidth h. $n = 100$ and 100 replications are used for the generation. $\hat{b}$ reports the linear regression coefficient of $g(\cdot)$ on $\hat{g}(\cdot)$.*

		Process A ($\beta = 0.7$)		Process B ($\beta = 0.5$)	
p	h	$\hat{b}$	$\hat{\beta}$	$\hat{b}$	$\hat{\beta}$
2	0.5	0.862 (0.311)	0.504 (0.266)	1.207 (0.328)	0.485 (0.182)
2	0.75	0.981 (0.451)	0.568 (0.314)	1.282 (0.376)	0.515 (0.194)
2	1.0	1.065 (0.559)	0.603 (0.337)	1.355 (0.415)	0.536 (0.195)
2	1.5	1.220 (0.681)	0.647 (0.356)	1.547 (0.498)	0.564 (0.187)
3	0.5	0.867 (0.325)	0.507 (0.275)	1.213 (0.330)	0.486 (0.183)
3	1.0	0.979 (0.568)	0.575 (0.347)	1.362 (0.418)	0.536 (0.197)
4	0.5	0.842 (0.338)	0.502 (0.274)	1.215 (0.327)	0.485 (0.181)
4	1.0	1.028 (0.600)	0.612 (0.362)	1.294 (0.483)	0.562 (0.200)

TABLE 5.6. *Notes as in Table 5.5, but $n = 500$.*

where $\mathcal{P}(z_t|x_t)$ denotes the best linear projection of z_t on a constant, x_t and x_t^2. Now the estimation of an additive model as in (5.37) with $p = 2$ leads to

$$g_1(x) = g(x) + \beta^2 \mathcal{P}[g(y_{t-3}) \mid y_{t-1} = x] + \dots \tag{5.40}$$

If $x^2 > \sigma^2$ then $g(x) > 0$, and if $x^2 < \sigma^2$ then $g(x) < 0$. But also the projections in (5.40) take the sign of the difference between x^2 and σ^2. Thus, for small x^2, the estimate $g_1(x)$ in (5.40) has a negative discrepancy as an estimator of $g(x)$, and a positive discrepancy for large x^2. The same holds for $g_2(x)$ as an estimate of $\beta g(x)$:

$$g_2(x) = \beta g(x) + \beta^2 \mathcal{P}[g(y_{t-3}) \mid y_{t-2} = x] + \dots \tag{5.41}$$

		Process A ($\beta = 0.7$)		Process B ($\beta = 0.5$)	
p	h	$\hat{b}$	$\hat{\beta}$	$\hat{b}$	$\hat{\beta}$
2	0.5	0.953 (0.158)	0.656 (0.146)	1.156 (0.131)	0.480 (0.077)
2	1.0	1.037 (0.182)	0.689 (0.154)	1.247 (0.150)	0.510 (0.075)
3	0.5	0.950 (0.155)	0.654 (0.146)	1.158 (0.131)	0.481 (0.076)
3	1.0	1.032 (0.179)	0.686 (0.156)	1.249 (0.151)	0.510 (0.075)

TABLE 5.7. *Notes as in Table 5.5, but* $n = 2000$.

If for every $k > 2$

$$| \mathcal{P}[g(y_{t-k}) \mid y_{t-2} = x] \,| \geq | \mathcal{P}[g(y_{t-k}) \mid y_{t-1} = x] \,|,$$

as it was shown for GARCH models in Section 4.11, then the discrepancy of $g_1(x)$ as an estimate of $g(x)$ is smaller than the discrepancy of $g_2(x)$ as an estimate of $\beta g(x)$. Now suppose β and $g(x)$, and thus also $g_1(x)$ and $g_2(x)$, are known. Then the OLS estimate in (5.38) is too large. However, when β and $g(x)$ are not known, the local linear estimation of (5.37) produces a positive bias for $g_1(x)$ and $g_2(x)$, because in the GARCH case both functions have positive second derivatives for all $x \in \mathbb{R}$, and the bias of $\hat{g}_2(x)$ is smaller than the bias of $\hat{g}_1(x)$.

Thus, there are two effects that affect the adequacy of the estimator of β in opposite direction: the model bias tends to overestimate, the statistical bias to underestimate β. It cannot be stated in general that one effect is larger than the other, or that both effects cancel. From the simulation results, however, it appears that the statistical bias outweighs the model bias, so β is in fact too small. This bias problem strongly affects the simulation results for $n = 500$. For $n = 2000$, however, the bias is rather small even for $p = 2$, as the simulation results in Table 5.7 show. In general, the estimates of β are better behaved for Process B, i.e. the process with smaller β. For Process A ($\beta = 0.7$), the estimates even for $n = 2000$ seem to be negatively biased.

In Figure 5.24 and Figure 5.25, the densities of the estimates of β are plotted for process A with bandwidths $h = 0.5$ and $h = 1.0$, respectively. For reasonable statistical inference, a sample size of order 2000 is required. Note that for the smaller sample sizes, the densities appear to be skewed. For $n = 2000$, however, the density is less skewed and clearly unimodal.

The corresponding results for process B in Figure 5.26 and 5.27 show that here the estimates of the smaller β are better behaved in the sense that standard deviations are smaller and densities are unimodal.

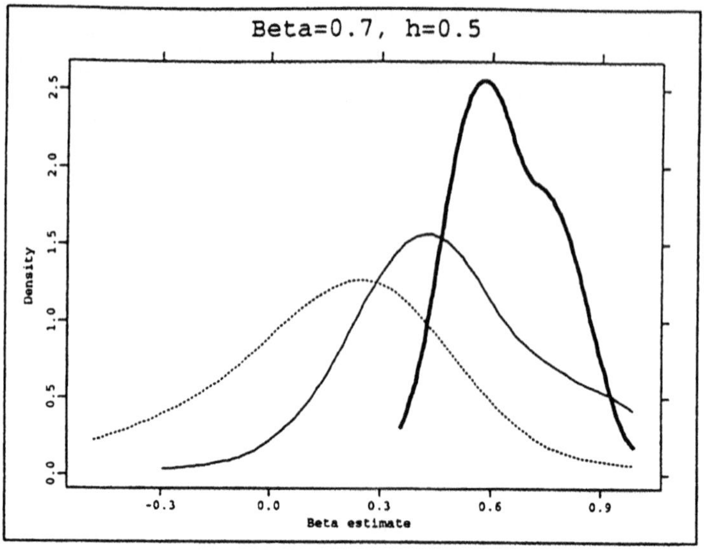

FIGURE 5.24. *The densities of the estimates of β for process A with $h = 0.5$. The dotted line corresponds to $n = 100$, the solid line to $n = 500$, and the thick line to $n = 2000$. A nonparametric kernel density estimator was used with Silverman's rule of thumb.*

5.5.3 FX Results

The nonparametric GARCH estimation outlined in the previous section shall be applied to the HFDF93 FX returns described in Section 2.4. As in Chapter 4, the residual series ε_t of the fitted AR models divided by its empirical standard deviation was chosen as the relevant series for ARCH modelling. Hence, the unconditional variance of ε_t is one. As for the simulation study in the last section, the backfitting procedure was used for estimation of the additive model. At each univariate smoothing step, the supersmoother of Friedman (1984) was used. This is basically a k-nearest neighbor estimator (see Section 3.4.4) with locally optimized span k. For details, see Friedman (1984) or Härdle (1990, pp.181). The supersmoother was chosen in favor of local linear estimation because of the high computational efficency. Unfortunately, the local linear estimation routine in the XploRe macro `gamnoid` was not fast enough to be used for more than 20000 data. For all results reported in the following, a bass enhancement factor of five (the default value in XploRe) was selected. This factor enlarges to some extent the original smoothing parameter and thus produces smoother estimates. It was seen in Section 2.4 that the FX return series on a high frequency scale contain many extreme

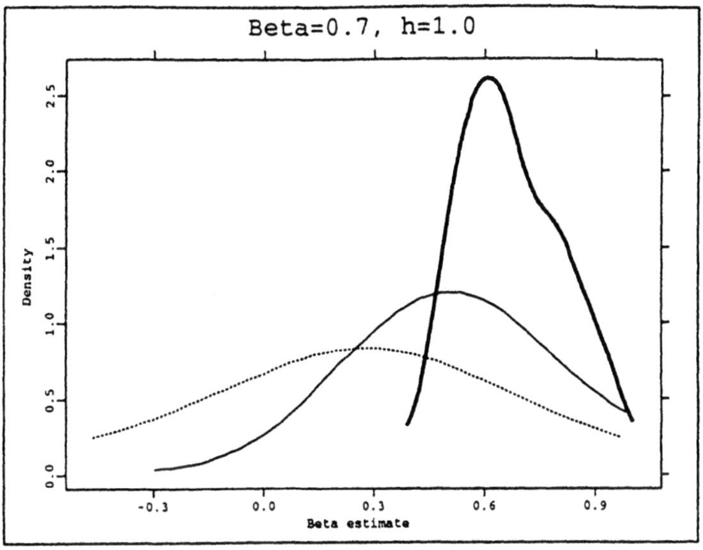

FIGURE 5.25. *The densities of the estimates of β for process A with $h = 1.0$. The dotted line corresponds to $n = 100$, the solid line to $n = 500$, and the thick line to $n = 2000$. A nonparametric kernel density estimator was used with Silverman's rule of thumb.*

outliers, i.e. returns more than five standard deviations from the mean. In order to prevent nonparametric estimation to fail at the boundaries, these observations were trimmed to the 1% and 99% quantile, respectively. The choice of the smoother, of the bass enhancement factor, and of the degree of trimming may appear to be somewhat arbitrary. However, experiments with the local linear estimator, various smoothing parameters and degrees of trimming revealed that the basic results reported in the following are quite robust.

An additive model of order $p = 5$ was estimated for each exchange rate, so that enough information of the news impact curves at different lags is obtained. Thus, the model is

$$\begin{aligned} \varepsilon_t &= \sigma_t \xi_t, \\ \sigma_t^2 &= \sigma^2 + \sum_{j=1}^{5} g_j(\varepsilon_{t-j}). \end{aligned}$$

The additional information contained in $g_j(\cdot), j > 2$ was used for the estimation of β as follows. First, four estimates of β_j are obtained by the

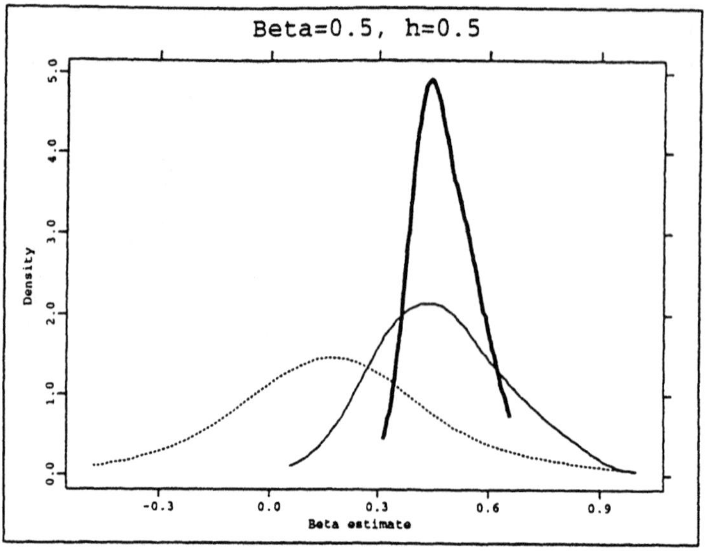

FIGURE 5.26. *The densities of the estimates of β for process B with $h = 0.5$. The dotted line corresponds to $n = 100$, the solid line to $n = 500$, and the thick line to $n = 2000$. A nonparametric kernel density estimator was used with Silverman's rule of thumb.*

regression

$$g_{j+1}(x) = \beta_{0,j} + \beta_j g_j(x), \ \ j = 1, \dots, 4,$$

and, second, the geometric mean is taken as

$$\bar{\beta} = (\beta_1 \cdots \beta_4)^{1/4}.$$

This $\bar{\beta}$ was then used to perform the autoregression of the conditional variance, so that

$$\hat{\sigma}_t^2 = \hat{\sigma}^2 + \sum_{i=0}^{t-2} \bar{\beta}^i g_1(\varepsilon_{t-i-1}). \tag{5.42}$$

The estimated functions $g_1(\cdot)$, $g_2(\cdot)$ and $g_3(\cdot)$ are plotted for each exchange rate in Figure 5.28, 5.29 and 5.30, respectively. Only the first three of five functions are shown for visual clarity. For DEM/USD, the type of asymmetry detected for the CHARN model in Section 5.2 is confirmed and is apparent for all three functions. For the Yen rates, on the other hand, the asymmetries reported in Section 5.2 are not homogenous for the first three news impact curves: for JPY/USD, the positive skewness of g_1 seems to dominate the negative skewness of g_2 and g_3, whereas for JPY/DEM the asymmetry of g_3 dominates the asymmetry of the first two functions.

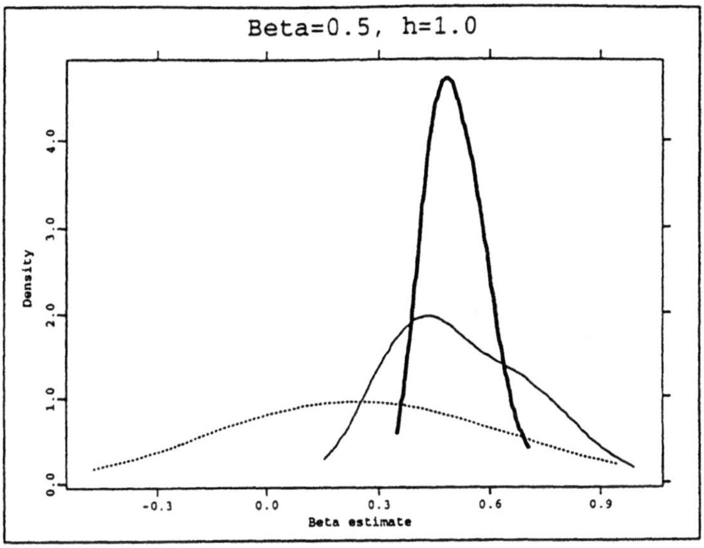

FIGURE 5.27. *The densities of the estimates of β for process B with $h = 1.0$. The dotted line corresponds to $n = 100$, the solid line to $n = 500$, and the thick line to $n = 2000$. A nonparametric kernel density estimator was used with Silverman's rule of thumb.*

Except for JPY/DEM, where g_3 on the positive part is slightly above g_2, the 'scaling property' of the functions is visually obvious. One question is, for instance, whether the scaling factors are robust across the functions $g_1, \cdots, g_p$.

Table 5.8 lists the estimation results for β_j and gives diagnostic statistics for the standardized residuals $\xi_t = \varepsilon_t/\sigma_t$. Surprisingly, the estimates of β are substantially smaller than the corresponding estimates obtained from parametric GARCH models (recall from Chapter 4 that parametric GARCH estimation provided $\beta \approx 0.84$ for DEM/USD and JPY/USD, and $\beta \approx 0.89$ for JPY/DEM). This holds especially for β_1. The residual diagnostics show that the fact that the geometric means $\bar{\beta}$ are relatively small has a negative influence on the fit, because the memory in estimated volatility is too short and thus squared residuals are still positively autocorrelated at higher lags. This holds for all rates, but particulary for the Yen rates, where the $\bar{\beta}$'s are smallest. Note that the kurtosis of standardized residuals is substantially smaller than it was before because, as noted above, outliers were trimmed, which reduces the kurtosis.

Concluding, the nonparametric GARCH model applied to the FX returns provides a fit that cannot compete with the fits of parametric models or

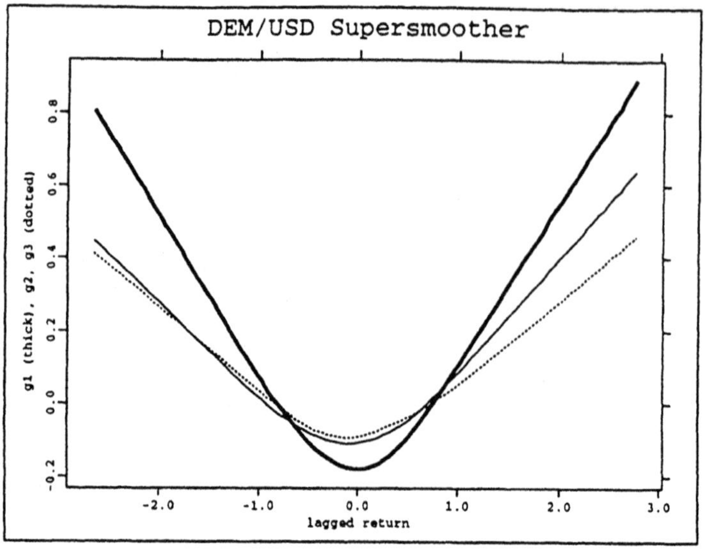

FIGURE 5.28. *The estimated functions* $g_1(\cdot)$ *(thick),* $g_2(\cdot)$ *(solid), and* $g_3(\cdot)$ *(dotted) for DEM/USD.*

the MNARCH model of high order. In the light of the simulation results of Section 5.5.2, this is very likely to be the result of a large 'true' autoregression coefficient β of order 0.9, in which case (in fact for the even moderate case $\beta = 0.7$) the suggested estimation procedure was seen to underestimate. In the simulation study with $n = 2000$ the absolute bias was not even large, so it was conjectured that for the much larger sample size of the FX returns this bias would not play a dominant role anymore. As the results show, this conjecture was misleading, but other factors might also have played a role such as the choice of the smoother. Even though in the experiments with the local linear estimator the results did not substantially differ, this smoother should still be preferred because of its better bias behavior. This, although promising, was not feasible due to the extreme requirements for computing power. A more exhaustive investigation of NGARCH estimates for the FX rates is therefore left to future research.

5.6 Conclusions

The demand for more flexible ways of modelling volatility has become important in current research since the well-known leverage effect in stock returns revealed standard GARCH models to be misspecified. In this chapter, some

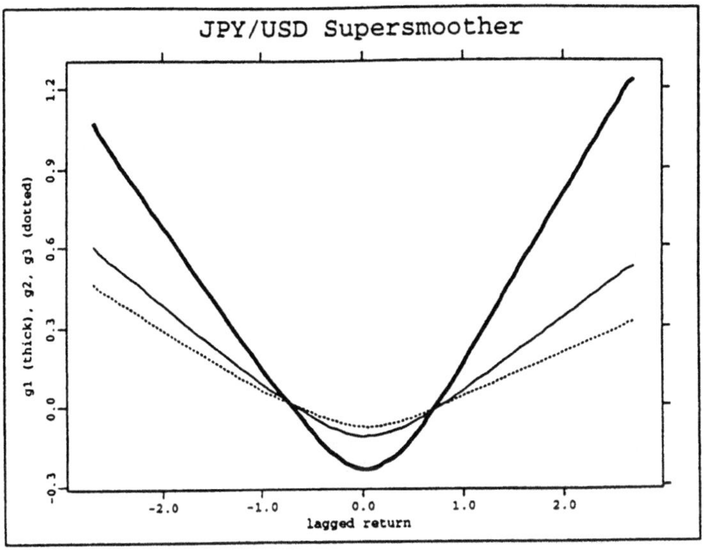

FIGURE 5.29. *The estimated functions* $g_1(\cdot)$ *(thick),* $g_2(\cdot)$ *(solid), and* $g_3(\cdot)$ *(dotted) for JPY/USD.*

new nonparametric approaches are discussed. A nonparametric ARCH model of order one was fitted to high–frequency FX rate series via local linear estimation. The volatility function is skewed, so asymmetry is apparent. By adding more lags, one is more able to cope with the long memory in volatility, as shown by the multiplicative nonparametric models. These models are relatively parsimonious and reveal individual nonlinearities of the lagged variables. This stands in contradiction to standard GARCH models. Particularly the EGARCH model as one of the standard parametric models allowing for asymmetry is not favored by the results. It appears to be a strong assumption that the news impact curve as defined by Engle and Ng (1993) increases exponentially, because the impact of outliers on volatility is overweighted. The news impact curves appear to have different shapes for different lags. This result can be used for subsequent parametric model selection and –refinement.

It was shown that the conditional skewness and kurtosis of the FX rates are not constant, but rather have a typical form: conditional skewness increases with lagged returns, and conditional kurtosis has a shape inverted to the conditional variance. Thus, there is a compensation for higher 'risk' (volatility) via higher order moments. A nonparametric stochastic volatility model was proposed that allows for heterogeneous conditional skewness and kurtosis.

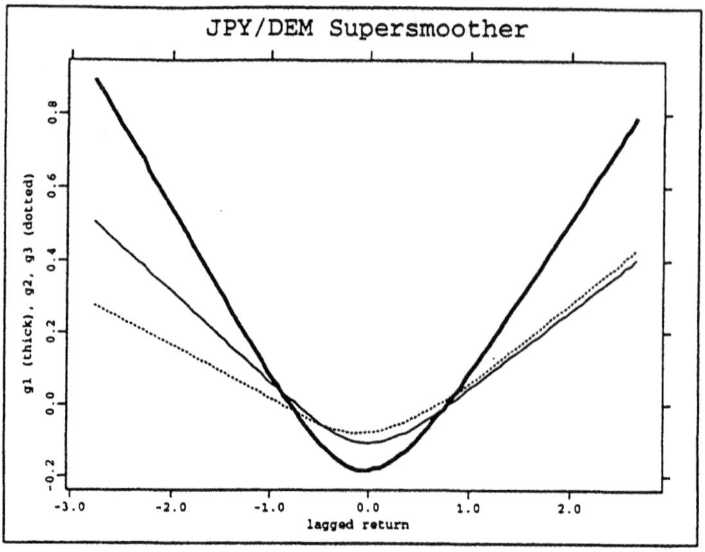

FIGURE 5.30. *The estimated functions* $g_1(\cdot)$ *(thick),* $g_2(\cdot)$ *(solid), and* $g_3(\cdot)$ *(dotted) for JPY/DEM.*

Nonparametric generalized ARCH models were introduced and estimated. A simulation study showed the convergence of the autoregression parameter to the true parameter. The NGARCH estimation for the FX rates with the supersmoother led to surprisingly small β–estimates, which implied significant ARCH–effects in the residuals at higher lags. The news impact curves of the additive model showed the expected scaling character.

In general, for nonparametric volatility estimation a large sample size is required, preferably more than 1000 observations.

	DEM/USD	JPY/USD	JPY/DEM
β_1	0.629	0.484	0.556
β_2	0.795	0.695	0.730
β_3	0.803	0.772	0.644
β_4	0.825	0.823	0.907
$\bar{\beta}$	0.759	0.680	0.699
$m(\xi_t)$	−0.005	−0.008	−0.016
$\text{Var}(\xi_t)$	1.029	1.011	0.997
$\text{Skew}(\xi_t)$	0.031	0.005	−0.033
$\text{Kurt}(\xi_t)$	4.050	4.450	3.880
$Q_2(10)$	33.69	60.57	67.38
$Q_2(100)$	221.40	752.01	821.59
$Q_2(1000)$	1702.23	4433.09	3691.61

TABLE 5.8. *Estimation results for the nonparameric GARCH model applied to the FX returns. $\bar{\beta}$ is the geometric mean of $\beta_1, \ldots, \beta_4$, and $Q_2(m)$ is the Portmanteau statistic of the squared standardized residuals with m lags. All statistics are significant at the 5% level.*

6
Conclusions and Outlook

Volatility is the predominant factor of financial decisions in present time. As was argued in the introduction of this thesis, one important reason is the general tendency towards liberalization of financial markets with free–floating asset prices and exchange rates. Even the currencies in the European Monetary System are effectively free–floating since August 1993, because the 15% variability band was more a symbol than a serious restriction. Of course this will change again, once the European Monetary Union will be established by political decisions. However, volatility of the three main currency blocks, i.e. Dollar, Euro and Yen, is very likely to remain on a high level due to the discrepancies of the macroeconomic policies in these regions. Therefore, a correct understanding of the dynamic properties of volatility is crucial for reliable prediction of financial time series, which serves as the basis for policy–making.

The general subject of this treatise was to find suitable time series models, which on the one hand are parsimonious, on the other hand flexible enough to account for the special features of financial time series. Because linear models of the Box–Jenkins type fail the second requirement, nonlinear time series models are needed. Within this new and very broad model class, just a few models can be chosen and checked for their adequacy. Throughout the book this was mainly the successful ARCH model class. However, the main goal was to detect anomalies of standard ARCH parametrizations and to introduce an alternative nonparametric ARCH model class that is more flexible and thus better able to deal with pecularities of the analyzed time series.

After some general remarks on uncertainty, risk and volatility in financial markets, it was shown in Chapter 2 that there is no unique risk measure available. Traditionally, in most economic and statistic models the standard deviation or alternatively the variance is used as a proxy for 'risk', and this also plays the major role throughout this work, even though the mean absolute value may be more appropriate, as the autocorrelation functions in Chapter 2 indicate. The generalization of risk by Rothschild and Stiglitz (1970) lacks the ability to be translated into a tractable statistical model with finite number of moments, as was shown at the beginning of Chapter 2.

Before going into details of FX rates, the second chapter briefly summarizes the specific properties of stock returns and interest rates. An empirical analysis of a Standard & Poors 500 series revealed a significant leverage–effect. Dealing with FX rates, the importance of high frequency data analysis and the resulting necessity to explicitly model seasonal volatility was underlined. The flexible activity–based time scale was shown to provide an elegant solution. Many high frequency FX rates with their different data sources and aggregations were described. Based on the operational time scale, typical properties of the series were investigated, two of which are the long memory of volatility and the fat tails of the return distribution compared with weekly FX returns and a normal distribution. It was possible to identify news to be responsible for shocks to the DEM/USD return series. News that can be predicted by their regular appearance such as announcements of economic indicators seemed to induce less persistent shocks to the FX rates than irregular news.

The survey of nonlinear time series models in Chapter 3 covers many important parametric and nonparametric models used in financial econometrics. It was seen that most of these models allow for conditional heteroskedasticity and that the most prominent and successful among these is the ARCH model. Bilinear models, for example, seem to be better suited for sudden outbursts of volatility, as in seismological time series. The survey of nonparametric time series analysis attempts to capture the most important approaches to nonparametric model building techniques. In order to avoid misspecification and spurious good fits of nonlinear models, nonlinearity tests are necessary. In the context of this work, mainly the Lagrange multiplier test against conditional heteroskedasticity, which is equivalent to Engle's ARCH test, is of importance. It was shown that the high frequency FX return series by far fail to pass this test. This was plausible on the ground of the ACF of squared returns reported in Chapter 2.

The first objective of Chapter 4 was to give a survey of ARCH models with its most important extensions and to categorize them according to their goal. A generalization of the news impact curve of Engle and Ng (1993) led to a new definition of *news impact function* where volatility depends on an isolated shock and the time lag of its occurence. Estimation results for the FX rates showed that a GARCH(1,1) model is to a large extent able to deal with the long memory of volatility. Parameter estimates implied a conditional variance close to the unit root. The integrated GARCH model, however, did not provide the same good fit. Here, the behavior of likelihood ratio tests has to be further investigated in order to distinguish between stationary and non-stationary volatility. Finally, the EGARCH model did not improve the results of the GARCH fit. Outliers seemed to be overweighed by this model due to the exponential increase of the news impact curve, in accordance to the results of Engle and Ng (1993). Also, the asymmetry parameter of the EGARCH model was not significant for all rates. This does not imply, of course, that volatility is symmetric. One goal of Chapter 5 was to show that there are asymmetries in volatility. For DEM/USD, this asymmetry is significant for large lagged returns, as based on uniform confidence bands. In particular, the impact of news on volatility of the DEM/USD rate is larger for positive returns than for negative ones. This was found by using local polynomial estimation in a CHARN model, and smoothing splines in a multiplicative nonparametric ARCH model.

With respect to the inherent long memory, however, low order models of the CHARN and MNARCH model class were shown to be insufficient. Therefore, a parsimonious nonparametric analogue to a GARCH model was formulated that can also be viewed as a semiparametric model. A procedure to estimate the nonparametric impact function as well as the autoregressive coefficient was suggested. A detailed simulation study for two generated GARCH processes showed that estimation is reliable only for large data sets, preferably more than 1000 observations. For high-frequency data analysis this will usually not be a serious restriction. Also, a procedure to correct for the bias due to truncation of a model with infinitely many lags was provided. As the application to the 20 minute FX series shows, the NGARCH model has potential to combine the simplicity and long-term dependence of a GARCH model with the flexibility of a CHARN model.

Our analysis has concentrated on statistical models for the volatility of financial time series. However, many related and complementary topics are not covered or only briefly sketched. In the following a few issues are named that are left for future research.

First, one has to investigate the out-of-sample prediction ability of existing volatility models. On the basis of a detailed prediction competition one would be able to evaluate advantages and deficencies of volatility models in a practical situation.

Second, as mentioned in the introduction, simulation studies will have to show how sensitive option prices are to misspecifications of the volatility model. It is conjectured, for example, that an erroneously specified EGARCH model predicts a too large volatility at the boundaries and thus overprices the option in turbulent periods. Nonparametric GARCH models that allow for volatility saturation may serve as better volatility models for option pricing.

Third, the issue of order- and lag-selection was left out for two reasons: on the one hand, this is only relevant for – parametric or nonparametric – ARCH models in this context, not for GARCH, because a GARCH(1,1) in most cases provided a sufficiently general lag structure. On the other hand, the findings in Section 2.4 suggest a homogeneous and monotonously declining impact of lagged returns on volatility. Recall that Engle (1982) suggested an ARCH(q) model with linearly declining coefficients. In other words, the evidence is such that Friday's volatility is dependent on Wednesday's and Monday's volatility in the same qualitative way, but the latter, of course, downscaled. This is the reason why the nonparametric GARCH model is so appealing: it uses the same impact function for every lag, only quantitatively scaled according to its time lag.

Last, but not least, ways to estimate multiple time series models for high frequency data have to be found. The activity based time scale used in Section 2.4 for the FX rates is incomplete in this respect, because the rates have different seasonal activity patterns and thus different time scales.

Financial volatility estimation with nonlinear time series models will remain an open research field in the future. Many unsolved questions have to be faced, and the relevance for macroeconomic policy–making will presumably even increase in line with the liberalization of financial markets. Higher and more complex volatility is the price for getting more liquid and efficient markets. The improved understanding of its dynamical properties will thus help to avoid panic reactions in turbulent markets. Also, the findings in recent literature on financial volatility and in this contribution may serve as a basis for the theory and practice of hedging risks.

A
The Moments of log $|\xi_t|$

In this chapter, results are derived, which are used in Section 5.4. For a reference to the integral expressions used here, see Bronstein, Semendjajev, Musiol, and Mühlig, Taschenbuch der Mathematik, Verlag Harri Deutsch, 2nd ed., 1995. It is shown that if $\xi_t \sim N.i.d.(0,1)$, then $E(\ln|\xi_t|) \approx -0.635$ and $\text{Var}(\ln|\xi_t|) = \pi^2/8$.

Let $y \equiv \ln|\xi_t|$, then it follows for the density of y

$$f(y) = \sqrt{\frac{2}{\pi}} \exp\left(y - \frac{1}{2}e^{2y}\right) \tag{A.1}$$

and

$$\begin{aligned} E(y) &= \sqrt{2/\pi} \int_{-\infty}^{\infty} y \exp\left(y - \frac{1}{2}e^{2y}\right) dy \\ &= \sqrt{2/\pi} \int_0^{\infty} \ln t \exp(-\frac{1}{2}t^2) dt \\ &= 2/\sqrt{\pi} \ln(\sqrt{2}) \int_0^{\infty} \exp(-u^2) du + 2/\sqrt{\pi} \int_0^{\infty} \ln u \exp(-u^2) du \\ &= \ln\sqrt{2} - (C + 2\ln 2) \\ &= -\ln\sqrt{2} - \frac{1}{2}C \approx -0.635 \end{aligned} \tag{A.2}$$

where $C \approx 0.577$ denotes Euler's constant.

Similarly,

$$\begin{aligned} E(y^2) &= \sqrt{\frac{2}{\pi}} \int_{-\infty}^{\infty} y^2 \exp(y - \frac{1}{2}\exp(2y)) dy \\ &= \sqrt{\frac{2}{\pi}} \int_0^{\infty} \ln^2 t \exp(-\frac{1}{2}t^2) dt \\ &= \frac{2}{\sqrt{\pi}} \ln^2\sqrt{2} \int_0^{\infty} \exp(-u^2) du \\ &\quad + \frac{4}{\sqrt{\pi}} \ln\sqrt{2} \int_0^{\infty} \ln u \exp(-u^2) du \\ &\quad + \frac{2}{\sqrt{\pi}} \int_0^{\infty} \ln^2 u \exp(-u^2) du \end{aligned}$$

$$= \ln^2(\sqrt{2} - \ln\sqrt{2}(C + 2\ln 2) + \frac{1}{4}(\frac{\pi^2}{2} + (C + 2\ln 2)^2)$$

$$= \frac{\pi^2}{8} + (-\ln\sqrt{2} - \frac{1}{2}C)^2 \qquad \text{(A.3)}$$

so that

$$\text{Var}(y) = \pi^2/8 \approx 1.23. \qquad \text{(A.4)}$$

B

times.lib – A Time Series Library for XploRe 4

times.lib is a new library for the interactive graphical computing environment XploRe, see Härdle et al. (1995) for basic information about this software package. XploRe is a matrix oriented programming language that additionally allows for interactive modification of graphics. All standard statistical tools and methods are available. XploRe 3 is a version developed for PCs under DOS. A Windows version is currently in development. Also, a UNIX version, i.e. XploRe 4, is in the beta stage. **times.lib** is developed for the UNIX version XploRe 4.

In the current state, **times.lib** allows fast calculation of the autocorrelation function (**acf**), the partial autocorrelation function (**pacf**), the correlation integral as described in Section 3.2 (**corrint**), and the generation and estimation of standard ARMA and GARCH models (**genarma**, **armacls**, **armalik**, **genarch** and **archest**). These macros are presented below. ACF and PACF are computed in the spectral domain via the Fast Fourier Transformation (FFT). For long time series this is considerably faster than the calculation of autocorrelations in the time domain. For the calculation of the likelihood function of ARMA models, the innovation algorithm was used in **armalik** as described in Brockwell and Davis: "Time Series: Theory and Methods", Springer Verlag, New York, 1991. The optimization of the likelihood functions in **armalik** and **archest** is based on the **nelmin** algorithm implemented in XploRe. It is basically a simplex algorithm that does not require first derivatives. For details, see Nelder and Mead, "A simplex method for function minimization", *Computer Journal*, 7, 308–313. Experiments have shown that this algorithm is appropriate for GARCH likelihood functions and is quite fast. More efficient gradient algorithms such as BFGS could be implemented as well. **archest** allows the estimation of GARCH(p, q) models with $0 < p, q < 3$. For general applications this will be sufficient. If models of higher order are required, the macro can easily be extended by adding the corresponding procedure with the likelihood function at the end of the macro. Extensions to allow for non-normal conditional densities are also possible by modifying the likelihood procedures.

```
proc (y) = acf (x)
; -----------------------------------------------------------------
; Library        times
; -----------------------------------------------------------------
;  See_also      pacf, fft, invfft
; -----------------------------------------------------------------
;   Macro        acf
; -----------------------------------------------------------------
;   Description  autocorrelation function for time series
; -----------------------------------------------------------------
;   Usage        y = acf(x)
;   Input
;     Parameter  x
;     Definition vector
;   Output
;     Parameter  y
;     Definition vector
; -----------------------------------------------------------------
;   Example      library("times")
;                randomize (0)
;                x=normal(100)
;                a1=acf(x)
;                a1[1:5]
; -----------------------------------------------------------------
;   Result
;                [1,]      1
;                [2,] -0.15902
;                [3,] -0.12114
;                [4,] 0.29794
;                [5,] -0.021693
; -----------------------------------------------------------------
;   Author       Christian Hafner, 960605
; -----------------------------------------------------------------
  n = rows(x)
  x = x-meanc(x)
  p = log(n) / log(2)
  p = rint(exp(log(2)*ceil(p)))          ; next power of 2
  if (n != p)
    x = x|(matrix(p-n)-1)                ; append series
  endif
  x=x~(matrix(p).*0)
  ftr = fft(x)                           ; fourier transform
  peri = (sumc((ftr.*ftr)')/p)'          ; periodogram
  peri=peri~matrix(p).*0
  y1 = invfft(peri)./sumc(x[,1]^2).*p    ; autocorr function
  y = y1[1:n,1]
endp
```

```
proc(y) = pacf(x, k)
; -----------------------------------------------------------------
; Library        times
; -----------------------------------------------------------------
;  See_also      acf, fft, invfft
; -----------------------------------------------------------------
;   Macro        pacf
; -----------------------------------------------------------------
;   Description  partial autocorrelation function
; -----------------------------------------------------------------
;   Usage        y = pacf(x,k)
;   Input
;     Parameter  x
;     Definition vector
;     Parameter  k
;     Definition positive integer < 100
;   Output
;     Parameter  y
;     Definition vector
; -----------------------------------------------------------------
;   Example      library("times")
;                randomize (0)
;                x=normal(100)
;                a2=pacf(x,20)
;                a2[1:5]
; -----------------------------------------------------------------
;   Result
;                [1,] -0.15902
;                [2,] -0.15022
;                [3,] 0.2644
;                [4,] 0.057189
;                [5,] -0.12492
; -----------------------------------------------------------------
;   Author       Christian Hafner, 960605
; -----------------------------------------------------------------
  p=1                    ; initialize corr matrix
  incr=1                 ; initialize increment vector
  a=acf(x)               ; compute autocorrelations
  y=matrix(k).*a[2]      ; initialize pacf-vector
  i=2
  while(i<=k)
      incr=a[i]|incr
      p=(p~incr[1:rows(incr)-1])|incr' ; denominator matrix
      pn=p[,1:cols(p)-1]~a[2:i+1]      ; nominator matrix
      y[i]=det(pn)/det(p)              ; Cramer's rule
      i=i+1
  endo
endp
```

```
proc(y) = genarma(a,b,eps)
; -----------------------------------------------------------------
; Library        times
; -----------------------------------------------------------------
;  See_also      genarch
; -----------------------------------------------------------------
;   Macro        genarma
; -----------------------------------------------------------------
;   Description  generates an ARMA process with mean zero
; -----------------------------------------------------------------
;   Usage        y = genarma(a, b, eps)
;   Input
;     Parameter  a
;     Definition p-vector of autoregressive parameters
;     Parameter  b
;     Definition q-vector of moving average parameters
;     Parameter  eps
;     Definition n-vector of noise
;   Output
;     Parameter  y
;     Definition n-vector, the ARMA process
; -----------------------------------------------------------------
;   Example      library("times")
;                randomize(0)
;                genarma(0.1,0.1,normal(5))
; -----------------------------------------------------------------
;   Result
;                [1,] -0.21293
;                [2,]  -1.0504
;                [3,]   1.7444
;                [4,] -0.93571
;                [5,]  -1.6582
; -----------------------------------------------------------------
;   Author       Christian Hafner, 960819
; -----------------------------------------------------------------
  p = rows(a)     ; autoregressive order
  q = rows(b)     ; moving average order
  n = rows(eps)   ; length of process
  y = matrix(n)
  ma=eps
  y[1] = eps[1]
  m = max(p|q)
  i = 1
  while(i<=m)     ; loop for starting values
    ma[i+1]=eps[i+1]+b[1:min(i|q)]'*eps[i:max(1|i-q+1)]
    y[i+1] = ma[i+1]+a[1:min(i|p)]'*y[i:max(1|i-p+1)]
    i = i+1
  endo
  j=1             ; loop for moving average
  while(j<=q)
    ma[m+2:n] = ma[m+2:n]+b[j].*eps[m+2-j:n-j]
    j=j+1
  endo
  y = genar(ma, y[1:p], a)
endp
```

```
proc(y,wnv) = armacls(zz,p,q)
; -----------------------------------------------------------
; Library        times
; -----------------------------------------------------------
;  See_also      armalik
; -----------------------------------------------------------
;   Macro        armacls
; -----------------------------------------------------------
;   Description  estimates an ARMA process with mean zero
;   by conditional least squares
; -----------------------------------------------------------
;   Usage        {y,wnv} = armacls(x,p,q)
;   Input
;     Parameter  x
;     Definition n-vector, the process
;     Parameter  p
;     Definition scalar, the autoregression order
;     Parameter  q
;     Definition scalar, the moving average order
;   Output
;     Parameter  y
;     Definition list containing 1. p+q-vector, the
;                estimated parameters, 2. the number of
;                iterations, and 3., a 0-1 scalar
;                indicating convergence
;     Parameter  wnv
;     Definition the estimate of the white noise variance
; -----------------------------------------------------------
;   Example      library("times")
;                randomize(0)
;                x = genarma(0.7,0.3,normal(500))
;                {y,wnv}=armacls(x,1,1)
;                y{1}
; -----------------------------------------------------------
;   Result
;                [1,]  0.70623
;                [2,]  0.27249
; -----------------------------------------------------------
;   Author       Christian Hafner, 960906
; -----------------------------------------------------------
  putglobal("zz")
  q = rint(q)      ; moving average order
  p = rint(p)      ; autoregression order
  error((p<1)&&(q<1), "one of p and q must be positive")
  putglobal("p")
  n = rows(zz)
  start = normal(p+q)./(p+q)    ; random starting values
  ; minimization of squared residuals:
  y = nelmin(start,"armapq",200,1e-5)
  ssr = getglobal("ssr")
  wnv = ssr/(n-p-q)      ; estimate of white noise variance
endp
;-----------------------------------------------------------
proc(ssr) = armapq(a)
  zz = getglobal("zz")
```

```
  p = getglobal("p")
  q = rint(rows(a)-p)
  switch
    case (p<=0)       ; the MA(q) case
      p = 1
      phi = 0
      theta = a
      break
    case (q<=0)       ; the AR(p) case
      q = 1
      theta = 0
      phi = a
      break
    case ((q>0) &&(p>0))  ; the ARMA(p,q) case
      phi = a[1:p]
      theta = a[p+1:p+q]
      break
  endsw
  n = rows(zz)
  ma = zz             ; initialize MA-vector
  m = max(p|q)
  u = matrix(n)       ; the residuals
  u[1] = zz[1]
  i = 1
  while(i<=m)         ; loop for starting values
    ma[i+1] = zz[i+1]-phi[1:min(i|p)]'* zz[i:max(1|i-p+1)]
    u[i+1] = ma[i+1]-theta[1:min(i|q)]'*u[i:max(1|i-q+1)]
    i = i+1
  endo
  j = 1               ; loop for moving average
  while(j<=p)
    ma[m+2:n] = ma[m+2:n]-phi[j].*zz[m+2-j:n-j]
    j = j+1
  endo
  u = genar(ma, u[1:q], -theta) ; generation of residuals
  ssr = sum(u.^2)     ; the sum of squared residuals
  putglobal("ssr")
endp
```

```
proc(a,stderr,covp,s2) = armalik(zz)
; -----------------------------------------------------------------
; Library          times
; -----------------------------------------------------------------
;  See_also        armacls
; -----------------------------------------------------------------
;   Macro          armalik
; -----------------------------------------------------------------
;   Description    estimates an ARMA(1,1) process with
;                  mean zero by maximum likelihood using
;                  the innovation algorithm
; -----------------------------------------------------------------
;   Usage          y = armalik(x)
;   Input
;     Parameter    x
;     Definition   n-vector, the process
;   Output
;     Parameter    y
;     Definition   list containing 1. the estimated
;                  parameters, 2. the corresponding
;                  asymptotic standard deviations, 3. the
;                  asymptotic covariance, and 4. the
;                  estimate of the white noise variance
; -----------------------------------------------------------------
;   Example        library("times")
;                  randomize(0)
;                  x = genarma(0.7,0.3,normal(100))
;                  y=armalik(x)
;                  y{1}
; -----------------------------------------------------------------
;   Result
;                  [1,]  0.87487
;                  [2,] -0.069252
; -----------------------------------------------------------------
;   Author         Christian Hafner, 960906
; -----------------------------------------------------------------
  putglobal("zz")
  n=rows(zz)
  start=normal(2)./3       ; starting values
  a=nelmin(start,"innova",50,1e-5)  ; likelihood max
  a=a{1}
  phi=a[1]                 ; autoregression parameter
  theta=a[2]               ; moving average parameter
;   asymptotic standard deviations :
  stdphi=(1+phi*theta)/(phi+theta)*sqrt(1-phi^2)/sqrt(n)
  stdtheta=(1+phi*theta)/(phi+theta)*sqrt(1-theta^2)/sqrt(n)
  stderr=stdphi|stdtheta
;   asymptotic covariance of phi and theta:
  covp=-(1/n)*(1+phi*theta)/(phi+theta)^2*(1-phi^2)*(1-theta^2)
  s2=getglobal("t1")       ; sum of squared residuals
  s2=s2/n                  ; estimate white noise variance
endp
;-----------------------------------------------------------------
proc(y)=innova(par)        ; the innovation algorithm
  phi=par[1]
```

```
  theta=par[2]
  if (abs(phi-theta)<1e-5)
    y = 1e+10
  else
    zz=getglobal("zz")
    n=rows(zz)
    y=0
    t1=0
    t2=0
    xhat=zz[1]
    r=(1+2*theta*phi+theta^2)/(1-phi^2)
    i = 1
    while(i<n)
      thin = theta/r
      r = 1 + theta^2 -theta^2 / r
      xhat = phi*zz[i]+thin * (zz[i]-xhat)
      t1=t1+((zz[i+1]-xhat)^2)/r
      t2=t2+log(r)
      i=i+1
    endo
    y=log(t1/n)+t2/n
    putglobal("t1")
  endif
endp
```

```
proc(y,s2) = genarch(a,b,n)
; ---------------------------------------------------------------
; Library        times
; ---------------------------------------------------------------
;  See_also      genarma
; ---------------------------------------------------------------
;   Macro        genarch
; ---------------------------------------------------------------
;   Description generates Gaussian GARCH processes
; ---------------------------------------------------------------
;   Usage        y = genarch(a, b, n)
;   Input
;     Parameter   a
;     Definition  (q+1)-vector of constant and ARCH
;                 parameters
;     Parameter   b
;     Definition  p-vector of GARCH parameters
;     Parameter   n
;     Definition  scalar, length of output process
;   Output
;     Parameter   y
;     Definition  n-vector, the GARCH process
;     Parameter   s2
;     Definition  n-vector, the volatility process
; ---------------------------------------------------------------
;   Example       library("times")
;                 randomize(0)
;                 y = genarch(0.1|0.2,0.7,5)
;                 y{1}
; ---------------------------------------------------------------
;   Result
;                 [1,]  0.87293
;                 [2,] -0.81784
;                 [3,]  -1.0228
;                 [4,]  0.56941
;                 [5,] -0.30926
; ---------------------------------------------------------------
;   Author        Christian Hafner, 960819
; ---------------------------------------------------------------
  q = rows(a)-1 ; order of ARCH without constant
  error(q<1, "a must contain at least 2 elements")
  error(sum(a[2:q+1])+sum(b)>=1, "Process nonstationary!")
  errtxt="Parameters must be nonnegative!"
  error(((sum(a<0))||(sum(b<0)))>=1, errtxt)
  p = rows(b)   ; order of GARCH
  m = p+q
  y = matrix(n+m)
    ; initialize conditional variance
  s2 = (a[1]/(sum(a[2:q+1])+sum(b))).*matrix(n+m)
    ; starting values
  y[1:m] = sqrt(s2[1:m]).*normal(m)
  i = m+1
  while (i<=n+m)
    s2[i] = a[1] + a[2:q+1]'*y[i-1:i-q]^2+b'*s2[i-1:i-p]
    y[i] = sqrt(s2[i])*normal(1)
```

```
    i = i+1
  endo
  y = y[m+1:m+n]
  s2 = s2[m+1:m+n]
endp
```

```
proc(cab,stderr,lik,s2)=archest(xx,q,p)
; -----------------------------------------------------------------
; Library        times
; -----------------------------------------------------------------
;  See_also      nelmin
; -----------------------------------------------------------------
;   Macro        archest
; -----------------------------------------------------------------
;   Description  QMLE of GARCH with mean zero
; -----------------------------------------------------------------
;   Usage        y = archest(xx,q,p)
;   Input
;     Parameter  xx
;     Definition vector
;     Parameter  q
;     Definition 1 or 2 (can be extended)
;     Parameter  p
;     Definition 1 or 2 (can be extended)
;   Output
;     Parameter  y
;     Definition list containing 1. parameter estimates, 2.
;                standard errors, 3. likelihood value, 4.
;                volatility estimate
; -----------------------------------------------------------------
;   Example      library("times")
;                randomize (0)
;                x=normal(100)
;                z=archest(x,1,1)
;                z{1}{1}
; -----------------------------------------------------------------
;   Result
;               [1,] 0.485276
;               [2,] 0.002673
;               [3,] 0.534511
; -----------------------------------------------------------------
;   Author     Christian Hafner, 960814
; -----------------------------------------------------------------
  putglobal("xx")
  n=rows(xx)
  q=rint(q)                                 ; ARCH order
  p=rint(p)                                 ; GARCH order
  m=p+q+1
  error((q<1)||(q>2), "q must be 1 or 2")
  error((p<1)||(p>2), "p must be 1 or 2")
  switch
      case ((p==1)&&(q==1))
fun="garch11"          break     ; GARCH(1,1) model
      case ((p==1)&&(q==2))
fun="garch21"          break     ; GARCH(2,1) model
      case ((p==2)&&(q==1))
fun="garch12"          break     ; GARCH(1,2) model
      case ((p==2)&&(q==2))
fun="garch22"          break     ; GARCH(2,2) model
  endsw
  start=uniform(m)./m                        ; starting values
```

```
  cab=nelmin(start,fun,200,1e-5)          ; likelihood max
  h1=cab[1]
  h2=matrix(m-1).*mean(xx^2)
  j=1
  while(j<=q)
      h1=h1+cab[1+j].*xx[q-j+1:n-j]^2
      j=j+1
  endo
  ex = h2[1:q]| h1
  s2 = genar(ex, h2[1:p], cab[q+2:m])  ; cond. variance
  s2der=matrix(n,m)
; generation of the derivative of s2 w.r.t.:
; the constant
  s2der[,1]=genar(matrix(n), matrix(p), cab[q+2:m])
  i=1
  while(i<=q)                  ; the ARCH parameters
    s2der[,i+1]=genar(h2[1:q]|xx[q-i+1:n-i]^2,h2[1:p],cab[q+2:m])
    i=i+1
  endo
  while(i<m)                   ; and the GARCH parameters
    s2der[,i+1]=genar( h2 | s2[m-i:n-i] , h2[1:p], cab[q+2:m])
    i=i+1
  endo
  ; unconditional kurtosis
  ku=mean((xx-mean(xx))^4)/(mean(xx^2))^2
  ; conditional kurtosis
  kc=ku.*((mean(s2))^2/mean(s2^2))
  ; Hessian matrix
  g1=(0.5/(s2^2).*s2der)' * s2der./n
  ; outer product
  g2=(0.25/(s2^2).*s2der.*(kc-1))' * s2der./n
  ; asymptotic covariance matrix
  ascov=inv(g1)*g2*inv(g1)
  stderr=matrix(m)
  i=1
  while(i<=m)
    stderr[i]=sqrt(ascov[i,i]/n)      ; standard errors
    i=i+1
  endo
  ; log likelihood value
  lik=-n/2*log(2*pi)-0.5*sum(log(s2)+(xx^2)./s2)
endp
;-----------------------------------------------------------------
proc(y)=garch11(a)
  xx=getglobal("xx")
  n = rows(xx)
  ex = 0 | a[1] + a[2].*xx[1:n-1]^2
  s2=genar(ex, mean(xx^2), a[3])
  if(sum((a<=0)>=1) ||  (sum(a[2:3])>=1))
    y=1e+10
  else
    y=sum(log(s2)+(xx^2)./s2)
  endif
endp
proc(y)=garch12(a)
```

```
  xx=getglobal("xx")
  n = rows(xx)
  ex = 0 | a[1] + a[2].*xx[1:n-1]^2
  s2 = genar(ex, matrix(2).*mean(xx^2), a[3:4])
  if(sum((a<=0)>=1) ||  (sum(a[2:4])>=1))
    y=1e+10
  else
    y=sum(log(s2)+(xx^2)./s2)
  endif
endp
proc(y)=garch21(a)
  xx = getglobal("xx")
  n = rows(xx)
  ex = 0|mean(xx^2)|a[1]+a[2].*xx[2:n-1]^2+a[3].*xx[1:n-2]^2
  s2 = genar(ex, mean(xx^2), a[4])
  if(sum((a<=0)>=1) ||  (sum(a[2:4])>=1))
    y=1e+10
  else
    y=sum(log(s2)+(xx^2)./s2)
  endif
endp
proc(y)=garch22(a)
  xx=getglobal("xx")
  n = rows(xx)
  ex = matrix(2)|a[1]+a[2].*xx[2:n-1]^2+a[3].*xx[1:n-2]^2
  s2 = genar(ex, matrix(2).*mean(xx^2), a[4:5])
  if(sum((a<=0)>=1) ||  (sum(a[2:5])>=1))
    y=1e+10
  else
    y=sum(log(s2)+(xx^2)./s2)
  endif
endp
```

```
proc(y) = corrint(x, m)
; -----------------------------------------------------------------
; Library          times
; -----------------------------------------------------------------
;  See_also        distance
; -----------------------------------------------------------------
;   Macro          corrint
; -----------------------------------------------------------------
;   Description    correlation integral for time series
; -----------------------------------------------------------------
;   Usage          y = corrint(x,m)
;   Input
;     Parameter    x
;     Definition   vector
;     Parameter    m
;     Definition   positive integer < 10 (embedding dimension)
;   Output
;     Parameter    y
;     Definition   array (first column: log epsilon,
;                  second column: log correlation integral)
; -----------------------------------------------------------------
;   Example        library("times")
;                  randomize (0)
;                  x=normal(100)
;                  y=corrint(x,2)
;                  y[1:2,1:2]
; -----------------------------------------------------------------
;   Result
;                  [1,] -0.67811 -1.0089
;                  [2,] -0.6487 -0.99557
; -----------------------------------------------------------------
;   Author         Christian Hafner, 960605
; -----------------------------------------------------------------
  error((m<2 || m>10), "m must be in (2,3,...,9)")
  error(cols(x)<>1, "X must be univariate!")
  std=sqrt(varc(x))
  dk=9
  k=matrix(dk)-1
  r=20*m                                ; number of m-histories
  df=matrix(r, m)                       ; matrix of m-histories
  t=floor(uniform(r).*(rows(x)-m))+m    ; index vector
  i=1
  while(i<m)
      t=t-1
      df[,i]=index(x, t)                ; generate m-histories
      i=i+1
  endo
  d=distance(df, "MAXIMUM")       ; compute r(r-1)/2 distances
  i = 1:rows(d)^2
  reshape ("i", #(rows(d), cols(d)))
  i = i<=i'
  d = paf (#(d), #(i))
  deps=1.5*std/99                 ; gap between two epsilons
  oeps=0.5*std                    ; origin of epsilons
  {xb,yb}=bindata(d, deps, oeps) ; bin the distances
```

```
  w=sort(xb~yb)                     ; sort the bins
  xc=conv(w[,1], w[,2], 0, 1)       ; avoid empty bins
  w = xc{1}~cumsum(xc{2})./sum(xc{2})
  w = paf (w, ((w[,1].>=0) && (w[,1].<=100)))
  epsk=log(0.5+(w[,1]+0.5).*1.5./99)~log(w[,2])
y=epsk
endp
```

References

Andersen, T.G. (1994). Stochastic autoregressive volatility: a framework for volatility modeling, *Mathematical Finance* **4**: 75–102.

Andersen, T.G. and Bollerslev, T.P. (1995). Intraday seasonality and volatility persistence in financial markets, *Proceedings of the First International Conference on High Frequency Data in Finance, Zürich*.

Ango Nze, P. (1992). Critères d'ergodicité de quelques modèles à représentation markovienne, *Technical Report 315, ser. 1*, C.R. Acad. Sci. Paris.

Auestad, B. and Tjøstheim, D. (1990). Identification of nonlinear time series: First order characterization and order estimation, *Biometrika* **77**: 669–687.

Bachelier, L. (1900). Théorie de la spéculation, *Annales de l'Ecole Normale Superieure, Series 3* **17**: 21–86.

Baillie, R.T. and Bollerslev, T.P. (1989). The message in daily exchange rates: A conditional variance tale, *Journal of Business and Economic Statistics* **7**: 297–305.

Baillie, R.T. and Bollerslev, T.P. (1990). Intra–day and inter–market volatility in foreign exchange rates, *Review of Economic Studies* **58**: 565–585.

Baillie, R.T., Bollerslev, T.P. and Mikkelsen, O. (1996). Fractionally integrated generalized autoregressive conditional heteroskedasticity, *Journal of Econometrics*. forthcoming.

Basawa, I.V. and Prakasa Rao, B.L.S. (1980). *Statistical inference for stochastic processes*, Academic Press, London.

Bera, A. and Higgins, M. (1993). A survey of ARCH models: properties, estimation and testing, *Journal of Economic Surveys* **7**: 305–366.

Berndt, E.K., Hall, B.H., Hall, R.E. and Hausman, J.A. (1974). Estimation inference in nonlinear structural models, *Annals of Economic and Social Measurement* **4**: 653–665.

Bessembinder, H. (1994). Bid–ask spreads in the interbank foreign exchange markets, *Journal of Financial Economics* **35**: 317–348.

Bickel, P.J. (1982). On adaptive estimation, *Annals of Statistics* **10**: 647–671.

Bickel, P.J. and Rosenblatt, M. (1973). On some global measures of the deviations of density function estimates, *Annals of Statistics* **1**: 1071–1091.

Bierens, H.J. (1983). Uniform consistency of kernel estimators of a regression function under generalized conditions, *Journal of the American Statistical Association* **78**: 699–707.

Billingsley, P. (1968). *Convergence of Probability Measures*, Wiley, New York.

Black, F. (1976). Studies in stock price volatility changes, *Proceedings of the 1976 Meeting of the Business and Economic Statistics Section*, American Statistical Association, pp. 177–181.

Black, F. and Scholes, M. (1973). The pricing of options and corporate liabilities, *Journal of Political Economy* **81**: 637–654.

Bollerslev, T.P. (1986). Generalized autoregressive conditional heteroscedasticity, *Journal of Econometrics* **31**: 307–327.

Bollerslev, T.P., Chou, R.Y. and Kroner, K. (1992). ARCH modelling in finance: a review of the theory and empirical evidence, *Journal of Econometrics* **52**: 5–59.

Bollerslev, T.P., Engle, R.F. and Wooldridge, J.M. (1988). A capital asset pricing model with time-varying covariances, *Journal of Political Economy* **96**: 116–131.

Bollerslev, T.P. and Mikkelsen, O. (1995). Modeling and pricing long-memory in stock market volatility, *Technical report*, Northwestern University, Department of Finance.

Boothe, P. and Longworth, D. (1986). Foreign exchange market efficency tests, implications of recent empirical findings, *Journal of International Money and Finance* **5**: 135–152.

Bossaerts, P., Hafner, C. and Härdle, W. (1996). A new method for volatility estimation with applications to foreign exchange rate series, *in* G. Bol, G. Nakhaeizadeh and K.H. Vollmer (eds), *Finanzmarktanalyse und -prognose mit innovativen quantitativen Verfahren*, Physica Verlag, pp. 71–83.

Bossaerts, P., Härdle, W. and Hafner, C. (1996). Foreign exchange rates have surprising volatility, *in* P. Robinson (ed.), *Athens Conference on Applied Probability and Time Series, vol.2*, number 115 in *Lecture Notes in Statistics*, Springer Verlag, pp. 55–72.

Bossaerts, P. and Hillion, P. (1996). Local parametric analysis of hedging in discrete time, *Journal of Econometrics*. forthcoming.

Box, G.E.P. and Jenkins, G.M. (1976). *Time Series Analysis: Forecasting and Control*, Holden-Day, San Fransisco.

Breckling, J. and Hillmer, M. (1996). Verschiedene verfahren zur zinsprognose: Ein methodischer prognosegütevergleich, *in* G. Bol, G. Nakhaeizadeh and K.H. Vollmer (eds), *Finanzmarktanalyse und -prognose mit innovativen quantitativen Verfahren*, Physica–Verlag.

Breiman, L. and Friedman, J.H. (1985). Estimating optimal transformations for multiple regression and correlations (with discussion), *Journal of the American Statistical Association* **80**: 580–619.

Breusch, T. and Pagan, A.R. (1979). A simple test for heteroskedasticity and random coefficient variation, *Econometrica* **47**: 1287–1294.

Brock, W.A. and Dechert, W.D. (1988). A general class of specification tests: The scalar case, *Proceedings of the Business and Economic Statistics Section*, American Statistical Association, pp. 70–79.

Brock, W.A., Dechert, W.D. and Scheinkman, J.A. (1987). A test for independence based on the correlation dimension, *Technical report*, University of Wisconsin, Social Systems Research Institute, Madison.

Brock, W.A., Hsieh, D.A. and LeBaron, B. (1991). *Nonlinear Dynamics, Chaos, and Instability: Statistical Theory and Economic Evidence*, MIT Press.

Chan, K.S. (1990). Testing for threshold autoregression, *Annals of Statistics* **18**: 1886–1894.

Chen, R. (1995). A nonparametric predictor for nonlinear linear time series, *Technical report*, Department of Statistics, Texas A&M University.

Chen, R. and Hafner, C. (1995). Nonlinear time series analysis, *in* W. Härdle, S. Klinke and B. Turlach (eds), *XploRe - an interactive statistical computing environment*, Springer Verlag, pp. 287–309.

Chen, R. and Tsay, R.S. (1993a). Functional-coefficient autoregressive models, *Journal of the American Statistical Association* **88**: 298–308.

Chen, R. and Tsay, R.S. (1993b). Nonlinear additive ARX models, *Journal of the American Statistical Association* **88**: 955–967.

Christie, A.A. (1982). The stochastic behavior of common stock variances: Value, leverage and interest rate effects, *Journal of Financial Economics* **10**: 407–432.

Cleveland, W.S. (1979). Robust locally weighted regression and smoothing scatterplots, *Journal of the American Statistical Association* **74**: 829–836.

Cleveland, W.S. and Devlin, S.J. (1988). Locally weighted regression: An approach to regression analysis by local fitting, *Journal of the American Statistical Association* **83**: 596–610.

Collomb, G. and Härdle, W. (1986). Strong uniform convergence rates in robust nonparametric time series analysis and prediction: Kernel regression estimation from dependent observations, *Stochastic Processes and their Applications* **23**: 77–89.

Cox, J.C., Ingersoll, Jr., J.E. and Ross, S.A. (1985). A theory of the term structure of interest rates, *Econometrica* **53**: 385–407.

Cox, J.C. and Ross, S.A. (1976). The valuation of options for alternative stochastic processes, *Journal of Financial Economics* **3**: 145–166.

Dacorogna, M.M., Müller, U.A., Nagler, R.J., Olsen, R.B. and Pictet, O.V. (1993). A geographical model for the daily and weekly seasonal volatility in the foreign exchange market, *Journal of International Money and Finance* **12**: 413–426.

Diebold, F.X. and Nason, J.M. (1990). Nonparametric exchange rate prediction ?, *Journal of International Economics* **28**: 315–332.

Diebolt, J. and Guégan, D. (1993). Tail behavior of the stationary density of general non-linear autoregressive processes of order 1, *Journal of Applied Probability* **30**: 315–329.

Ding, Z., Granger, C.W.J. and Engle, R.F. (1993). A long memory property of stock market returns and a new model, *Journal of Empirical Finance* **1**: 83–106.

Domowitz, I. and Hakkio, C.S. (1985). Conditional variance and the risk premium in the foreign exchange market, *Journal of International Economics* **19**: 47–66.

Drost, F. and Nijman, T. (1993). Temporal aggregation of GARCH processes, *Econometrica* **61**: 909–927.

Duan, J.C. (1995). The GARCH option pricing model, *Mathematical Finance* **5**: 13–32.

Engel, C. and Hamilton, J.D. (1990). Long swings in the dollar: Are they in the data and do markets know it?, *American Economic Review* **80**: 689–713.

Engle, R.F. (1982). Autoregressive conditional heteroscedasticity with estimates of the variance of U.K. inflation, *Econometrica* **50**: 987–1008.

Engle, R.F. and Bollerslev, T.P. (1986). Modelling the persistence of conditional variances, *Econometric Reviews* **5**: 1–50, 81–87.

Engle, R.F. and Gonzalez-Rivera, G. (1991). Semiparametric ARCH models, *Journal of Business and Economic Statistics* **9**: 345–360.

Engle, R.F., Lilien, D.M. and Robins, R.P. (1987). Estimating time varying risk premia in the term structure: The ARCH-M model, *Econometrica* **55**: 391–407.

Engle, R.F. and Ng, V.K. (1993). Measuring and testing the impact of news on volatility, *Journal of Finance* **48**: 1749–1778.

Fama, E.F. (1965). The behavior of stock market prices, *Journal of Business* **38**: 34–105.

Fama, E.F. (1970). Efficient capital markets: A review of theory and empirical work, *Journal of Finance* **25**: 383–420.

Fama, E.F. (1991). Efficient capital markets: Ii, *Journal of Finance* **46**: 1575–1617.

Fan, J. (1993). Local linear regression smoothers and their minimax efficency, *The Annals of Statistics* **21**: 196–216.

Fan, J. and Gijbels, I. (1995). Data–driven bandwidth selection in local polynomial fitting: variable bandwidth and spatial adaptation, *Journal of the Royal Statistical Society B* **57**: 349–350.

Fan, J. and Gijbels, I. (1996). *Local polynomial modeling and its application - Theory and methodologies*, Chapman and Hall.

Frankel, J. (1986). The implication of mean–variance optimization for four questions in international finance, *Journal of International Money and Finance* **5**: Supplement, S53–S75.

Friedman, J.H. (1984). A variable span smoother, *Technical Report LCS5*, Department of Statistics, Stanford University, Stanford, CA.

Friedman, J.H. and Stuetzle, W. (1981). Projection pursuit regression, *Journal of the American Statistical Association* **76**: 817–823.

Gallant, A., Hsieh, D.A. and Tauchen, G. (1995). Estimation of stochastic volatility models with diagnostics, *Technical report*, Duke University, Durham.

Geweke, J. (1986). Comment on modeling the persistence of conditional variances, *Econometric Reviews* **5**: 57–62.

Glassman, D. (1987). Exchange rate risk and transaction costs: Evidence from bid–ask spreads, *Journal of International Money and Finance* **6**: 479–490.

Goodhart, C. and Figliuoli, L. (1991). Every minute counts in financial markets, *Journal of International Money and Finance* **10**: 23–52.

Gouriéroux, C. (1992). *Modèles ARCH et Applications Financières*, Economica.

Gouriéroux, C. and Monfort, A. (1992). Qualitative threshold ARCH models, *Journal of Econometrics* **52**: 159–199.

Gouriéroux, C. and Monfort, A. (1995). *Statistics and Econometric Models: General Concepts, Estimation, Prediction and Algorithms*, Vol. 1, Cambridge University Press.

Gouriéroux, C., Monfort, A. and Trognon, A. (1984). Pseudo maximum likelihood methods: Theory, *Econometrica* **52**: 681–700.

Granger, C.W.J. and Anderson, A.P. (1978). *An Introduction to Bilinear Time Series Models*, Vandenhoeck & Ruprecht, Göttingen and Zürich.

Granger, C.W.J. and Teräsvirta, T. (1993). *Modelling Nonlinear Economic Relationships*, Academic Press, Oxford.

Grassberger, P. and Procaccia, I. (1983). Measuring the strangeness of strange attractors, *Physica* **9D**: 189–208.

Guillaume, D., Dacorogna, M.M., Davé, R.D., Müller, U.A., Olsen, R.B. and Pictet, O.V. (1994). From the bird's eye to the microscope: A survey of new stylized facts of the intra–daily foreign exchange market, *Technical report*, Olsen & Associates.

Györfi, L., Härdle, W., Sarda, P. and Vieu, P. (1989). *Nonparametric Curve Estimation from Time Series*, Vol. 60 of *Lecture Notes in Statistics*, Springer Verlag, Heidelberg.

Hafner, C. (1996). Kernel estimation of financial time series, *in* M. Schröder (ed.), *Quantitative Verfahren im Finanzmarktbereich*, number 5 in *ZEW Wirtschaftsanalysen*, Nomos Verlagsgesellschaft, Baden–Baden, pp. 223–239.

Hafner, C. (1997). Estimating high frequency foreign exchange rate volatility with nonparametric ARCH models, *Journal of Statistical Planning and Inference*. forthcoming.

Hafner, C. and Herwartz, H. (1997). Structural analysis of multivariate GARCH models using impulse response functions, *Technical report*, CORE, Louvain-la-Neuve.

Hafner, C., Tjøstheim, D. and Yang, L. (1997). Estimation of nonparametric generalized ARCH models, *Technical report*, SFB 373, Humboldt–Universität zu Berlin.

Haggan, V. and Ozaki, T. (1981). Modeling nonlinear vibrations using an amplitude-dependent autoregressive time series model, *Biometrika* **68**: 189–196.

Hall, P. and Heyde, C.C. (1980). *Martingale Limit Theory and Its Applications*, Academic Press, New York.

Hall, P., Matthews, D. and Platen, E. (1995). Algorithms for analyzing nonstationary time series with fractal noise, *Technical report*, Centre for Mathematics and its Applications, Australian National University, Canberra, Australia.

Hamilton, J.D. (1989). A new approach to the economic analysis of nonstationary time series and the business cycle, *Econometrica* **57**: 357–384.

Hamilton, J.D. (1994). *Time Series Analysis*, Princeton University Press.

Härdle, W. (1990). *Applied Nonparametric Regression*, Cambridge University Press, Cambridge.

Härdle, W. and Hafner, C. (1996). Zinsprognose mit univariater nichtparametrischer zeitreihenanalyse, *in* G. Bol, G. Nakhaeizadeh and K.H. Vollmer (eds), *Finanzmarktanalyse und -prognose mit innovativen quantitativen Verfahren*, Physica–Verlag, pp. 329–333.

Härdle, W. and Hafner, C. (1997). Discrete time option pricing with flexible volatility estimation, *Technical report*, CORE, Louvain-la-Neuve.

Härdle, W., Klinke, S. and Turlach, B. (1995). *XploRe - An Interactive Statistical Computing Environment*, Springer Verlag.

Härdle, W., Lütkepohl, H. and Chen, R. (1997). A review of nonparametric time series analysis, *International Statistical Review*. forthcoming.

Härdle, W. and Mammen, E. (1993). Comparing nonparametric versus parametric regression fits, *Annals of Statistics* **21**: 1926–1948.

Härdle, W. and Tsybakov, A. (1997). Local polynomial estimation of the volatility function, *Journal of Econometrics*. forthcoming.

Härdle, W., Tsybakov, A. and Yang, L. (1997). Nonparametric vector autoregression, *Journal of Statistical Planning and Inference*. forthcoming.

Härdle, W. and Vieu, P. (1992). Kernel regression smoothing of time series, *Journal of Time Series Analysis* **13**: 209–232.

Hart, J. (1994). Automated kernel smoothing of dependent data by using time series cross–validation, *Journal of the Royal Statistical Society* **56**: 529–542.

Hastie, T.J. and Tibshirani, R.J. (1990). *Generalized Additive Models*, Vol. 43 of *Monographs on Statistics and Applied Probability*, Chapman and Hall, London.

Hinich, M.J. (1982). Testing for gaussianity and linearity of a stationary time series, *Journal of Time Series Analysis* **3**: 169–176.

Hinich, M.J. and Patterson, D.M. (1980). Identification of the coefficient in a nonlinear time series of the quadratic type, *Journal of Econometrics* **30**: 269–288.

Hjellvik, V. and Tjøstheim, D. (1995). Nonparametric tests of linearity for time series, *Biometrika* **82**: 351–368.

Hsieh, D.A. (1989). Modelling heteroskedasticity in daily foreign exchange rates, *Journal of Business and Economic Statistics* **7**: 307–317.

Hsieh, D.A. (1991). Chaos and nonlinear dynamics: Application to financial markets, *Journal of Finance* **46**: 1839–1878.

Hull, J. and White, A. (1987). The pricing of options on assets with stochastic volatilities, *Journal of Finance* **42**: 281–300.

Ingersoll, Jr., J.E. (1987). *Theory of Financial Decision Making*, Rowman & Littlefield.

Jones, D.A. (1978). Non-linear autoregressive processes, *Journal of the Royal Statistical Society, Series A* **360**: 71–95.

Keenan, D.M. (1985). A tukey nonadditivity-type test for time series non-linearity, *Biometrika* **72**: 39–44.

Kim, T.Y. and Cox, D.D. (1996). Bandwidth selection in kernel smoothing of time series, *Journal of Time Series Analysis* **17**: 49–63.

Klimko, L.A. and Nelson, P.I. (1978). On conditional least squares estimation for stochastic processes, *Annals of Statistics* **6**: 629–643.

Lai, T.L. and Wei, C.Z. (1983). Asymptotic properties of general autoregressive models and strong consistency of the least squares estimates of their parameters, *Journal of Multivariate Analysis* **13**: 1–23.

Lasota, A. and Mackey, M.C. (1989). Stochastic perturbation of dynamical systems: the weak convergence of measures, *Journal of Mathematical Analysis and Applications* **138**: 232–248.

Lawrance, A.J. (1991). Directionality and reversibility in time series, *International Statistical Review* **59**: 67–79.

LeBaron, B. (1995). Chaos and nonlinear forecastability in economics and finance, *in* H. Tong (ed.), *Chaos and Forecasting - Proceedings of the Royal Society Meeting*, World Scientific Publishing, Singapore.

LeRoy, S.F. (1989). Efficient capital markets and martingales, *Journal of Economic Literature* **27**: 1583–1621.

Lintner, J. (1965). Security prices, risk and maximal gains from diversification, *Journal of Finance* **20**: 587–615.

Linton, O. (1992). The shape of the risk premium: Evidence from a semiparametric, mean- exponential GARCH model, *Technical report*, Yale University.

Linton, O. (1993). Adaptive estimation in ARCH models, *Econometric Theory* **9**: 539–569.

Linton, O. and Nielsen, J.P. (1994). A multiplicative bias reduction method for nonparametric regression, *Statistics and Probability Letters* **19**: 181–187.

Linton, O. and Nielsen, J.P. (1995). A kernel method of estimating structured nonparametric regression based on marginal integration, *Biometrika* **82**: 93–100.

Ljung, G.M. and Box, G.E.P. (1978). On a measure of lack of fit in time series models, *Biometrika* **65**: 297–303.

Lütkepohl, H. (1991). *Introduction to Multiple Time Series Analysis*, Springer Verlag.

Luukkonen, R., Saikkonen, P. and Teräsvirta, T. (1988). Testing linearity against smooth transition autoregressive models, *Biometrika* **75**: 491–499.

Mahieu, R. (1995). *Financial Market Volatility - Statistical Models and Empirical Analysis*, PhD thesis, Universitaire Pers Maastricht.

Mahieu, R. and Schotman, P. (1995). Stochastic volatility and the distribution of exchange rate news, *Technical report*, Limburg Institute of Financial Economics (LIFE), University of Limburg.

Mandelbrot, B. (1963). The variation of certain speculative prices, *Journal of Business* **36**: 394–419.

Mandelbrot, B. and Taylor, H. (1967). On the distribution of stock price differences, *Operations Research* **15**: 1057–1062.

Maravall, A. (1983). An application of nonlinear time series forecasting, *Journal of Business and Economic Statistics* **1**: 66–74.

Marron, S. and Härdle, W. (1986). Random approximations to an error criterion of nonparametric statistics, *Journal of Multivariate Analysis* **20**: 91–113.

Masry, E. and Tjøstheim, D. (1995). Nonparametric estimation and identification of nonlinear ARCH time series: Strong convergence and asymptotic normality, *Econometric Theory* **11**: 258–289.

McLeod, A.I. and Li, W.K. (1983). Diagnostic checking ARMA time series models using squared residual autocorrelations, *Journal of Time Series Analysis* **4**: 269–273.

Meese, R.A. and Rogoff, K. (1983). Empirical exchange rate models of the seventies: Do they fit out of sample?, *Journal of International Economics* **14**: 3–24.

Melino, A. and Turnbull, S.M. (1990). Pricing foreign currency options with stochastic volatility, *Journal of Econometrics* **45**: 239–265.

Melvin, M. (1985). *Currency Substitution and Western European Monetary Unification*, Economica 52:205.

Mills, T. (1993). *The econometric modelling of financial time series*, Cambridge University Press, Cambridge.

Mossin, J. (1966). Equilibrium in a capital asset market, *Econometrica* **34**: 768–783.

Müller, U.A., Dacorogna, M.M., Davé, R.D., Olsen, R.B., Pictet, O.V. and Weizsäcker, J.E.v. (1995). Volatilities of different time resolutions – analyzing the dynamics of market components, *Proceedings of the First International Conference on High Frequency Data in Finance, Zürich.*

Müller, U.A., Dacorogna, M.M., Olsen, R.B., Pictet, O.V., Schwarz, M. and Morgenegg, C. (1990). Statistical study of foreign exchange rates, empirical evidence of a price change scaling law, and intraday analysis, *Journal of Banking and Finance* **14**: 1189–1208.

Müller, U.A., Dacorogna, M.M. and Pictet, O.V. (1995). The error of statistical volatility of intra–daily quoted price changes observed over a time interval, *Technical report*, Olsen & Associates.

Nadaraya, E. (1964). On estimating regression, *Theory of Probability and its Applications* **9**: 141–142.

Nelson, D.B. (1990a). ARCH models as diffusion approximations, *Journal of Econometrics* **45**: 7–38.

Nelson, D.B. (1990b). Stationarity and persistence in the GARCH(1,1) model, *Econometric Theory* **6**: 318–334.

Nelson, D.B. (1991). Conditional heteroskedasticity in asset returns: A new approach, *Econometrica* **59**: 347–370.

Neumann, J.v. and Morgenstern, O. (1944). *Theory of Games and Economic Behavior*, Princeton University Press, Princeton, N.J.

Nicholls, D. and Quinn, B. (1982). *Random Coefficient Autoregressive Models: An Introduction*, Vol. 11 of *Lecture Notes in Statistics*, Springer Verlag.

Pagan, A.R. and Hong, Y.S. (1991). Nonparametric estimation and the risk premium, *in* W.A. Barnett, J. Powell and G. Tauchen (eds), *Nonparametric and semiparametric methods in econometrics and statistics, Proceedings of the fifth international symposium in economic theory and econometrics*, Cambridge University Press, Cambridge.

Pagan, A.R. and Schwert, G.W. (1990). Alternative models for conditional stock volatility, *Journal of Econometrics* **45**: 267–290.

Pantula, S.G. (1988). Estimation of autoregressive models with ARCH errors, *Sankhya: The Indian Journal of Statistics B* **50**: 119–138.

Petruccelli, J. and Davies, N. (1986). A portmanteau test for self-exciting threshold autoregressive-type nonlinearity in time series, *Biometrika* **73**: 687–694.

Pham, D.T. (1985). Bilinear markovian representations and bilinear models, *Stochastic Processes and their Applications* **20**: 295–306.

Priestley, M.B. (1988). *Non-linear and Non-stationary Time Series Analysis*, Academic Press, New York.

Rabemananjara, R. and Zakoian, J.M. (1993). Threshold ARCH models and asymmetries in volatility, *Journal of Applied Econometrics* **8**: 31–49.

Ramsey, J.B. (1969). Tests for specification errors in classical linear least–squares regression analysis, *Journal of the Royal Statistical Society B* **31**: 350–371.

Ramsey, J.B. and Rothman, P. (1991). Time irreversibility of stationary time series: Estimators and test statistics, *Technical report*, Department of Economics, New York University and University of Delaware.

Robinson, P.M. (1977). The estimation of a nonlinear moving average model, *Stochastic Processes and Applications*.

Robinson, P.M. (1983). Non-parametric estimation for time series models, *Journal of Time Series Analysis* **4**: 185–208.

Rosenblatt, M. (1956). Remarks on some nonparametric estimates of a density function, *Annals of Mathematical Statistics* **27**: 832–837.

Ross, S.A. (1976). The arbitrage theory of capital asset pricing, *Journal of Economic Theory* **13**: 341–360.

Rothman, P. (1994). The time reversibility test with applications to financial data, *in* W. Semmler (ed.), *Business Cycles: Theory and Empirical Methods*, Kluwer Academic Publishers, chapter 15, pp. 389–403.

Rothschild, M. and Stiglitz, J.E. (1970). Increasing risk I: A definition, *Journal of Economic Theory* **3**: 225–243.

Schnidrig, R. and Würtz, D. (1995). Investigation of the volatility and autocorrelation function of the USDDEM exchange rate on operational time scales, *Technical Report 95-04*, ETH Zürich.

Schwarz, G. (1978). Estimating the dimension of a model, *Annals of Statistics* **6**: 461–464.

Sentana, E. and Wadhwani, S. (1991). Semi-parametric estimation and the predictability of stock market returns: Some lessons from japan, *Review of Economic Studies* **58**: 547–563.

Sharpe, W.F. (1964). Capital asset prices: A theory of market equilibrium under conditions of risk, *Journal of Finance* **19**: 425–442.

Silverman, B.W. (1984). Spline smoothing: the equivalent variable kernel method, *Annals of Statistics* **12**: 898–916.

Sims, C. (1980). Macroeconomics and reality, *Econometrica* **48**: 1–48.

Stoll, H.R. (1989). Inferring the components of the bid–ask spread: Theory and empirical evidence, *Journal of Finance* **44**: 115–134.

Subba Rao, T. (1981). On the theory of bilinear time series models, *Journal of the Royal Statistical Society, Series B* **43**: 244–255.

Subba Rao, T. and Gabr, M.M. (1980). *An introduction to bispectral analysis and bilinear time series models*, Vol. 24 of *Lecture Notes in Statistics*, Springer Verlag, New York.

Sugihara, G. and May, R.M. (1990). Nonlinear forecasting as a way of distinguishing chaos from measurement error in time series, *Nature* **344**: 734–741.

Tapia, R.A. and Thompson, J.R. (1978). *Nonparametric Probability Density Estimation*, John Hopkins University Press, Baltimore.

Teräsvirta, T. (1994). Specification, estimation, and evaluation of smooth transition autoregressive models, *Journal of the American Statistical Association* **89**: 208–218.

Tibshirani, R.J. (1988). Estimating transformations for regression via additivity and variance stabilization, *Journal of the American Statistical Association* **83**: 394–405.

Tjøstheim, D. (1986). Estimation in nonlinear time series models, *Stochastic Processes and Applications* **21**: 251–273.

Tjøstheim, D. (1990). Nonlinear time series and markov chains, *Advances in Applied Probability* **22**: 587–611.

Tjøstheim, D. (1994). Non–linear time series: a selective review, *Scandinavian Journal of Statistics* **21**: 97–130.

Tong, H. (1978). On a threshold model, *in* C.H. Chen (ed.), *Pattern Recognition and Signal Processing*, Sijthoff and Noordholf, The Netherlands.

Tong, H. (1983). *Threshold Models in Nonlinear Time Series Analysis*, Vol. 21 of *Lecture Notes in Statistics*, Springer Verlag, Heidelberg.

Tong, H. (1990). *Nonlinear Time Series Analysis: A Dynamic Approach*, Oxford University Press, Oxford.

Truong, Y.K. (1993). A nonparametric framework for time series analysis, *New Directions in Time Series Analysis*, Springer Verlag, New York.

Tsay, R.S. (1986). Nonlinearity tests for time series, *Biometrika* **73**: 461–466.

Tsay, R.S. (1989). Testing and modeling threshold autoregressive processes, *Journal of the American Statistical Association* **84**: 231–240.

Tsay, R.S. (1991). Detecting and modeling nonlinearity in univariate time series analysis, *Statistica Sinica* **1**: 431–451.

Tschernig, R. (1995). Long memory in foreign exchange rates revisited, *Journal of International Financial Markets, Institutions and Money* **5**: 53–78.

Tsybakov, A. (1986). Robust reconstruction of functions by the local-approximation method, *Problems of Information Transmission* **22**: 133–146.

Tweedie, R.L. (1975). Sufficient conditions for ergodicity and recurrence of markov chains on a general state space, *Stochastic Processes and their Applications* **3**: 385–403.

Venables, W.N. and Ripley, B.D. (1994). *Modern Applied Statistics with S-Plus*, Springer Verlag.

Visser, H. (1991). *Modern Monetary Theory*, Edward Elgar.

Wasserfallen, W. and Zimmermann, H. (1985). The behavior of intra-daily exchange rates, *Journal of Banking and Finance* **9**: 55–72.

Watson, G. (1964). Smooth regression analysis, *Sankhya A* **26**: 359–372.

Weiss, A.A. (1986a). ARCH and bilinear time series models; comparison and combination, *Journal of Business and Economic Statistics* **4**: 59–70.

Weiss, A.A. (1986b). Asymptotic theory for ARCH models: Estimation and testing, *Econometric Theory* **2**: 107–131.

White, H. (1980). A heteroskedasticity-consistent covariance matrix estimator and a direct test for heteroskedasticity, *Econometrica* **48**: 817–838.

White, H. (1982). Maximum likelihood estimation of misspecified models, *Econometrica* **50**: 1–25.

Yakowitz, S. (1987). Nearest-neighbour methods for time series analysis, *Journal of Time Series Analysis* **8**: 235–247.

Yang, L. and Hafner, C. (1997). Nonparametric estimation of a stochastic volatility model, *Technical report*, SFB 373, Humboldt–Universität zu Berlin.

Yang, L. and Härdle, W. (1997). Nonparametric autoregression with multiplicative volatility and additive mean, *Journal of Time Series Analysis*. forthcoming.

Zakoian, J.M. (1994). Threshold heteroskedastic functions, *Journal of Economic Dynamics and Control* **18**: 931–955.

Zhang, X. (1994). *Analyse Numérique des Options Américaines dans un Modèle de Diffusion avec des Sauts*, PhD thesis, Ecole Nationale des Ponts et Chaussées, Paris.

Author Index

Subject Index

GPSR Compliance

The European Union's (EU) General Product Safety Regulation (GPSR) is a set of rules that requires consumer products to be safe and our obligations to ensure this.

If you have any concerns about our products, you can contact us on ProductSafety@springernature.com

In case Publisher is established outside the EU, the EU authorized representative is:

Springer Nature Customer Service Center GmbH
Europaplatz 3
69115 Heidelberg, Germany

Batch number: 10725973

Printed by Printforce, the Netherlands